ADAPTIVENESS

Rapid and transformational actions are evermore urgently needed to achieve a just, resilient, and ecologically sustainable global society, as envisioned and supported by the Sustainable Development Goals. Moreover, dynamic governance approaches are vital for addressing changing and uncertain conditions. At many levels, governance needs to be responsive and flexible, in one word, adaptive. This book provides a state-of-the-art review of the conceptual development of adaptiveness as a key concept in the environmental governance literature, complemented by applications from global, regional, and national levels. It reviews the politics of adaptiveness, investigates which governance processes foster adaptiveness, and discusses how, when, and why adaptiveness influences earth system governance. It is a timely synthesis for students, researchers, and practitioners interested in environmental governance, sustainability, and social change processes. This is one of a series of publications associated with the Earth System Governance Project. For more publications, see www.cambridge.org/earth-system-governance.

BERND SIEBENHÜNER is Professor of Ecological Economics at Carl von Ossietzky University of Oldenburg, Germany. He has also held positions at the Potsdam Institute for Climate Impact Research (PIK), Harvard University, and the Nelson Mandela University, South Africa. As a member of the Scientific Steering Committee of the Earth System Governance Project, he contributed to its first Science Plan. In his current research, he focuses, among other things, on social learning, international organisations, climate adaptation, and transdisciplinarity.

RIYANTI DJALANTE is the academic programme officer at the United Nations University – Institute for the Advanced Study of Sustainability (UNU-IAS). She has 10 years of scientific research and professional experience in the field of governance, development, disaster risk reduction, and climate change management. She is a lead author of the 2018 Earth System Governance Project Science Plan, the IPCC Sixth Assessment Report, and the Global Environmental Outlook (GEO-6) Report. She is also a Steering Committee member of the Integrated Research on Disaster Risk programme.

CAMBRIDGE
UNIVERSITY PRESS

University Printing House, Cambridge CB2 8BS, United Kingdom

One Liberty Plaza, 20th Floor, New York, NY 10006, USA

477 Williamstown Road, Port Melbourne, VIC 3207, Australia

314–321, 3rd Floor, Plot 3, Splendor Forum, Jasola District Centre, New Delhi – 110025, India

79 Anson Road, #06–04/06, Singapore 079906

Cambridge University Press is part of the University of Cambridge.

It furthers the University's mission by disseminating knowledge in the pursuit of education, learning, and research at the highest international levels of excellence.

www.cambridge.org
Information on this title: www.cambridge.org/9781108479028
DOI: 10.1017/9781108782180

© Cambridge University Press 2021

First published 2021

A catalogue record for this publication is available from the British Library.

ISBN 978-1-108-47902-8 Hardback
ISBN 978-1-108-74914-5 Paperback

Cambridge University Press has no responsibility for the persistence or accuracy of URLs for external or third-party internet websites referred to in this publication and does not guarantee that any content on such websites is, or will remain, accurate or appropriate.

ADAPTIVENESS

Changing Earth System Governance

Edited by

BERND SIEBENHÜNER

Carl von Ossietzky University of Oldenburg

RIYANTI DJALANTE

United Nations University – Institute for the Advanced Study of Sustainability

CAMBRIDGE
UNIVERSITY PRESS

Contents

Figures

Tables

Contributors

Guy Chiasson teaches political science and regional studies at the Université du Québec en Outaouais, Canada. His main research interests are municipal politics and urban governance in mid-sized Canadian cities as well as politics related to natural resources. His most recent research projects relate to municipal participation in forest governance and its implication for regional development. He published *Minorités francophones et Gouvernance urbaine* (Francophone minorities and urban governance) with Greg Allain in 2017 and co-authored *L'économie politique des ressources naturelles au Québec* (The political economy of natural resources in Quebec) in 2018.

Riyanti Djalante is an academic programme officer at the United Nations University – Institute for the Advanced Study of Sustainability (UNU-IAS), Japan. She coordinates research and policy development on global change and resilience, particularly those related to disaster risk reduction (DRR), climate change adaptation (CCA), and Sustainable Development Goals (SDGs). In the Earth System Governance (ESG) Project, she is a research fellow and contributing author for the 2018 Science and Implementation Plan. Dr Djalante is a visiting associate professor at Keio University, Japan. She serves as a member of the Scientific Committee for the Integrated Research on Disaster Risks (IRDR), lead author of IPCC Assessment Report 6 and Special Report on the impacts of 1.5°C global warming, and UNEP Global Environmental Outlook 6. Dr Djalante has also consulted international agencies on issues related to governance, DRR, and CCA.

Frédérik Doyon is a professor at the Department of Natural Sciences at the Université du Québec en Outaouais, Canada, and a researcher at the Institute of Temperate Forest Sciences. His research uses fundamentals from forest ecology, landscape ecology, and socio-ecological systems, addressing scientific questions using field experiments, action research, and simulation models. Many of his scientific achievements have been in applying process and empirical modelling for developing decision-making tools aimed at designing promising sustainable forest management strategies. His recent work focuses on the impacts of climate change on the southern forests of Quebec and the vulnerability and adaptation of communities who depend on them.

Pedro Fidelman is an Australia-based scholar interested in understanding the role of institutions (e.g. rules, norms, and decision-making processes) in addressing pressing contemporary environmental issues. This involves understanding how institutions create enabling and disabling conditions for society to respond and adapt to global environmental change. Particular areas of experience include marine social-ecological systems, climate change adaptation, and natural resource management in Australia, Brazil, and South East Asia. A senior research fellow with the University of Queensland Centre for Policy Futures, Dr Fidelman also serves as a senior research fellow with the ESG Project.

Torsten Grothmann is an environmental psychologist and sustainability scientist, and works as a senior scientist in the interdisciplinary Ecological Economics Department at the Carl von Ossietzky University of Oldenburg, Germany. His current research focuses on social, psychological, and methodological aspects of sustainability transformations, particularly of strategies for fostering climate change mitigation and adaptation. For almost 20 years he has investigated vulnerability, resilience, and adaptation to climate change and published numerous articles and book chapters in this research field. Grothmann studied psychology, philosophy, and business administration at the University of Bielefeld, Germany, the Free University of Berlin, Germany, and the University of California, Irvine, USA.

Dave Huitema is a professor of environmental policy at the Netherlands Open University. He also works at the Institute for Environmental Studies (IVM) at the VU University of Amsterdam (VUA), the Netherlands. Huitema focuses on the adaptability of policy systems. For policy systems to be adaptable, learning needs to take place and agency needs to be developed to translate learning in policy change. This is why the team is analysing, for example, the role of experiments, evaluation, and entrepreneurs in learning and policy innovation.

Nicolas W. Jager is a postdoctoral researcher at the Department of Ecological Economics at Carl von Ossietzky University, Oldenburg, Germany. In his work, he centres on issues of environmental and sustainability governance, public participation, institutional change, and policy failure and decline. His studies span a variety of regions in Europe and beyond, and cover diverse issues such as water, biodiversity, agriculture, or energy, and the nexus between these. In his current work, he assesses in what ways policy systems are subject to lock-ins preventing them from further climate adaptation activities.

Julie P. King, MA, is a doctoral researcher at the Department of Ecological Economics at Carl von Ossietzky University, Oldenburg, Germany. Her research focuses on climate change adaptation policy at the state level in Germany. Within this context, her dissertation focuses on the adaptation deficit in certain problem domains and regions. King is part of the international 'ADAPT Lock-In' project team that examines how systemic forces may hinder more effective climate adaptation activities. King has a master's degree in sustainability economics and management and has worked at a regional development organisation in the north-west of Germany.

Louis Lebel is the director of the Unit for Social and Environmental Research at Chiang Mai University, Thailand. His research interests include social justice, global environmental change, livelihoods, public health, gender norms, development studies, adaptation, aquaculture, consumption, flood disaster politics, and water governance. A current theoretical and empirical research focus is on the role of narratives in policy change and persistence. He helps edit the journals *Global Environmental Change*, *Ecology & Society*, and *Aquaculture Environment Interactions*. He is a research associate of the Stockholm Environment Institute.

Annie Montpetit is a PhD candidate in applied social sciences at the Université du Québec en Outaouais, Canada. She is conducting a thesis on climate change adaptive capacity of Canadian forest collectives. Her research interests relate to the intertwined relations between social-ecological systems, forest governance, and climate change adaptation. In parallel to her research, she is an independent consultant who advises local governance organisations on public participation in forest management.

Angela Oels works as a postdoctoral researcher in the climate and energy group at the Institute for Ecological Economic Research (IÖW) in Berlin, Germany. She holds a PhD in environmental sciences from the University of East Anglia, UK, and a postdoctoral qualification in political science from Hamburg University, Germany. She is an adjunct lecturer for political science at Hamburg University. At IÖW, Oels researches social acceptance of demand-side flexibility in the energy transition. In other work, she develops visions for resilient urban neighbourhoods, facilitates consultation processes for Germany's Adaptation Strategy, and does work on digitisation and 'smart cities'.

H. Carolyn Peach Brown is an Associate professor and Director of Environmental Studies at the University of Prince Edward Island, Canada. She holds a PhD in Natural Resource Policy and Management from Cornell University, USA. Prior to her PhD she lived for over 10 years in a small village in the Democratic Republic of Congo and worked in agricultural and community development. Peach Brown's research focuses on environmental governance and how it contributes to the goals of sustainable resource management and improved livelihoods, in the context of a changing climate. She has research projects in Central Africa, Atlantic Canada, and the Caribbean.

Tim Rayner is a research fellow in the School of Environmental Sciences, University of East Anglia, UK. Part of the Tyndall Centre for Climate Change Research, since 2006 he has participated in a range of European Union (EU) and national research council–funded projects covering climate change governance and policy, particularly from EU and UK perspectives. He has published on mitigation- and adaptation-related policy areas, and emerging debates over climate engineering and the potential for greenhouse gas removal. He is currently participating as a consortium partner in the Jean Monnet Network 'Governing the EU's Climate and Energy Transition in Turbulent Times' (GOVTRAN).

Courtney Schultz is an associate professor of forest and natural resource policy at Colorado State University, USA. She investigates environmental governance challenges at the science–policy–management interface, and her recent work has focused on policy innovations to support collaborative landscape restoration, effective fire management, and climate change adaptation on US forestlands. She directs the Public Lands Policy Group, a research group that produces original research to inform the practice of natural resource management and advance understanding of policy developments that affect public lands.

Bernd Siebenhüner is chair of Ecological Economics at Carl von Ossietzky University of Oldenburg, Germany and director of the master's Sustainability Economics and Management Programme. After earning degrees in economics and political science from the Free University of Berlin, Germany, and a PhD from the University of Halle-Wittenberg, Germany, he held positions at the Potsdam Institute for Climate Impact Research (PIK), Harvard University, USA, and the Nelson Mandela University, South Africa. He served in the Scientific Steering Committee of the ESG Project from 2008 to 2014 and headed numerous research projects in the fields of social learning, international organisations, global environmental governance, corporate sustainability strategies, climate adaptation, biodiversity governance, and the role of science in global environmental governance.

Peter Stoett is dean of the Faculty of Social Science and Humanities at Ontario Tech University, Canada. Previously, he directed the Loyola Sustainability Research Centre at Concordia University in Montreal, Canada. He is a senior research fellow with the ESG Project and has published widely in international environmental policy and human rights issues.

John Turnpenny is a senior lecturer in public policy in the School of Politics, University of East Anglia, UK. His research interests include the politics of public policymaking, especially the relationship between evidence and policy formulation, policy analysis tools, and construction and deployment of scientific evidence. He has recently worked on the politics of valuing nature, and previously researched policy appraisal, use of analytical tools in policy, climate change and society, scenario creation and futures communication, and knowledge brokerage.

Joanna Vince is a senior lecturer in politics and international relations at the School of Social Sciences in the College of Arts, Law, and Education at the University of Tasmania, Australia. Her research focuses on international, domestic, and comparative oceans governance; marine resource management; marine plastic pollution and governance solutions; non-state market driven governance in fisheries and aquaculture; and the effectiveness of governance arrangements in deterring illegal, unregulated, and unreported fishing.

Zachary Wurtzebach is a social scientist and programme manager at the Center for Large Landscape Conservation in Bozeman, Montana. His recent research has investigated how policies, organisational structures, and social processes influence the co-production and application of scientific information in public land management. In his current position, he is currently co-ordinating and conducting applied research on policy tools and collaborative governance for connectivity conservation in the United States and internationally.

Asim Zia is a professor of public policy and computer science at the University of Vermont (UVM), USA. He is director of the Institute for Environmental Diplomacy and Security (IEDS) and co-director of the Social Ecological Gaming and Simulation (SEGS) laboratory at UVM. He has a PhD in public policy from the Georgia Institute of Technology, is a recipient of a postdoctoral fellowship from the National Center for Atmospheric Research (2004–2006), a fellow at the Gund Institute for Environment, a senior research fellow for the ESG Project, and an academic editor at *PLoS ONE* since 2013.

Foreword

Adaptiveness has been a core concept in the global research community on earth system governance since its very beginning. All 11 global conferences on earth system governance that have been held so far included a dedicated stream of panels on adaptiveness, and numerous publications have referred to this concept and the more detailed research questions that were laid down in the first Science and Implementation Plan of the Earth System Governance (ESG) Project.

This success of the adaptiveness strand in the ESG Project was not foreseeable when the project was founded in the mid-2000s. In fact, the concept of adaptiveness was introduced in the first science plan rather as a compromise – as a new umbrella term to bring together strong communities of scholars that all operated under different conceptual terms, and that we hoped to attract to the inclusive global network that the ESG Project was envisioned to become. There were, to name just a few, the prolific community of scholars working around the concept of *resilience*, as well as the many colleagues looking into questions of *adaptive governance* or *adaptive management*. Scholars of *anticipatory governance* tried to explore how current institutions can be made more adaptive to future changes and to better understand the inherent dynamics of socio-ecological systems. A different, even though overlapping, community studied *adaptation*, mainly to the emerging threat of climate change. Further widely used terms in these debates were the *vulnerability* and *adaptive capacity* of communities, regions, and countries. A separate but equally large group of sustainability scholars investigated *social learning* and *institutional dynamics*, and what is today often known as *governance for transformation*.

All these communities looked into ways of how societies and governance systems can adapt to a dynamic environment, anticipate future changes, and learn. *Adaptiveness* became the umbrella concept that brought these communities together.

When we introduced the term 'adaptiveness' in the first ESG Science and Implementation Plan, it was of course not a neologism as such; the word adaptiveness has been used in the English language for at least 150 years (following the *Collins Dictionary*). But none of the main research communities at that time worked with explicit reference to adaptiveness. This term, once accepted in the new science plan, thus allowed all communities to join the ESG Project and to find their place in the larger and integrative scientific framework that the first science plan offered. Students of resilience, adaptation, vulnerability, adaptive governance, and social learning could all present their research, engage in fruitful dialogue, and learn from different research traditions in the adaptiveness stream that the ESG Project organised at its annual conferences, at the many smaller workshops, and in its publication outlets. The concept of adaptiveness even helped to organise the research community very practically: research fellows and lead faculty of the project who worked on resilience or adaptive governance were all internally labelled in the project's databases as part of the adaptiveness stream, and then brought together in specialised mailing lists or other activities by the ESG International Project Office.

The 2009 Science and Implementation Plan also helped to raise attention in the adaptiveness research community about other analytical themes that the plan emphasised.

The analytical theme of 'architecture', for example, brought the adaptiveness research community in conversations around the institutional hardware of governance (see *Architectures of Earth System Governance*, Cambridge University Press, 2020). What are the institutional arrangements, for instance, that help foster resilience in local communities? Which institutional arrangements advance social learning, and how can such arrangements be made more dynamic and adaptive? Or, what types of global regimes can best support global adaptation governance, for example when it comes to increasing migration pressures or food crises because of climate change?

The analytical theme of 'agency', on its part, supported a more sophisticated analysis of the actors and agents that were influential in earth system governance, including when it comes to adaptiveness (see *Agency in Earth System Governance*, Cambridge University Press, 2019). The 'agency' research programme brought a new focus on actors and agency beyond national governments; the debate now focused more on the agency of non-state actors, from environmentalist organisations, business actors, or cities to the many public–private partnerships or private governance schemes, such as the Forest Stewardship Council. All this proved to be highly important for adaptiveness research, where national governments are still important but often need to work in collaboration with private actors, at local, national, and transnational levels.

Finally, the 2009 Science and Implementation Plan of the ESG Project added new normative considerations that other sustainability research programmes – such as the International Human Dimensions Programme on Global Environmental Change – had not emphasised much at that time. One more normative line of investigation was the research theme of 'accountability and legitimacy' in the 2009 Science and Implementation Plan, which also covered questions of legitimacy, transparency, and more broadly democracy. Here again, links to the adaptiveness research programme – and related themes of resilience, adaptation, or adaptive governance – proved highly fruitful. At earth system governance conferences, for instance, scholars were able to debate the democratic quality of local adaptation policies or the legitimacy of novel types of adaptive governance that often grant a more limited role to state actors. How can we understand the democratic legitimacy, for example, of the increasing role of private governance mechanisms in local adaptation to climate change? Who takes decisions there, with what legitimacy, and with accountability to whom?

The second more normative line that the ESG Project has prioritised from the start is research on questions of justice. In the 2009 Science and Implementation Plan, research on justice was framed under the heading of 'access and allocation'; more recently, the terminological debate moved towards a new notion of 'planetary justice'. Again, the relevance of justice research to questions of adaptive governance, resilience, or adaptation is evident. Adaptation and adaptive governance are, like all political processes, activities that allocate values and goods in societies, from local to global. Adaptation and adaptive governance generate losers and winners: having brought adaptiveness research in dialogue with research on justice within the ESG Project proved tremendously fruitful for both.

The first Science and Implementation Plan of the ESG Project was not implemented until 2018. Since then, multiple harvesting activities have been underway. It is wonderful to see, in this volume, the breadth and depth of the adaptiveness stream in earth system governance research as it has developed over the last decade. Our community is grateful to this volume's editors – both leading scholars of adaptiveness in earth system governance for over a decade – for having compiled this harvesting volume, a major milestone in its field.

And there is little doubt: this line of research will continue to flourish, be it simply because the planetary crisis of earth system transformations accelerates. The global mean temperature is more than 1°C above pre-industrial levels, and the first impacts of a global climate crisis are widely documented. The loss of biodiversity, the destruction of ecosystems, the expanding gap between rich and poor on this planet, and now added the global pandemic of COVID-19 that is accelerating at the time of writing: all this shows that the adaptiveness of our societies, and of the governance systems that we have put into place to steer societal behaviour, is still as relevant as it has been in the mid-2000s when the ESG Project was set up. This adaptiveness of governance will be a key variable in humankind's increasingly stormy voyage into an Anthropocene that is full of uncertainties, risks, and dynamics, but also still hope and promise.

Frank Biermann, founding chair, Earth System Governance Project,
Utrecht University, the Netherlands

Preface and Acknowledgements

It has been a long journey to conceptualise, bring together, and finalise this book. Its origins can be traced back to a memorable workshop in 2008 in New Delhi, India, when the Earth System Governance (ESG) Project was officially adopted. It was at this workshop that the project's first Science Plan was finalised by the Scientific Planning Committee and welcomed by the Steering Committee of the International Human Dimensions Programme on Global Environmental Change. In the following year, the implementation of the Science Plan began with an international conference of the ESG Project held in Amsterdam. Since then, the ESG community has grown substantially to be the largest global social science research alliance in the area of governance and global environmental change to date.

Subsequent to the launch of the ESG Project, the idea was born to synthesise major research strands and findings concerning the analytical theme of adaptiveness. During the 2016 Conference on Earth System Governance in Nairobi, Kenya, the editors drafted and submitted a first proposal for the initiative. Like similar processes reaping the fruits of research on the themes of architecture and agency, this book contributes to the larger ESG Harvesting Initiative. After the Scientific Steering Committee and in particular Frank Biermann had welcomed the initiative, we outlined a draft concept of the harvesting process in the theme of adaptiveness as one of the core analytical themes of the 2008 ESG Science and Implementation Plan. It was over a hearty African lunch when the idea of an edited book on adaptiveness in the framework of the Harvesting Initiative came into being.

The chapters have been sourced by two calls sent out in January and April 2017 that resulted in a first list of book chapters and authors. The majority of the writing processes took place during 2017 and 2018. During the 2018 Utrecht Conference on Earth System Governance, we presented the initial findings from our synthesis chapter that is now Chapter 2 in this book. There, the author workshop resulted in the list of guiding questions for the individual chapters and the proposed title of the book. Various authors of this book's chapters presented their ideas and chapter concepts. In a separate meeting with book authors, we presented the progress and discussed lingering research topics and remaining gaps in the literature on adaptiveness. Moreover, together we drafted a new set of forward-looking questions and research agendas on adaptiveness condensed in the so-called Utrecht Questions, as presented in the concluding chapter of the book.

This book was finalised during the first half of 2020 when the World Health Organisation declared COVID-19 a pandemic, affecting almost all nations and communities. These conditions call even louder for the need to strengthen our efforts to create a more sustainable, equitable, and adaptive global society with suitable governance modes and structures. Individuals as well as governments have adapted rapidly, shifting to new modes of life and governance. Privately, we have changed to doing almost everything online. Many governments have demonstrated a high responsiveness towards new data and the urgency of the situation by often drastic measures that have led to the hitherto most effective and fastest emission reductions locally as well as globally. Here again, we need to learn to live with changes and risks, be they dramatic or slow, simple or complex, localised or global, and navigate through them to maintain continuity and progress, and to advance towards the global goals of sustainability. As the concept of adaptiveness is understood and discussed in this book, it can help to manoeuvre through crises such as COVID-19, challenging governance approaches and systems to respond to dramatically changing conditions in socio-ecological systems. The 'new normal' is a dynamic change and it is here with us for years to come. Thus adaptive governance will remain urgent and essential to effectively find and implement solutions.

We would like to thank all of the authors of the 10 chapters who have been actively involved in writing and reviewing the chapters since 2017 and for patiently supporting the publication process. All authors not only contributed their chapters and participated in meetings but also peer reviewed other chapters. In particular, we thank H. Carolyn Peach Brown from the University of Prince Edward Island, Canada, for her continuous support and the expeditious reviews of numerous chapters. As co-author of the first ESG Science Plan chapter on adaptiveness, Louis Lebel supported the process as author and by providing most helpful comments to chapters. Susi Moser gave much appreciated comments during the Utrecht meeting and Raffaela Kozar of the United Nations University – Institute for the Advanced Study of Sustainability (UNU-IAS) in Japan contributed to a chapter, but got interrupted by the COVID-19 crisis. Rakhyun Kim of Utrecht University, who is also the co-author of the new Science Plan, reviewed one of the chapters almost overnight. We remain most grateful for his efforts.

The majority of the editing progress took place in 2019 and 2020. As editors, we wish to express our sincere gratitude to Nicolas W. Jager and Julie P. King who came on board in 2019 as authors and were involved in the editorial process. We are particularly indebted to Julie P. King for coordinating and facilitating the communication and the submission processes in an extremely well-organised and friendly manner. Without her, the book would have hardly come together. We also gratefully acknowledge the research assistance provided by Franziska Beck, Anna Krämer, and André Meinhard, graduate students from Carl von Ossietzky University of Oldenburg, Germany, in helping conduct the data collection for the systematic literature review of the adaptiveness literature as presented in Chapter 2 and reformatting the references for the whole book.

We are greatly indebted to Cambridge University Press, particularly Sarah Lambert in assisting the submission processes until this book came into fruition. Also thanks to Emma Kiddle and Sai Priya Katta at Cambridge University Press for their assistance, patience, and support at different stages of the process. To the three anonymous reviewers of the book proposal, we are grateful for your early input and thoughtful comments. Many thanks also go to Ruben Zondervan, who coordinated the Harvesting Initiative during his term as executive director of the ESG Project. Finally, we would like to warm-heartedly thank our colleague and friend Frank Biermann of the Copernicus Institute of Sustainable Development at Utrecht University, the Netherlands, for his enthusiasm and leadership in the entire ESG Project, for pushing and supporting us in the Harvesting Initiative and for contributing the foreword to this book.

1

On Adaptiveness

Changing Earth System Governance

RIYANTI DJALANTE, BERND SIEBENHÜNER, JULIE P. KING,
NICOLAS W. JAGER, AND LOUIS LEBEL

1.1 Introduction

The year 2020 was advocated to be the 'super year for sustainability', in which the United Nations (UN) sought to launch a 'decade of action' for implementing the Sustainable Development Goals (SDGs) within the Agenda 2030 (UN, 2020). Supplementing the SDGs, the Paris Agreement on Climate Change, Sendai Framework for Disaster Risk Reduction, and the New Urban Agenda were all adopted in 2015 and 2016. In order to achieve these goals and thus more sustainable development, global efforts need to be strengthened, to accelerate, and to gain more transformative dynamics (UN, 2020). However, reports have regularly documented that global environmental changes and their impacts have been enormous, while the speed and scale of necessary progress for managing the global challenges have remained insufficient (IPBES, 2019; IPCC, 2018, 2019a, 2019b).

By 2020, the level of global warming was at 1.1°C above pre-industrial levels (IPCC, 2018), and began to seriously impact the world's natural and human systems (IPCC, 2018, 2019a, 2019b). Humankind has thus far failed to achieve the Paris Agreement goal of limiting warming to 2°C (UNEP, 2019). Rapid and transformative actions are increasingly called for to reduce greenhouse gases emissions by 2030 and achieve net-zero emissions by 2050. Such actions not only include processes such as decarbonisation, implementation of bioenergy and carbon capture and storage (BECCS), but also behavioural changes (IPCC, 2018). Nature and its vital resources and services used by humans, including biodiversity and ecosystem functions and services, are deteriorating worldwide (IPBES, 2019). These reports document that we are not on course to achieve the SDGs by 2030 and that governance responses have neither been adequate nor adaptive vis-à-vis the dynamics of the challenges at hand.

As this book was finalised, COVID-19 was pronounced a global pandemic by the World Health Organisation (WHO, 2020) in March 2020. The virus and its consequences wrought havoc on global health, disrupted education systems, and brought tourism and aviation industries to a halt (UN, 2020). The COVID-19 virus spread globally virtually overnight with the number of people affected and dying increasing exponentially on a daily basis. Governments immediately ordered people to work from, study, and stay at home; wash their hands more regularly; and practise social distancing. From January to April 2020, global aviation was largely grounded, countries' borders closed, jobs lost overnight, and companies declared bankrupt. National economies suffered as the virus spurred economic recession. In response, economic stimulus packages were rolled out in countries around the world. Within a few months, government and institutional responses, as well as public behaviour, were forced to adapt and change practices at extraordinary speeds. Such quick and widespread responses were unprecedented, especially when compared to the pace and scale of the responses to reduce carbon emissions and manage climate change. Driven by the problem at hand and informed by science, governance and institutional responses to the COVID-19 pandemic demonstrate what adaptive governance responses can look like.

Similarly, rapid and transformational actions become ever more urgent to achieve a just, resilient, and ecologically sustainable global society. In particular, governance approaches are called upon that respond to address the respective problem dynamics and are effective to align social, economic, and ecological developments towards the sustainability goals. These governance approaches for rapid and transformational actions have to address changing and uncertain conditions and need to be responsive, flexible, and, in that sense, adaptive.

The Earth System Governance (ESG) Project as a global alliance of social science researchers in the area of governance and global environmental change evaluates current governance practices and explores novel proposals in the search for more effective governance mechanisms to address major changes and transitions in the biogeochemical systems of the planet (Biermann, 2019). In doing so, the ESG Project conceptualised earth system governance as 'the interrelated and increasingly integrated system of formal and informal rules, rule-making systems, and actor-networks at all levels of human society (from local to global) that are set up to steer societies towards preventing, mitigating, and adapting to global and local environmental change and, in particular, earth system transformation, within the normative context of sustainable development' (Biermann et al., 2009: 4). In its Science Plan of 2009, the project developed a core research focus around five analytical themes (5As) – namely, architecture, agency, adaptiveness, accountability, and allocation and access (Figure 1.1) (Biermann et al., 2009). To continue the process, the ESG Project prepared a new

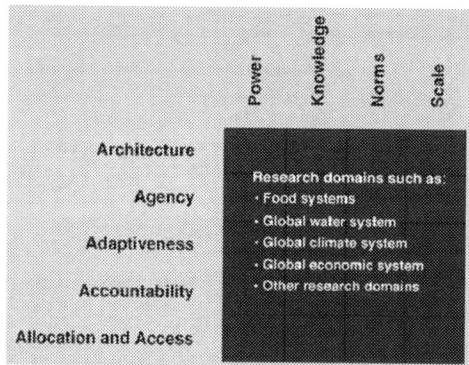

Figure 1.1 Adaptiveness in the 5As within the ESG Project Science Plan 2009.
Source: Biermann et al. (2009: 28)

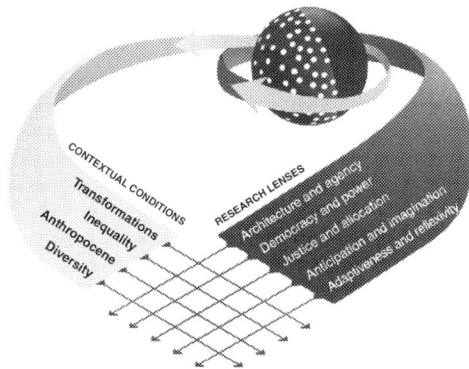

Figure 1.2 Adaptiveness and reflexivity as research lenses in the new ESG Project Science Plan 2018.
Source: ESG (2018: 19)

Science and Implementation Plan in 2018, which combined adaptiveness with reflexivity as a core theme for future research in the field organised around five research lenses and four contextual conditions (Figure 1.2) (ESG, 2018).

The Harvesting Initiative within the ESG Project aims to review the results of a decade of research on these themes and compiles key research findings in books or journal contributions (ESG, 2020). This initiative has resulted in a number of publications, special issues, and edited volumes on agency (Betsill et al., 2019); agency and empowerment (van der Heijden et al., 2019); and architecture (Biermann & Kim, 2020). This book is an outcome of this Harvesting Initiative, focusing on the analytical theme of adaptiveness.

Throughout the book, we follow the initial understanding of adaptiveness as 'an umbrella term for a set of related concepts – vulnerability, resilience, adaptation, robustness, adaptive capacity, social learning and so on – to describe changes made by social groups in response to, or in anticipation of, challenges created through environmental change' (Biermann et al., 2009: 45). Understanding adaptiveness as an umbrella for these key concepts, harvesting related research thus could draw on the related outcomes from the related fields of study. However, in this book we seek to draw connections between the respective fields among themselves and towards adaptiveness and adaptive governance in earth system governance. Thus, it is our goal to not only repeat what has been discussed in the respective fields, but also to synthesise and relate the findings to each other and to the challenges of adaptive governance. In doing so, we avoid positing one concept against another in the interest of carving out overarching insights and lessons. However, the challenge arises where to draw the boundaries of the umbrella and to scrutinise the multiple connections and relationships within or under the umbrella, including those that are implicit or not explicitly referring to adaptiveness per se. This book thus followed a pragmatic approach combining a bird's-eye perspective to see the whole picture largely with the means of a systematic literature review with a bottom-up perspective from selective discussions and empirical case studies.

Since the 2009 Science Plan postulated this notion of adaptiveness in the attempt to bring together different research strands, our interest in this book was to analyse how far it has been taken up and brought to fruition in the scholarly community and beyond. Thus, the overarching research question addressed in this book is: *How has adaptiveness, as an umbrella concept, been developed and applied in the context of earth system governance in the first decade after its inception, and what insights and practical solutions has it yielded?* Following the ESG 2009 Science Plan, this broad question will be approached by addressing four specific questions:

1. What are the politics of adaptiveness?
2. Which governance processes foster adaptiveness?
3. What attributes of governance systems enhance capacities to adapt?
4. How, when, and why does adaptiveness influence earth system governance?

Thus, this book brings together the threads of a debate that has been gaining societal relevance and academic traction throughout the last decade. This work is a collaboration written by eminent authors in the related fields and documents experiences from different world regions as well as different levels of decision-making. The 10 chapters discuss recent trends in the literature on adaptiveness and the utilisation of adaptiveness concepts and draw on case studies examining challenges and solutions requiring aspects of adaptiveness.

The structure for this chapter is as follows. Based on the introduction to the motivation and rationale for the whole book in Section 1.1, Section 1.2 examines the concept of adaptiveness by summarising the latest debates, the links to related concepts and its interlinkages with other analytical issues. The following Section 1.3 reflects on research methods to explore themes of adaptiveness. Section 1.4 presents the book structure as well as key findings from the individual book chapters. Finally, Section 1.5 discusses synthesis findings from this volume, how they relate to the 2009 Science Plan questions on adaptiveness, and the role of adaptiveness in the future of earth system governance. In this section, we put forward the findings from the chapters on the four ESG 2009 Science Plan questions listed in Section 1.1.

1.2 Adaptiveness: Related Concepts and Interlinkages

Within the context of earth system governance, adaptiveness is a catch-all term to describe changes generally made by actor groups or institutions in anticipation of or responding to risks, disruptions, or challenges resulting from environmental change. It thus relates to concepts of adaptive management, adaptive governance, vulnerability, resilience, robustness, adaptive capacity, and social learning. These concepts represent larger research traditions that overlap in parts and all address dynamics in socio-ecological systems. However, they are not identical and have partly complementary and partly divergent research foci. Acknowledging these differences, the overarching notion of adaptiveness seeks to bring together the commonalities and connections between the concepts as outlined in the following.

1.2.1 Adaptive Management and Adaptive Governance

Adaptive management is one of the most utilised concepts in the research related to adaptiveness in the sense of the 2009 ESG Science Plan. It is considered a management approach for responding to ecosystem change (Folke, 2006). It aims at maintaining and managing dynamic and at the same time resilient systems that can withstand stresses of climate change, habitat fragmentation, and other anthropogenic effects without losing its capabilities to provide essential ecosystem services (Chazdon, 2008). Active adaptive management and governance of resilience (Lebel et al., 2006) are essentially tasked with sustaining desired ecosystem states and transforming degraded ecosystems into fundamentally new and more desirable configurations (Folke, 2006). Through feedback learning and structured scenarios, actors can tackle uncertainty and unpredictability intrinsic to all socio-ecological systems (Berkes et al., 2000; Folke et al., 2002). Adaptive management, adaptive co-management, and anticipatory governance share numerous similarities with adaptive governance

(Huitema et al., 2009; Hurlbert & Gupta, 2018) that brings them together metaphorically and practically underneath the umbrella of adaptiveness.

Adaptive governance has emerged as a framework to proactively and flexibly deal with increasingly uncertain, systemic, complex problems (Dietz et al., 2003). Such governance approaches connect individuals, organisations, agencies, and institutions at multiple levels (Folke et al., 2005), and are often facilitated by key leaders and shadow networks (Olsson et al., 2006). Adaptive governance encompasses a range of interactions between actors, networks, organisations, and institutions emerging in pursuit of a desired state for social-ecological systems (SES) (Chaffin et al., 2014). They seek to align the ecosystem dynamics with governance responses, trying to match scales, complexity, and intensity between governance and SES-related problems (Termeer et al., 2010).

1.2.2 Resilience

The concept of resilience has evolved considerably since Holling's (1973) seminal paper. Resilience is proposed as 'the capacity of a system to absorb disturbance and reorganize while undergoing change so as to still retain essentially the same function, structure, identity, and feedback' (Walker et al., 2004: 5). Like adaptiveness, the concept builds on the insight into non-linear dynamics, thresholds, uncertainty, and surprise. It analyses how periods of gradual change interact with periods of rapid change, and the interaction of dynamics across temporal and spatial scales (Folke, 2006). Resilience, adaptability, and transformability are three related attributes of SES that largely determine their future trajectories (Walker et al., 2004). Adaptability refers to the capacity of actors in the system to influence resilience, while transform-ability is the capacity to create a fundamentally new system when ecological, economic, or social structures make the existing system untenable (Walker et al., 2004). With its origin in ecology, the field of study has evolved to address core social science topics of governance, power, and learning (Olsson et al., 2014). Resilience has multiple levels of meaning: as a metaphor related to sustainability, as a property of dynamic models, and as a measurable quantity that can be assessed in field studies of SES (Carpenter et al., 2001). There is a vast breadth of literature proposing various resilience frameworks and attempts to operationalise the concept into specific applications, such as the food system (e.g. Hodbod & Eakin, 2015), urban planning (Davoudi et al., 2012; Lloyd et al., 2013), and disaster management (Chang & Shinozuka, 2004; Cutter et al., 2008; Djalante et al., 2013).

1.2.3 Vulnerability

Vulnerability is defined by the Intergovernmental Panel on Climate Change (IPCC) as 'the propensity or predisposition to be adversely affected. Vulnerability encompasses a variety of concepts and elements including sensitivity or susceptibility to harm and lack of capacity to cope and adapt' (IPCC, 2014: 1775). Its key components include exposure, sensitivity, and adaptive capacity (IPCC, 2014). Miller et al. (2010) discuss whether resilience and vulnerability are complementary or conflicting concepts. They argue that resilience and vulnerability represent two related yet different approaches to understanding how systems and actors respond to change, to shocks and surprises, as well as to slow creeping changes. Vulnerability research poses many challenges including how to develop robust and credible measurements, how to incorporate diverse methods that include perceptions of risk and vulnerability, and how to incorporate governance research on the mechanisms that mediate vulnerability and promote adaptive action and resilience (Adger, 2006). General conditions of vulnerability are characterised by multiple contexts, multiple dimensions, temporal variability, multiple scales, and scale interdependency (Hufschmidt, 2011). In discussing social vulnerability, Cutter et al. (2012) proposed three main tenets for vulnerability research: (1) the identification of conditions that make people or places vulnerable to extreme natural events (i.e. an exposure model), (2) the assumption that vulnerability is a social condition (i.e. a measure of societal resistance or resilience in regard to hazards), and (3) the integration of potential exposures and societal resilience with a specific focus on particular places or regions. There is a vast number of frameworks available to assess the vulnerability of coupled human–environment systems (Turner et al., 2003) to climate change (Füssel, 2007), to natural hazards (Birkmann, 2006), or to livelihoods (Yaro, 2004).

1.2.4 Adaptive Capacity

As a component of vulnerability (Kelly & Adger, 2000; Smit et al., 2000), the IPCC defines adaptive capacity as 'the characteristics of communities, countries and regions that influence their propensity or ability to adapt' (IPCC, 2001: 882). The adaptive capacity of SES is related to the existence of social, economic, or political mechanisms for coping with (climatic) change. Even though the debate is ongoing about how to conceptualise adaptive capacity, there is broad understanding of its multidimensional character, determined by complex inter-relationships of numerous factors at different scales, and based on institutional collective responses as well as the availability of and access to resources (Cinner et al., 2018; Vincent, 2007).

Central elements of adaptive capacity are common at different scales, although the structure of each index is scale-specific (Gupta et al., 2010; Vincent, 2007). Collective action and social capital have been identified as pertinent elements of adaptive capacity in relation to the performance of institutions that cope with the risks of changes in climate (Adger, 2003). What seems to be a strongly related message for adaptiveness research is that adaptive capacity requires a diversity of responses to cope with complex systems, high dynamics, and substantial uncertainty in human-dominated environments (Elmqvist et al., 2003).

1.2.5 Robustness

Studies on robustness are commonly discussed in terms of 'network robustness' (e.g. Klau & Weiskircher, 2005) or 'modelling robustness' (e.g. Hinrichsen & Pritchard, 2011; Kuorikoski et al., 2010). Robustness can be seen as an antonym to (static) vulnerability. It is related to general resilience, which includes coping with the unknown (Scholz et al., 2012). Robustness and resilience are necessary for maintaining the adaptive capacity and work through preserving a balance among heterogeneity, modularity, and redundancy, and tightening feedback loops to provide incentives for sound stewardship (Levin & Lubchenco, 2008).

1.2.6 Social Learning

Literature on social learning has emerged rapidly in recent years, mainly originating from the field of psychology (e.g. Bandura, 1977; Mischel, 1973). Social learning is a broad concept encompassing multifaceted, more specific types and levels of learning and knowledge in relation to SES (Reed et al., 2010). These include collective or group learning and social memory, mental models and knowledge-system integration, visioning and scenario building, leadership, agents and actor groups, social networks, institutional and organisational inertia and change, adaptive capacity, transformability, and systems of adaptive governance that allow for the management of essential ecosystem services (Folke, 2006). Of particular relevance is the question of how far knowledge and learning relate to practical behaviour of actors and societies. The process of social learning involves change at and beyond the individual level to change within broader social units by way of social integrations within social networks (Reed et al., 2010). Thus, 'communities of practice' (Wenger, 2010) became a popular research focus. Through successive rounds of learning and problem-solving, these learning networks can incorporate new knowledge and related new or altered practices to deal with problems at increasingly larger scales, ideally arriving at adaptive co-management arrangements (Berkes, 2009). Through problem-sharing perspectives and working with different kinds of knowledge and competencies, multiple actors or stakeholder parties co-construct a social learning process in an emerging community of practice (Bouwen & Taillieu, 2004).

A core question in social learning studies is which organisational or societal level is concerned. Within organisations such as municipalities or corporations, organisational learning can take different forms drawing on organisational sociology (Siebenhüner & Arnold, 2007). On a national level, social learning processes have been found to relate largely to political cultures among other factors (Social Learning Group, 2001). In global environmental governance, organisations are observed to engage in one of three forms of learning: reflexive learning, adaptive learning, and no learning depending on specific learning mechanisms, change agents in leadership functions, and external triggers such as pressures from governments or non-governmental actors (Siebenhüner, 2008). Reflexive social learning informed by policy and programme evaluation constitutes an increasingly important basis for 'interactive governance' (Sanderson, 2002).

Social learning processes are crucial for building adaptiveness, since they help to cope with informational uncertainty, reduce normative uncertainty, build consensus on criteria for monitoring and evaluation, empower stakeholders to take adaptive actions, reduce conflicts and identify synergies between adaptations, and improve fairness of decisions and actions (Lebel et al., 2010). Informal networks are considered to play a crucial role in such learning processes (Pahl-Wostl, 2009). Transformative change building on fundamental social learning processes towards adaptive management have even been described as 'learning to manage by managing to learn' (Pahl-Wostl, 2007: 49).

1.3 Reflection on Research Methods

Both ESG Project Science Plans of 2009 and 2018 discuss the use and development of adequate methods for addressing the challenges and issues of earth system governance research. While Biermann et al. (2009) discuss various social science methods and stress, in particular the role and benefit of interdisciplinary research methods at the interface of the social and natural sciences, the 2018 Science Plan goes one step further. Beyond the suggestion of a set of new, innovative methods for analysing matters of earth system governance, it outlines the ontological and epistemological foundations of the research agenda and argues for a wide diversity of the ways of knowing and representing the world (ESG, 2018). Additionally, it extends the methodological portfolio and explicitly includes transdisciplinary research methods 'noting the need for engagement with broader societal actors outside of academia who also hold key knowledge and perspectives on what is both feasible and desirable as solutions to societal problems' (ESG, 2018: 84).

Among the ESG analytical problems, the theme of adaptiveness poses some particular methodological challenges. Most of the phenomena subsumed under adaptiveness are intangible and not directly measurable. Vulnerability, resilience, and robustness, for example, are inherent to a (socio-ecological) system and become only apparent when their limits are tested in times of pressure, stress, or crisis. Hence, studies around these phenomena are often placed within such settings of increased stress, describing systems responses to perturbations (see e.g. McGreavy et al., 2016). As another strategy, governance researchers try to approach resilience, for example, through the institutional and governance principles that attempt to shape the resilience of SES. In this vein, analysts take advantage of the inter-relatedness of those different concepts by relating, for instance, the adaptive capacities or arrangements for adaptive governance to the resilience of the underlying SES (e.g. Gunderson & Light, 2006). However, such a research strategy may also appear problematic because it rests on often implicit normative assumptions about those governance models, remains under-specified as to how governance modes and system properties are linked, and hence, may paint an overall simplistic picture (Biesbroek et al., 2017). In this light, the ESG Project's explicit inclusion of interdisciplinary approaches linking social and natural systems, as well as of the critical realist approaches 'to study and seek to understand generative causal mechanisms that produce events, processes and phenomena' (ESG, 2018: 78) appears particularly relevant for the study of adaptiveness.

Beyond these more general methodological issues, the study of adaptation faces some more practical methodological challenges, which could be tackled by a diversity of methodological approaches. Here, we provide a few examples.

Case studies are among the most popular research methods for studying questions of earth system governance, as the contributions of this volume highlight. In the social sciences, case studies are employed for a variety of purposes, including the detailed assessment of a phenomenon under study, the development of explanations for social outcomes and the broader generalisation of those, or the application of more general concepts in specific cases (George & Bennett, 2005).

While case studies are hardly an innovative or overlooked method, they offer great potential for the in-depth study of multifaceted issues, such as adaptiveness, as they allow for the consideration of context and place the research object within its wider social, environmental, and cultural context to trace processes in their historical evolution and to re-draw causal chains linking to specific outcomes. One great advantage here is their versatility to be combined with a magnitude of different methods and analysis techniques. Counterfactual analysis, for example, may provide one fruitful avenue to tackle the intangibility of various phenomena of adaptiveness. A counterfactual is a 'subjunctive conditional in which the antecedent is known or supposed for purposes of argument to be false' (Tetlock & Belkin, 1996: 4). In case-study research, counterfactual analysis is used to help with assessing the effect of an actual event by asking what would have happened if the event did not take place or occurred differently (Mahoney & Barrenechea, 2019). For example, in his analysis of the effectiveness of international fishing regimes, Stokke (2012) uses counterfactual analysis to assess what would have been if there was no fishing regime. This way of thinking may also prove beneficial in the study of adaptiveness as it may be used to, for instance, examine *ex post* the robustness of a specific governance solution if specific decisions were taken differently. However, *ex ante* case studies will require different complementary methods such as integrative modelling, scenario techniques, or backcasting approaches.

Counterfactual analysis can be enriched through the adept use of longitudinal within-case analysis or by comparison to others (Goertz, 2017). In longitudinal within-case analysis, a researcher takes a case where a specific phenomenon is given and goes back in time until it was not. This strategy enables the assessment of the circumstances under which a phenomenon occurred or did not occur and the significance of changes to those circumstances. For example, to analyse the effects of specific adaptive capacities on the effectiveness of a governance regime, one could trace back when specific governance measures were developed and how they affected regime effectiveness (e.g. reducing vulnerability vis-à-vis climatic changes). However, cases where these changes occur over time and can be traced back to single governance measures may be hard to find in reality. Hence, counterfactual thinking of that kind may provide a useful tool for case selection and for cross-case analysis.

The widespread use of *single- or small-N* case studies, however, may lead to a scattered research field characterised by many dispersed only loosely connected insights – a common problem in many fields of political research (Ryan, 2017). Hence, meta-reviews and analyses may be warranted, also in the study of adaptiveness, to synthesise the knowledge that is already there, and to generate new insights that go beyond the findings of the single (case) studies (Cook, 2014). One way to accumulate existing knowledge lies in reviewing and harvesting the insights produced in the various studies in the field, which is the aim of this book and especially the subject of the systematic review in Chapter 2. Another synthesis approach lies in the transformation of qualitative case studies into quantitative data through structured coding procedures, as envisioned by the case-survey meta-analysis method (Lucas, 1974). Under this method, qualitative case narratives are translated into quantitative data through coding – based on an analytical coding scheme and typically done by multiple raters – allowing for statistical analysis. For example, in their study tracing the processes and environmental impacts of social learning in participatory governance, Newig et al. (2019) draw conclusions from more than 300 cases of participatory environmental governance. Thus, the method provides for much wider generalisation over diverse settings and contexts (Jensen & Rodgers, 2001).

In general, the specific focus on governance responses and measures in relation to highly dynamic socio-ecological system developments calls for methods addressing these dynamics and temporal developments. As in anticipatory governance (ESG, 2018), forward-looking methods and approaches can help governance actors to better understand current dynamics in their future consequences and thus to act in an adaptive mode. For instance, *backcasting approaches* start out from a desired state of the respective socio-ecological system at some point in the future, and deduce specific steps and trajectories that would be required to take place before this point in time to make the desired state happen (Robinson, 2003; Quist & Vergragt, 2006). Alternatively, *foresight studies* (Meissner, 2012) or *futures studies* (Sardar, 2010) enable actors to acquire understanding of multiple future developments in complex systems. In a similar vein, *scenario techniques* have been used to involve stakeholders or various experts in the analysis of possible future developments linking it to actual and current decision-making (e.g. Bishop et al., 2007). Probably the most used method for analysing future developments, however, are *modelling approaches* of various kinds including system dynamic modelling (e.g. Kwakkel & Pruyt, 2013; Sterman, 2001), agent-based modelling (e.g. Patt & Siebenhüner, 2005), or integrative assessment (e.g. Scheuer et al., 2017). With growing interactive computing powers and social media experiences of users, serious gaming approaches gain prominence in forward-looking studies that explore problem situations and help to analyse decision-making under conditions of complexity and uncertainty (e.g. Mangnus et al., 2019; Vervoort et al., 2010). Even though these methods have not been in much use in earth system governance-related adaptiveness research yet, these methods can prove helpful in addressing the research challenges in the field in the future.

1.4 Book Structure

Subsequent to this introduction and discussion of the umbrella concept of adaptiveness the book structure starts out with the broad picture and the general concepts and progresses to more concrete case studies and practical applications. It thus runs from the general aspects to the more specific. Chapter 2 (Siebenhüner & Djalante) thus comprises a comprehensive analysis of the term 'adaptiveness' in most frequently cited research papers and shows how the theme has emerged and developed in the related literature from 1998 to 2018 (a decade before and after the first Science Plan). The particular focus of this chapter is to answer the four central research questions on adaptiveness posed in the 2009 ESG Science Plan. The next chapters add to the conceptual discussion and undertake the complex task of assessing adaptiveness. Chapter 3 (Montpetit et al.) proposes an operational framework to assess adaptive capacity, and thus suggests a method for identifying governance processes and attributes that foster adaptiveness. Chapter 4 (Fidelman) examines collaborative governance and its relationship to adaptive capacity drawing on examples from coastal resource management in the Western Pacific. Moving to the concrete applications of adaptiveness research, the following chapters focus on the governance of climate change-related challenges. Chapter 5 (Stoett & Vince) presents the cross-cutting nature of global challenges and presents an issue at the nexus between climate change, health, and biodiversity as a problem requiring collective action and adaptation. A cross-scale analysis follows in Chapter 6 (Zia), which applies the SES analytical approach to mitigation and adaptation policy instruments and sheds light on their synergies but also trade-offs. Chapter 7 (Siebenhüner et al.) applies the concept of 'lock-in' to explain how institutional, behavioural, and infrastructural factors can hinder adaptiveness in preparing for or responding to risks caused by climate change.

Subsequent chapters connect global challenges to the governance and management of landscapes and resources at different scales from international, to regional and national levels. Chapter 8 (Peach Brown) calls for more adaptiveness among the responsible international organisations after assessing mixed results of forest management instruments and development interventions in the Democratic Republic of Congo and the Central African Republic. Chapter 9 (Wurtzebach & Schultz) looks at forestry management in the United States in an analysis of the importance of multifaceted policy capacity in designing policy instruments that strike the balance between the stability and flexibility necessary for adaptive governance. Finally, Chapter 10 (Siebenhüner et al.) discusses the relevance of the book's findings for the 2018 Science Plan, the so-called Utrecht Questions formulated in 2018, and their relevance for global sustainability agendas. In some greater detail, the chapters discuss the following aspects.

Chapter 2, 'Synthesising and Identifying Emerging Issues in Adaptiveness Research within the Earth System Governance Framework (1998–2018)', by Siebenhüner and Djalante, synthesises related publications and identifies emerging issues in adaptiveness research within the earth system governance framework (1998–2018). They find that adaptiveness has not been taken up as a term in the earth system governance literature as such, but rather as linked to or implied in related concepts as mentioned earlier in this chapter. Addressing the research questions of the 2009 ESG Science Plan, the scholarly literature reports about specific attributes of governance systems at various levels and whether they propel adaptiveness. The political nature and the conflicts of adaptiveness constitute one current of this debate with remaining gaps (e.g. with regard to distributive impacts of adaptation policies). Other findings relate to the essential role of knowledge and learning in governance approaches towards adaptiveness.

Chapter 3, 'Climate Change Adaptive Capacity Assessments: Conceptual Approaches and Operational Process', by Montpetit et al., contributes to the research on adaptive capacity in three ways: first, by presenting an operational design of adaptive capacity in a diversity of contexts; second, by providing guidance on how to build an operational definition of the term coherent with the research questions and objectives at stake; and, third, by demonstrating how an operational framework of climate change adaptive capacity that integrates multiple epistemic, spatial, and temporal dimensions can be developed. The authors find that the diverse conceptualisations of adaptive capacity serve different purposes and shape the assessment criteria accordingly. They suggest that this plurality can be seen positively rather than as a challenge.

Chapter 4, 'Assessing Adaptive Capacity of Collaborative Governance Institutions', by Fidelman, explores the influence of governance institutions on adaptive capacity. Based on evidence drawn from examples of collaborative governance of coastal resources in Vietnam and Cambodia, as well as the international governance of seascape ecosystems in the Coral Triangle in the South-West Pacific, the author illustrates that institutions can both enable and disable adaptive capacity and consist of interconnected dimensions. Fidelman also supports the arguments that contextual factors matter, and power relations can be a constraining factor. Given these findings, complexity emerges as a defining property of institutional adaptive capacity. Hence, efforts aiming to assess institutional adaptive capacity should consider the relationships between types of rules and attributes of adaptive capacity, while also appraising the power relations and the surrounding social, cultural, and political context.

Chapter 5, 'The Marine Debris Nexus: Plastic, Climate Change, Biodiversity, and Human Health', by Stoett and Vince, describes the threats posed by the abundance of marine plastic pollution and links it to broader issues such as climate change, biodiversity conservation, and their impacts on human health. Current international agreements are non-binding and rely on nations to adopt their own laws and regulations and the slow or absent implementation of market-based instruments indicate that they will not suffice to reduce macro- and microplastics. Stoett and Vince suggest that most institutions seem better equipped to address single-issue problems. Currently, global political will and the technical sophistication to apply legal frameworks to multiple-issue problems are missing links. Large knowledge gaps and other unanswered questions are further obstacles to overcome, but a cross-cutting, nexus approach could push progress and enhance the adaptive capacity necessary for this wicked issue. The policy suggestions are seen as adaptive measures, which would constitute collective adaptation to mitigate plastic waste and climate change and protect marine ecosystems and with them global health necessary for moving toward the SDGs.

Chapter 6, 'Synergies and Trade-Offs Between Climate Change Adaptation and Mitigation Across Multiple Scales of Governance', by Zia, uses adaptive governance of SES as a framework to evaluate the mitigation and adaptation synergies and trade-offs through the United Nations Framework Convention on Climate Change (UNFCCC) policy mechanisms – namely, REDD+, the Clean Development Mechanisms (CDM), and the Adaptation Fund. The author argues that integrated adaptive governance of SES may provide a coherent framework to systematically assess the synergies and trade-offs of different policy mechanisms ensuing from the Paris Agreement and other global to local climate policy and governance actions.

Chapter 7, 'Lock-Ins in Climate Adaptation Governance: Conceptual and Empirical Approaches', by Siebenhüner et al., builds on the growing body of literature on barriers to adaptation to climate change, this chapter focuses on 'lock-ins' as a particular conceptual approach to understanding path dependencies. The chapter discusses, first, how lock-ins can be conceptualised, what indicators might identify them, and how they can be detected and described. Second, it postulates the emergence of lock-ins in climate adaptation policies by reference to central mechanisms originating from: (1) knowledge, discourses, and expertise; (2) physical infrastructures; (3) institutions and past policy tools; and (4) actors and their respective mental frames. In summary, the chapter illuminates lock-ins as phenomena that embody the opposite of adaptiveness and finds that institutional, infrastructural, and behavioural attributes of systems may individually or collectively prevent that system from changing.

Chapter 8, 'Governance and Climate Change Mitigation and Adaptation in Conflict-Affected Countries of Central Africa', by Peach Brown, identifies types of conflicts based on four initiatives in reducing emissions from deforestation and land degradation (REDD+) in the Democratic Republic of Congo and Central African Republic. This chapter connects adaptiveness to good governance, which is associated with a lower probability of conflict-related violence at the subnational level. The chapter discusses how by working with national governments to reform the forest management, address issues of tenure security, engage diverse stakeholders, and require accountability and transparency in the REDD+ process, these initiatives are generally promoting essential elements of good governance.

Chapter 9, 'Policy Tools and Capacities for Adaptiveness in US Public Land Management', by Wurtzebach and Schultz, analyses examples from federal forestry and land management in the United States and applies the concepts of adaptive governance and adaptive management. While adaptive governance theorists have outlined candidate legal tools for improved adaptiveness, the authors point out that less attention has been given to the resources and capacities needed to design and operationalise policy across multiple levels of governance. Wurtzebach and Schultz find that innovative policy changes allow for novel and more adaptive approaches to governing issues of larger scale, but recognise a need for better understanding of how new institutions interact with old ones and where and which new capacities could further progress.

Finally, Chapter 10, 'Adaptiveness in Earth System Governance: Synthesis, Policy Relevance, and the Way Forward', by Siebenhüner et al., revisits adaptiveness as an umbrella concept and its relations to the new 2018 Science Plan. Following our quest to address the four questions on adaptiveness in Chapter 1, we note that these answers may never be conclusively answered and the answers themselves may evolve. The chapter synthesises findings from the chapters of this book, particularly in regard to five key questions that all authors were invited to answer in their respective chapters. The concluding chapter thus brings together responses to these so-called Utrecht Questions. These questions were identified during the 2018 ESG Conference in Utrecht, the Netherlands, where the editors organised a meeting to discuss the progress of each chapter and discussed how the concept of adaptiveness has developed over time, remaining research gaps, and future research agendas.

1.5 Addressing the Four Adaptiveness Questions from the 2009 ESG Science Plan: Looking Back to Move Forward

The discussions and findings collected for this book are only a small portion of the research and discourse surrounding the theme of adaptiveness. Metaphorically, we attempt to weave threads gathered to form strands of common themes that will join many others to continue strengthening the network of ideas and lessons through the ESG Project and for more sustainable progress and problem-solving of global challenges.

In this section, we aim to summarise the insights collected within the Harvesting Initiative on the theme of adaptiveness to address questions from Biermann et al. (2009: 28) and ESG (2018: 19). Although these answers may never be conclusively answered and the answers themselves may evolve, at the end of this volume we will move on to subsequent questions (called the 'Utrecht Questions' because of their origin at an ESG conference) on adaptiveness to be addressed in the concluding chapter.

1.5.1 *What Are the Politics of Adaptiveness?*

The politics of adaptiveness refer to the political nature and the conflicts of adaptiveness, recognising that responses to massive changes in the ecological systems substantially impact political relations and power structures on different governance levels. At the same time, political factors and power relations themselves constitute factors that affect the adaptiveness of socio-ecological systems. Decisions about the necessity of intervention, choices on the direction of change in adaptation processes, and *what or who* should adapt are all inherently political matters. As such, the determination of the questions as to if, what, and how systems adapt may be contentious. Also, the time frames can be considered a political matter with large discrepancies between the pace of environmental change and long-term planning for adaptation and comparatively short electoral cycles.

Findings from Chapter 2 suggest that much of the literature is dominated by assessment tools and indicators for vulnerability, resilience, and adaptive capacity while conflictive and distributive effects tend to be neglected. In the interest of strengthening socio-ecological system capacities against climate or other environmental impacts, the political nature of adaptation measures and supportive policies is not in the core focus of the literature. Thus, consequences (e.g. for poor or other marginalised groups) remain out of sight and deserve more research attention in the future.

While Montpetit et al. in Chapter 3 focus on the indicator and the analytical rather than the power-related dimension of adaptiveness, they explain the political nature of the diverse adaptive capacity concepts and definitions. In doing so, they link the perspective on indicators and assessment tools with the political and power-focused view on whose interests are being served by which assessment tool. Likewise, Fidelman in Chapter 4 finds in the analysis of three case studies that power relations can impede adaptation efforts. The same seems to hold true for conflicts particularly in conflict-ridden areas and countries such as the Democratic Republic of Congo, as Peach Brown in Chapter 8 carves out.

What is more, the political conflicts and power relations from other policy fields, particularly climate mitigation, seem to impact on adaptation governance as well. Zia highlights this special relationship in Chapter 6, and in Chapter 5 Stoett and Vince describe relationships between different policy domains and the overlaps between them.

1.5.2 *Which Governance Processes Foster Adaptiveness?*

In the 2009 ESG Science Plan, Biermann et al. (2009: 48) emphasise the need to better understand the 'extent to which governance systems are adaptive and evolve in response to earth system challenges'. Thus, success of policies and governance processes cannot only be measured in actual environmental or social improvements in the short term, but need to be understood in relation to a dynamically changing socio-ecological system environment. This aspect of almost constant change implies that a governance response that was once effective might no longer be useful in the resulting, changed system environment. Thus, in Chapter 2, we find that monitoring these system changes is almost as essential as the capacity of governance systems to learn and reverse the course based on knowledge and new insights. Similarly, social learning at different scales has proven to be a pivotal governance process to address this dynamic nature of socio-ecological systems. If successful, it will lead into larger-scale transformative change towards adaptiveness at different levels of governance including national jurisdictions and international governance processes. In this volume, these processes are only touched upon implicitly, particularly in Chapter 8, which calls for international organisations that intervene in environmental matters in developing countries to be more reflective and learn from their mistakes, while dealing with complex issues in regions with weak governance structures and in some cases violent conflicts.

Scrutinising specific governance processes towards adaptiveness, Chapter 4 highlights collaborative governance institutions as one approach to bring together different actors as well as governance processes to tackle climate impacts. Another essential capacity of adaptive governance systems is identified by Wurtzebach and Schultz in Chapter 9. They find that modern adaptive forestry governance approaches and policies need to be compatible with older pieces of legislation and need to comply with rules and norms at other governance levels, such as the national level.

By contrast, Chapter 7 develops a conceptualisation of non-successful adaptiveness by highlighting lock-in effects. Siebenhüner et al. stress the need to better understand these rigidities and self-reinforcing mechanisms of governance decisions, instruments, and practices that inhibit flexibility and reduce the likelihood of change and adaptation to altered environmental conditions.

1.5.3 *What Attributes of Governance Systems Enhance Capacities to Adapt?*

The 2009 ESG Science Plan also seeks to better understand specific attributes of governance systems at various levels, but mainly whether and how they propel adaptiveness. The review of the most cited papers in Chapter 2 revealed that key attributes include participation, multilayered institutions, and knowledge-based deliberative governance approaches. However, several studies indicate that it is not essential to involve everybody, but to be thematically selective and to design the participatory processes well. In particular, real participation in decision-making has been valued most by participants and leads to effective outcomes. Also, learning and knowledge sharing requires a structured and well-moderated process to advance adaptive capacities and practical change.

Discussions relating to this question also recur throughout the other chapters in this volume. Here, the array of attributes relating to adaptiveness are often sorted into various categories from adaptive capacity to analytical, operational, and political capacities and how they manifest at the individual, organisational, and systemic levels. Together the attributes enable governing institutions to strike the right balance of stability and flexibility for adaptiveness supported by well-designed and implemented policies and tools. Among these attributes are leadership, communication, networking, and analytical skills; public trust-building and learning capacity; accountability mechanisms, inter-organisational social capital, and effective resource management. Adaptive management and adaptive governance may look or function differently in different contexts, but generally speaking, attributes that help governance systems reconcile multiple interests, deal with uncertainty and complexity, make informed decisions, and solve problems are also the traits that enhance their ability to adapt.

1.5.4 How, When, and Why Does Adaptiveness Influence Earth System Governance?

Findings from Chapter 2 suggest that positive answers to this question refer to the diversity of sectors relevant and involved in adaptiveness in general and into climate adaptation in particular. For instance, the water sector is involved as well as coastal protection, agriculture, urban planning, the health sector, and others. These connections are described in Chapter 5 addressing links between plastic, climate change, and biodiversity that are often overlooked, but are there and require common approaches considering the nexus between the problem and issue areas. Through this cross-sectoral nature of the topic of adaptation, connections to other issue areas and policy fields lie in the concept itself. However, the chances of concepts and insights on adaptiveness to reach out to other fields hinges on the absence of barriers that have been intensively discussed in the related literature. Some criticism and a conceptual way forward can be found in Chapter 7, which focuses on climate adaptation lock-ins.

Recapitulating these insights and reflecting on the chapters ahead has demonstrated that researchers continually advance their understanding of adaptiveness, the processes and characteristics which promote it, and its necessity for sustainable developments and problem-solving. At the same time, observing the current developments in response to a global pandemic has shown that decision makers and many citizens around the world themselves can adapt to sudden and extreme threats. However, it is imperative to recognise that the pandemic is not analogue to other environmental, wicked problems and that the adaptive actions to prevent its further spread are neither sustainable nor come from democratic decisions. This example shows the difficulty in balancing effectiveness and timeliness with accountability and acceptance (Weible et al., 2020). Nevertheless, it offers lessons on the vulnerability of global societies and particular groups, may help to build resilience among neighbours and communities, and acts as a window of opportunity to reflect on and learn from our practices and choices. Against this backdrop, adaptiveness emerges as highly relevant and omnipresent.

In summary, this chapter has discussed the rationale and motivation for the book, which correspond to the ESG Project Harvesting Initiatives, but also academic interest in conceptualising and comprehending adaptiveness as a theme. We have introduced the conceptual development of adaptiveness, its related concepts, and their junctures, which will be discussed in further depth in the next chapter.

References

Adger, W.N. (2003). Social aspects of adaptive capacity. In J.B. Smith, R.J.T. Klein, & S. Huq, eds., *Climate Change, Adaptive Capacity and Development*. London: Imperial College Press, 29–49.

(2006). Vulnerability. *Global Environmental Change*, 16(3), 268–81.

Bandura, A. (1977). *Social Learning Theory*. Englewood Cliffs, NJ: Prentice Hall.

Berkes, F. (2009). Evolution of co-management: role of knowledge generation, bridging organizations and social learning. *Journal of Environmental Management*, 90(5), 1692–702.

Berkes, F., Folke, C., & Colding, J. (eds.). (2000). *Linking Social and Ecological Systems: Management Practices and Social Mechanisms for Building Resilience*. Cambridge, UK: Cambridge University Press.

Betsill, M.M., Benney, T.M., & Gerlak, A.K. (eds.). (2019). *Agency in Earth System Governance*. Cambridge, UK: Cambridge University Press.

Biermann, F. (2019). Editorial to the inaugural issue of 'Earth System Governance'. *Earth System Governance*, 1, 100001.

Biermann, F., Betsill, M.M., Gupta, J. et al. (2009). *Earth System Governance: People, Places, and the Planet: Science Implementation Plan of the Earth System Governance Project*. Bonn: International Human Dimensions Programme on Global Environmental Change.

Biermann, F. & Kim, R.E. (eds.). (2020). *Architectures of Earth System Governance: Institutional Complexity and Structural Transformation*. Cambridge, UK: Cambridge University Press.

Biesbroek, G.R., Dupuis, J., & Wellstead, A. (2017). Explaining through causal mechanisms: resilience and governance of social-ecological systems. *Current Opinion in Environmental Sustainability*, 28, 64–70.

Birkmann, J. (2006). Measuring vulnerability to promote disaster-resilient societies: conceptual frameworks and definitions. In J., Birkmann, ed., *Measuring Vulnerability to*

Natural Hazards: Towards Disaster Resilient Societies. Tokyo and New York: United Nations University Press, 9–54.

Bishop, P., Hines, A., & Collins, T. (2007). The current state of scenario development: an overview of techniques. *Foresight*, 9(1), 5–25.

Bouwen, R. & Taillieu, T. (2004). Multi-party collaboration as social learning for interdependence: Developing relational knowing for sustainable natural resource management. *Journal of Community and Applied Social Psychology*, 14(3), 137–53.

Carpenter, S., Walker, B., Anderies, J.M., & Abel, N. (2001). From metaphor to measurement: resilience of what to what? *Ecosystems*, 4(8), 765–81.

Chaffin, B.C., Gosnell, H., & Cosens, B.A. (2014). A decade of adaptive governance scholarship: synthesis and future directions. *Ecology and Society*, 19(3), 56.

Chang, S.E. & Shinozuka, M. (2004). Measuring improvements in the disaster resilience of communities. *Earthquake Spectra*, 20(3), 739–55.

Chazdon, R.L. (2008). Beyond deforestation: restoring forests and ecosystem services on degraded lands. *Science*, 320(5882), 1458–60.

Cinner, J.E., Adger, W.N., Allison, E.H. et al. (2018). Building adaptive capacity to climate change in tropical coastal communities. *Nature Climate Change*, 8, 117–23.

Cook, T.D. (2014). Generalizing causal knowledge in the policy sciences: external validity as a task of both multi-attribute representation and multi-attribute extrapolation. *Journal of Policy Analysis and Management*, 33(2), 527–36.

Cutter, S.L., Barnes, L., Berry, M. et al. (2008). A place-based model for understanding community resilience to natural disasters. *Global Environmental Change*, 18(4), 598–606.

Cutter, S.L., Boruff, B.J., & Shirley, W.L. (2012). Social vulnerability to environmental hazards. In S.L. Cutter, ed., *Hazards, Vulnerability and Environmental Justice*. London: Routledge, 143–60.

Davoudi, S., Shaw, K., Haider, J. et al. (2012). Resilience: a bridging concept or a dead end? 'Reframing' resilience: challenges for planning theory and practice interacting traps: resilience assessment of a pasture management system in Northern Afghanistan urban resilience: what does it mean in planning practice? Resilience as a useful concept for climate change adaptation? The politics of resilience for planning: a cautionary note. *Planning Theory & Practice*, 13(2), 299–333.

Dietz, T., Ostrom, E., & Stern, P.C. (2003). The struggle to govern the commons. *Science*, 302(5652), 1907–12.

Djalante, R., Holley, C., Thomalla, F., & Carnegie, M. (2013). Pathways for adaptive and integrated disaster resilience. *Natural Hazards*, 69(3), 2105–35.

Elmqvist, T., Folke, C., Nyström, M. et al. (2003). Response diversity, ecosystem change, and resilience. *Frontiers in Ecology and the Environment*, 1(9), 488–94.

Earth System Governance (ESG) Project. (2018). *Earth System Governance: Science and Implementation Plan of the Earth System Governance Project*. Utrecht: ESG Project.
   (2020). Research findings. Retrieved from www.earthsystemgovernance.org/research-findings/.

Folke, C. (2006). Resilience: the emergence of a perspective for social-ecological systems analyses. *Global Environmental Change*, 16(3), 253–67.

Folke, C., Carpenter, S., Elmqvist, T. et al. (2002). Resilience and sustainable development: building adaptive capacity in a world of transformations. *AMBIO: A Journal of the Human Environment*, 31(5), 437–40.

Folke, C., Hahn, T., Olsson, P., & Norberg, J. (2005). Adaptive governance of social-ecological systems. *Annual Review of Environment and Resources*, 30, 441–73.

Füssel, H.M. (2007). Vulnerability: a generally applicable conceptual framework for climate change research. *Global Environmental Change*, 17(2), 155–67.

George, A.L. & Bennett, A. (2005). *Case Studies and Theory Development in the Social Sciences*. Cambridge, MA: MIT Press.

Goertz, G. (2017). *Multimethod Research, Causal Mechanisms, and Case Studies: An Integrated Approach*. Princeton, NJ: Princeton University Press.

Gunderson L.H. & Light. S.S. (2006). Adaptive management and adaptive governance in the Everglades ecosystem. *Policy Sciences*, 39, 323–34.

Gupta, J., Termeer, C., Klostermann, J. et al. (2010). The adaptive capacity wheel: a method to assess the inherent characteristics of institutions to enable the adaptive capacity of society. *Environmental Science & Policy*, 13(6), 459–71.

Hinrichsen, D. & Pritchard, A.J. (2011). *Mathematical Systems Theory I: Modelling, State Space Analysis, Stability and Robustness* (Vol. 48). Berlin: Springer Science & Business Media.

Hodbod, J. & Eakin, H. (2015). Adapting a social-ecological resilience framework for food systems. *Journal of Environmental Studies and Sciences*, 5(3), 474–84.

Holling, C.S. (1973). Resilience and stability of ecological systems. *Annual Review of Ecology and Systematics*, 4(1), 1–23.

Hufschmidt, G. (2011). A comparative analysis of several vulnerability concepts. *Natural Hazards*, 58(2), 621–43.

Huitema, D., Mostert, E., Egas, W. et al. (2009). Adaptive water governance: assessing the institutional prescriptions of adaptive (co-)management from a governance perspective and defining a research agenda. *Ecology and Society*, 14(1), 26.

Hurlbert, M.A. & Gupta, J. (2019). An institutional analysis method for identifying policy instruments facilitating the adaptive governance of drought. *Environmental Science & Policy*, 93, 221–31.

Intergovernmental Panel on Climate Change (IPCC). (2001). Adaptation to climate change in the context of sustainable development and equity. In J.J. McCarthy, O.F. Canziani, N.A. Leary, D.J. Dokken, & K.S. White, eds., *Climate Change 2001: Impacts, Adaptation and Vulnerability*. Retrieved from https://archive.ipcc.ch/ipccre ports/tar/wg2/pdf/wg2TARchap18.pdf.

Intergovernmental Panel on Climate Change (IPCC). (2014). Annex II: glossary. In V.R. Barros, C.B. Field, D.J. Dokken et al., eds., *Climate Change 2014: Impacts, Adaptation, and Vulnerability. Part B: Regional Aspects. Contribution of Working Group II to the Fifth Assessment Report of the Intergovernmental Panel on Climate Change*. Cambridge, UK: Cambridge University Press, 1757–76.

Intergovernmental Panel on Climate Change (IPCC). (2018). *Global Warming of 1.5°C: An IPCC Special Report on the Impacts of Global Warming of 1.5°C above Pre-Industrial Levels and Related Global Greenhouse Gas Emission Pathways, in the Context of Strengthening the Global Response to the Threat of Climate Change, Sustainable Development, and Efforts to Eradicate Poverty*. Geneva: IPCC.

Intergovernmental Panel on Climate Change (IPCC). (2019a). *Climate Change and Land: An IPCC Special Report on Climate Change, Desertification, Land Degradation, Sustainable Land Management, Food Security, and Greenhouse Gas Fluxes in Terrestrial Ecosystems*. Geneva: IPCC.

Intergovernmental Panel on Climate Change (IPCC). (2019b). *IPCC Special Report on the Ocean and Cryosphere in a Changing Climate*. Geneva: IPCC.

Intergovernmental Science-Policy Platform on Biodiversity and Ecosystem Services (IPBES). (2019). *Summary for Policymakers of the Global Assessment Report on*

Biodiversity and Ecosystem Services of the Intergovernmental Science-Policy Platform on Biodiversity and Ecosystem Services. Bonn: IPBES Secretariat.

Jensen, J.L. & Rodgers, R. (2001). Cumulating the intellectual gold of case study research. *Public Administration Review*, 61(2), 235–46.

Kelly, P.M. & Adger, W.N. (2000). Theory and practice in assessing vulnerability to climate change and Facilitating adaptation. *Climatic Change*, 47(4), 325–52.

Klau, G.W. & Weiskircher, R. (2005). Robustness and resilience. In U. Brandes & T. Erlebach, eds., *Network Analysis: Lecture Notes in Computer Science* (Vol. 3418). Berlin: Springer, 417–37.

Kuorikoski, J., Lehtinen, A., & Marchionni, C. (2010). Economic modelling as robustness analysis. *British Journal for the Philosophy of Science*, 61(3), 541–67.

Kwakkel, J.H. & Pruyt, E. (2013). Exploratory modeling and analysis: an approach for model-based foresight under deep uncertainty. *Technological Forecasting and Social Change*, 80(3), 419–31.

Lebel, L., Anderies, J.L., Campbell, B. et al. (2006). Governance and the capacity to manage resilience in regional social-ecological systems. *Ecology and Society*, 11(11), 19.

Lebel, L., Grothmann, T., & Siebenhüner, B. (2010). The role of social learning in adaptiveness: insights from water management. *International Environmental Agreements: Politics, Law and Economics*, 10(4), 333–53.

Levin, S.A. & Lubchenco, J. (2008). Resilience, robustness, and marine ecosystem-based management. *Bioscience*, 58(1), 27–32.

Lloyd, M.G., Peel, D., & Duck, R.W. (2013). Towards a social-ecological resilience framework for coastal planning. *Land Use Policy*, 30(1), 925–33.

Lucas, W.A. (1974). *The Case Survey Method: Aggregating Case Experience*. Santa Monica, CA: Rand Corporation.

McGreavy, B., Calhoun, A., Jansujwicz, J., & Levesque, V. (2016). Citizen science and natural resource governance: program design for vernal pool policy innovation. *Ecology and Society*, 21(2), 48.

Mahoney, J. & Barrenechea, R. (2019). The logic of counterfactual analysis in case-study explanation. *British Journal of Sociology*, 70, 306–38.

Mangnus, A.C., Vervoot, J.M., McGreevy, S.R. et al. (2019). New pathways for governing food system transformations: a pluralistic practice-based futures approach using visioning, back-casting, and serious gaming. *Ecology and Society*, 24(4), 2. doi: https://doi.org/10.5751/ES-11014-240402.

Meissner, D. (2012). Results and impact of national foresight studies. *Futures*, 44(10), 905–13.

Miller, F., Osbhar, H., Boyd, E. et al. (2010). Resilience and vulnerability: complementary or conflicting concepts? *Ecology and Society*, 15(3), 11.

Mischel, W. (1973). Toward a cognitive social learning reconceptualization of personality. *Psychological Review*, 80(4), 252.

Newig, J., Jager, N.W., Kochskämper, E., & Challies, E. (2019). Learning in participatory environmental governance – its antecedents and effects: findings from a case survey meta-analysis. *Journal of Environmental Policy & Planning*, 21(3), 213–27.

Olsson, P., Galaz, V., & Boonstra, W. (2014). Sustainability transformations: a resilience perspective. *Ecology and Society*, 19(4), 1.

Olsson, P., Gunderson, L.H., Carpenter, S.R. et al. (2006). Shooting the rapids: navigating transitions to adaptive governance of social-ecological systems. *Ecology and Society*, 11(1), 18.

Pahl-Wostl, C. (2007). Transitions towards adaptive management of water facing climate and global change. *Water Resources Management*, 21(1), 49–62.
   (2009). A conceptual framework for analysing adaptive capacity and multi-level learning processes in resource governance regimes. *Global Environmental Change*, 19(3), 354–65.
Patt, A. & Siebenhüner, B. (2005). Agent-based modeling and adaptation to climate change. *DIW-Vierteljahresheft*, 74(2), 310–20.
Quist, J. & Vergragt, P. (2006). Past and future of backcasting: the shift to stakeholder participation and a proposal for a methodological framework. *Futures*, 38(9), 1027–45.
Reed, M.S., Evely, A.S., Cundill, G. et al. (2010). What is social learning?. *Ecology and Society*, 15(4), r1.
Robinson, J. (2003). Future subjunctive: backcasting as social learning. *Futures*, 35(8), 839–56.
Ryan, M. (2017). Using cases in political science: reflections on Keith Dowding's 'The Philosophy and Methods of Political Science'. *Political Studies Review*, 15(2), 194–200.
Sanderson, I. (2002). Evaluation, policy learning and evidence-based policy making. *Public Administration*, 80(1), 1–22.
Sardar, Z. (2010). The namesake: futures; futures studies; futurology; futuristic; foresight – what's in a name? *Futures*, 42(3), 177–84.
Scheuer, S., Haase, D., & Volk, M. (2017). Integrative assessment of climate change for fast-growing urban areas: measurement and recommendations for future research. *PloS One*, 12(12), e0189451.
Scholz, R.W., Blumer, Y.B., & Brand, F.S. (2012). Risk, vulnerability, robustness, and resilience from a decision-theoretic perspective. *Journal of Risk Research*, 15(3), 313–30.
Siebenhüner, B. (2008). Learning in international organizations in global environmental governance. *Global Environmental Politics*, 8(4), 92–116.
Siebenhüner, B. & Arnold, M. (2007). Organizational learning to manage sustainable development. *Business Strategy and the Environment*, 16(5), 339–53.
Smit, B., Burton, I., Klein, R. & Wandel, J. (2000). An anatomy of adaptation to climate change and variability. *Climatic Change*, 45, 223–21.
Social Learning Group. (2001). *Learning to Manage Global Environmental Risks: A Comparative History of Social Responses to Climate Change, Ozone Depletion, and Acid Rain*. Cambridge, MA: MIT Press.
Sterman, J.D. (2001). System dynamics modeling: tools for learning in a complex world. *California Management Review*, 43(4), 8–25.
Stokke, O. (2012). *Disaggregating International Regimes*. Cambridge, MA: MIT Press.
Termeer, C.J., Dewulf, A., & van Lieshout, M. (2010). Disentangling scale approaches in governance research: comparing monocentric, multilevel, and adaptive governance. *Ecology and Society*, 15(4), 29.
Tetlock, P.E. & Belkin, A. (1996). *Counterfactual Thought Experiments in World Politics: Logical, Methodological, and Psychological Perspectives*. Princeton, NJ: Princeton University Press.
Turner, B.L., Kasperson, R.E., Matsone, P.A. et al. (2003). A framework for vulnerability analysis in sustainability science. *Proceedings of the National Academy of Sciences*, 100(14), 8074–9.
United Nations (UN). (2020). Coronavirus global health emergency. Retrieved from www.un.org/en/coronavirus/.

United Nations Environment Programme (UNEP). (2019). *UNEP Global Environment Outlook (GEO-6): Healthy Planet, Healthy People*. Nairobi: UNEP.

van der Heijden, J., Bulkeley, H., & Certomà, C. (eds.) (2019). *Urban Climate Politics: Agency and Empowerment*. Cambridge, UK: Cambridge University Press.

Vervoort, J.M., Kok, K., van Lammeren, R., & Veldkamp, T. (2010). Stepping into futures: exploring the potential of interactive media for participatory scenarios on social-ecological systems. *Futures*, 42(6), 604–16.

Vincent, K. (2007). Uncertainty in adaptive capacity and the importance of scale. *Global Environmental Change*, 17(1), 12–24.

Walker, B., Holling, C.S., Carpenter, S.R., & Kinzig, A. (2004). Resilience, adaptability and transformability in social-ecological systems. *Ecology and Society*, 9(2), 5.

Weible, C.M., Nohrstedt, D., Cairney, P. et al. (2020). COVID-19 and the policy sciences: initial reactions and perspectives. *Policy Sciences*. doi: https://doi.org/10.1007/s11077-020-09381-4.

Wenger, E. (2010). Communities of practice and social learning systems: the career of a concept. In C. Blackmore, ed., *Social Learning Systems and Communities of Practice* . London: Springer, 179–98.

World Health Organization (WHO). (2020). Coronavirus disease 2019. Retrieved from www.who.int/emergencies/diseases/novel-coronavirus-2019.

Yaro, J.A. (2004). Theorizing food insecurity: building a livelihood vulnerability framework for researching food insecurity. *Norwegian Journal of Geography*, 58(1), 23–37.

2

Synthesising and Identifying Emerging Issues in Adaptiveness Research within the Earth System Governance Framework (1998–2018)

BERND SIEBENHÜNER AND RIYANTI DJALANTE

2.1 Introduction

The Earth System Governance (ESG) Project developed a Science and Implementation Plan in 2008 and put forward a research agenda revolving around five analytical themes (Biermann et al., 2009) (Figure 1.1 in Chapter 1). As one of these core research themes, 'adaptiveness' has been introduced as an umbrella term embracing a set of related concepts: vulnerability, resilience, adaptation, robustness, adaptive capacity, and social learning. In essence, the notion of adaptiveness refers to governance processes and changes created by social groups in response to, or in anticipation of, challenges through social-ecological change. Thus adaptiveness 'refers to governance of adaptation to social-ecological change as well as the processes of change and adaptation within governance systems' (Biermann et al., 2009: 45). Giving it academic traction, the ESG Science Plan 2009 phrased four questions related to adaptiveness: 'First, what are the politics of adaptiveness? Second, which governance processes foster adaptiveness? Third, what attributes of governance systems enhance capacities to adapt? Fourth, how, when and why does adaptiveness influence earth system governance?' (Biermann et al., 2009: 45).

Building on the research addressing these questions, the earth system governance community has decided to keep the topic of adaptiveness also in the second Science Plan as of 2018 (ESG, 2018). Here, adaptiveness has been combined with the research lens on reflexivity. According to the new Science Plan, adaptiveness emphasises responses to changing social and ecological conditions (which may be coordinated, self-organised, or emergent), while reflexivity emphasises the centrality of critical scrutiny of prevailing values and practices in governing processes of change (ESG, 2018).

In this chapter, we take stock of what has been studied in the broader field of adaptiveness following the publication of the ESG 2009 Science Plan. We seek to examine how the concept has been taken up by researchers in the community and how adaptiveness research in the decade after the first Science Plan has influenced subsequent research particularly in helping to understand governance of global environmental change. It is based on a systematic literature review (SLR) of the relevant contributions in the years between 1998 and 2018 (a decade before and after the ESG Science Plan). We selected this time period considering a decade before and a decade after the work and publication of the 2009 Science Plan and its implementation phase until December 2018. While the main analysis focuses on the literature in this time range (2008–2018), we initially did a quick review on how adaptiveness has been considered as a single term in the literature.

In the course of this chapter, we first outline the method for a SLR (Section 2.2). Section 2.3 discusses the results based on the frequent and keywords analysis within the period of 1998–2018. In Section 2.4, we discuss key findings in the literature on adaptiveness based on the most-cited literature within the period between 2008 and 2018. This discussion is organised based on the four questions on adaptiveness within the 2009 Science Plan. In Section 2.5, we identify central strands of this research on adaptiveness including cross-cutting issues within the earth system governance community and bring together essential findings concerning the four guiding research questions from the most influential publications in the field. It then seeks to develop ideas for future research agendas and implementation needs in the field of adaptiveness. We complement this with a discussion on the policy relevance and future research needs.

2.2 Method of the SLR

Following our objective to arrive at a better oversight over the adaptiveness-related literature, we conducted a multilayered SLR using the Scopus research engine. A SLR is characterised by clearly formulated questions that use systematic and explicit methods to identify, select, and appraise relevant research (Robinson & Lowe, 2015; Xiao & Watson, 2019). When there is a fast-growing number of literature and empirical studies, SLR is an important method to assess and aggregate research outcomes through a balanced and objective summary of research (Brereton et al., 2007; Xiao & Watson, 2019). With recognition of the literature comparing strengths and weaknesses of different academic databases such as PubMed, Scopus, Web of Science, and Google Scholar (Bakkalbasi et al., 2006; Bar-Ilan, 2008; Falagas et al., 2008; Kulkarni et al., 2009), we chose the Scopus research engine since it is considered the largest database of the peer-reviewed literature (Burnham, 2006; De Moya-Anegón et al., 2007; Leydesdorff et al., 2010). It includes the social as well as the natural sciences and is internationally recognised. Based on a systematic search on the methodology of literature reviews, Xiao and Watson (2019) develop a typology and suggest steps in conducting a SLR that we use in this chapter (Table 2.1).

We chose the cut-off date of the search to be 31 December 2018. The *first* search we employed the terms 'Adaptive*' and 'Govern*' and 'Manag*'. More specifically, our search string was '(TITLE-ABS-KEY (Adaptive*) AND TITLE-ABS-KEY (Governance*) OR TITLE-ABS-KEY (Management*))', which resulted in a total hit of 67,389 publications as for 31 December 2018. Due to the wide search terms, further steps to narrow down the search were necessary in order to achieve more precise and appropriate results relevant for the thematic interest of our search. In the *second* stage, we thus applied several exclusions specified towards the subject area of governance research, document types, and source titles. As less than 5 per cent of the total literature are non-English literature, we also restricted the search to English-language publications. After the refinement of the broader time frame, there were overall results of 9,859 publications (1998 to 2018). These publications were then analysed quantitatively with bibliometric methods as documented in the following section. In doing so, the publications were examined in terms of authorships, references, citations, keywords, places of focus, types of publications, impact factors, time of publications and topics and sub-topics of research.

In a *third* stage, we narrowed down the time frame to publications that appeared between 2008 and 2018 after the first ESG Science Plan was published. Among the resulting hits, we identified initially 50 of those publications that have the highest citations from which we sorted out another 15 that were not thematically or disciplinarily relevant. There are 35 most-cited and most-relevant publications included in the final list (Table 2.2 in the Annex). Thereby, a qualitative analysis of the abstracts and the full texts became possible that will be presented and discussed in the later part of this chapter. The discussion also refers to more recent and thematically relevant literature that have not yet received high citation numbers due to their novelty.

2.3 An Overview of Progress of Research on Adaptiveness

2.3.1 'Adaptiveness' as a Single Term since 1900

The first question that we sought answers to was whether and how the term 'adaptiveness' as such has been used in the scientific literature in general and whether it has been taken up in the field of environmental governance research. Our bibliometric research on adaptiveness as a single word revealed that there are 7,297 articles using the term in the title, keyword, and/or abstract (between 1900 and 2018). Scopus has a feature that allows users to analyse the results in graphic form, as those shown in Figures 2.1 and 2.2. Figure 2.1 shows the use of

Table 2.1. *Key steps in the SLR (following Yu & Watson, 2019) and results of this study*

Category	Key steps	Notes on questions, dates/periods, key discussions	Keywords, inclusions, and exclusions	Results
Planning the review	1. Formulate the problem	How has adaptiveness as an umbrella concept been taken in the literature related to earth system governance?		
	2. Develop and validate the review protocol	Led by the authors, supported by two research assistants		
Conducting the review	3. Search the literature	Cut-off date 31 December 2018. Adaptiveness as a single term (1900–2018) (Section 2.3.1)	(ALL [Adaptiveness] AND YEAR [1900 to 2018])	7,297
		Cut-off date 31 December 2018. Adaptiveness as an umbrella term (1998–2018) (Section 2.3.2)	(TITLE-ABS-KEY (Adaptive*) AND TITLE-ABS-KEY (Governance* OR TITLE-ABS-KEY (Management*	67,389
			Further inclusion of year (2008–2018), subject areas (those related to environmental governance), document types (journal articles and book chapters), and language (English only)	9,859
		Key themes and discussions on adaptiveness in the literature (Section 2.4)	Further inclusion of most-cited and most-relevant articles	35
	4. Assess quality	Lead by the authors, supported by two research assistants		
	5. Extract data	Data is transferred to Excel format		
	6. Analyse and synthesise data	Frequency and keyword analysis		
		Adaptiveness as a single term in the literature overtime (1900–2018)		

Table 2.1. (*cont.*)

Category	Key steps	Notes on questions, dates/periods, key discussions	Keywords, inclusions, and exclusions	Results
		Frequency and keyword analysis Adaptiveness as an umbrella term in the literature related to ESG and environmental governance a decade before and a decade after the ESG Science Plan (1998–2018) Analysis of key themes and discussions on adaptiveness in most-cited literature a decade after ESG Science Plan (2008–2018)		
Reporting the review	7. Report findings	Section 2.3 on progress on research on adaptiveness Section 2.4 addressing the ESG Science Plan 2008 questions		

'adaptiveness' over time. There was no publication found from 1900 to 1926. The first publication mentioning adaptiveness in its abstract was authored by Eggen (1926) entitled 'Is Instinct an Entity?' in the *Journal of Abnormal and Social Psychology*. A considerable increase started in 2000, which led us to look deeper into the literature from this year onwards. Between 2000 and 2008 we found a gradual growth of the use of the term in the academic literature. From 2008 until 2018, however, the curve shows a steep growth with a small sloping curve in 2014.

2.3.2 'Adaptiveness' as an Umbrella Term (1998–2018, a Decade before and after the 2008 ESG Science Plan)

The next interest pursued with the frequency analysis was to analyse the number of publications between 1998 and 2018 using related search terms within the field of earth system governance and environmental governance. This timeline is selected to analyse progress a decade before and a decade after the 2018 ESG Science Plan. This is to determine the extent by which 'adaptiveness' as an umbrella term for related concepts such as vulnerability, resilience, adaptive capacity, and sustainability has been taken up in the literature in the last two decades. An initial search using keywords 'adaptive', 'governance', and 'management' resulted in 67,389 hits.

Figure 2.2 shows that the publication numbers increased slightly in the period between 1998 and 2008 and rose quite rapidly between 2008 and 2018 indicating a vastly accelerating publication activity in this thematic field. The first mention of adaptiveness in the context of earth system governance can be found in Wollenberg et al. (2000) in a paper entitled 'Using Scenarios to Make Decisions About the Future: Anticipatory Learning for the Adaptive Co-Management of Community

Documents by year

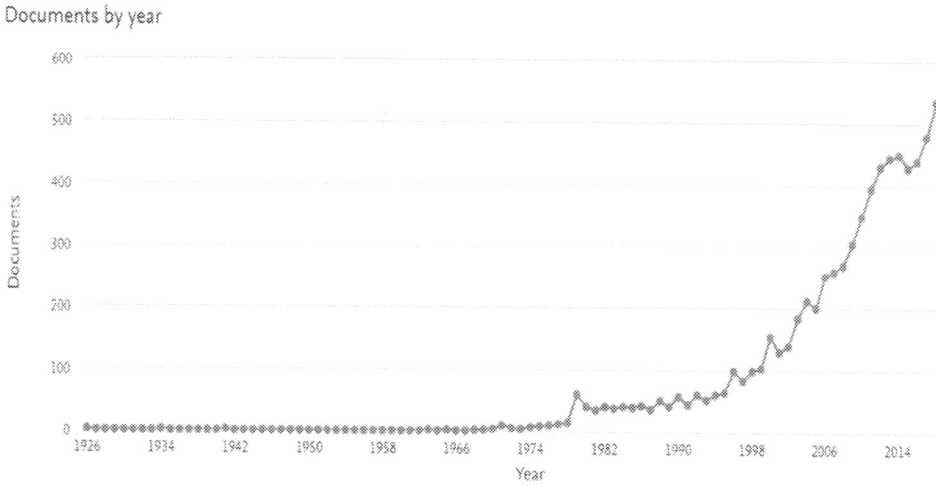

Figure 2.1 Use of the single term 'adaptiveness' in the literature since 1900 with the first appearance in 1926.
Source: Downloaded from Scopus in 2018

Documents by year

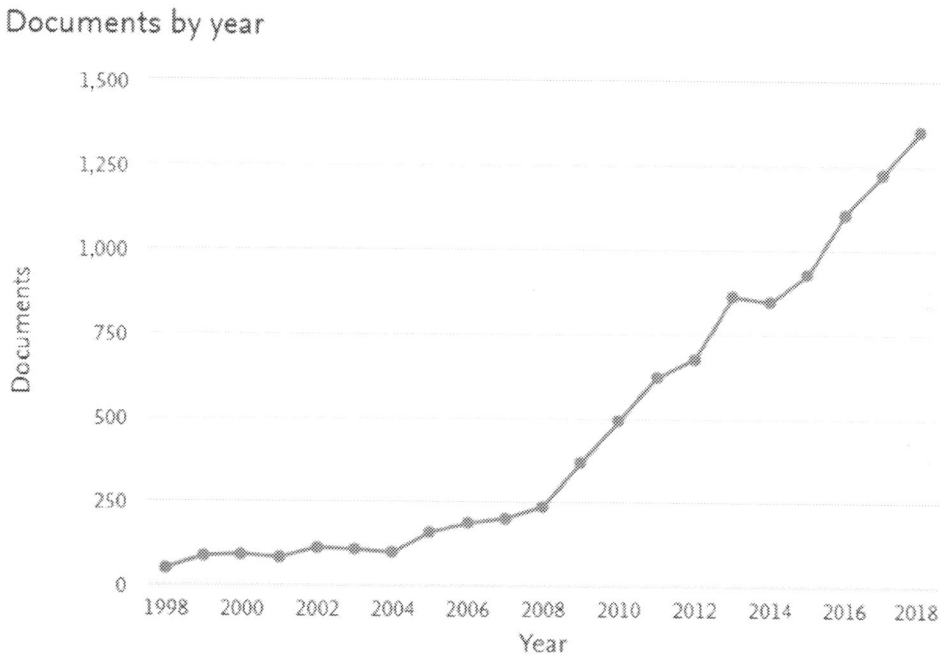

Figure 2.2 'Adaptiveness' as an umbrella term in the literature from 1998 to 2018.
Source: Based on data from Scopus (2018)

Bernd Siebenhüner and Riyanti Djalante

Forests'. In this paper, the authors argue that adaptiveness of community forest management requires a monitoring of past actions to not only respond to changes, but also to anticipate them. The first time it was proposed as an umbrella term for adaptation, adaptive capacity, and others was by Biermann (2007) who proposed four overarching principles for earth system governance as political practice – namely, credibility, stability, adaptiveness, and inclusiveness. Here, the term was employed as a meta-category or quality for the study of governance processes, not as the contents of governance processes (e.g. in the field of climate adaptation). We further found that adaptiveness has been discussed in key subject areas of environmental science, social science, agriculture, and earth and planetary science. Taken together, the notion of adaptiveness in environmental governance is not without precedence, but it was more popular in other scientific disciplines than in the context of earth system governance.

While 'adaptiveness' as a single term is not commonly used in the literature, related concepts and respective keywords were used in the search string. It employed the terms listed in Biermann et al. (2009) as elements under the umbrella of adaptiveness including resilience, vulnerability, adaptation, sustainability, adaptive management, and adaptive capacity. In Figure 2.3, we see that these concepts have been used much more frequently than the concept of adaptiveness as a keyword. 'Adaptive management', 'adaptation', and 'vulnerability' are the most often used keywords in this literature, while none of the literature uses 'robustness' or 'reflexivity' as keywords. We can see that the keyword 'adaptive management' is used most frequently by more than 5,000 articles, while 'climate change' and 'adaptation' are the second and third most used keywords. This confirms the observation made in the

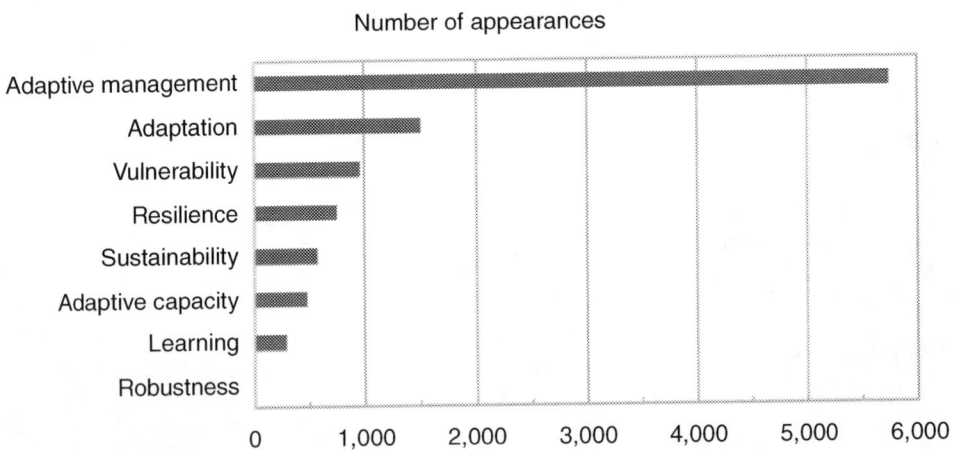

Figure 2.3 Total number of key concepts related to adaptiveness listed as keywords.
Source: Based on data from Scopus (2018)

second Science Plan that over time, the concept of adaptiveness has been used a lot in the studies related to climate change adaptation (ESG, 2018).

One area of interest is the field of climate change adaptation governance where significant conceptual and empirical work has been advanced on international, national-level, and countless local and community-based activities. 'Climate change' is the second most used keyword of around 3,500 articles, almost half of all articles included. The topic is largely dominant among the selected publications with almost half of the publications selected through the research string being linked to climate change. Climate adaptation could thus be identified as the prevailing sub-discourse. Related keywords such as 'impacts' and 'climate variation' would also fall into this discourse arena. We continued to assess the key sectors that are addressed in the literature. Through the keyword analysis, we found that water, the ecosystem, land, disaster, and coastal areas are the most common sectors or issue areas that the sampled papers focus on.

2.4 Addressing the ESG Science Plan 2008: Research Questions Based on the Most-Cited Papers (2008–2018)

This subsection presents an in-depth qualitative analysis of the content and key discussions within the most-cited publications for the four guiding research questions of the ESG Science Plan of 2008. Therefore, we selected and analysed the 35 most-cited references (Table 2.2 in the Annex) under the search string on 'adaptive governance' or 'adaptive management' within the social science literature at large and related to environmental governance more specifically that was published between 2008 and 2018. On the basis of the titles and the journal name, out of the 50 initially selected, we had to take out 15 of them as thematically or disciplinarily not relevant. The following discussion of the resulting list of papers is organised along the four guiding research questions and condenses the key results of the selected most-cited papers in the field.

2.4.1 What Are the Politics and Conflictive Dimensions of Adaptiveness?

The first question addressed the political nature and the conflicts of adaptiveness recognising that responses to massive changes in the ecological systems substantially impact, on political relations and power structures on different governance levels as well as social relations in general. What can generally be concluded from the most-cited papers in the field is that these issues of the politics of adaptiveness are being addressed, but that they stand behind other issues like adaptive capacity, effective data management, and sector-specific approaches as more popular topics in the field.

There are a number of conceptual contributions that address issues of power and conflict in relation to adaptiveness. In their paper on the relevance of adaptation to the development debate, Cannon and Müller-Mahn (2010: 2–3) state this relationship most explicitly: 'Adaptation to climate change should also be treated as being socially constructed. In doing so, we will assert that the resort to the language of "governance" (... especially as in "adaptive governance") disguises the essence of the issue: power relations and the behaviour of different actors with differing levels of power.' Vis-à-vis a rather technical and scientific approach of reducing risks and vulnerabilities, they call for a stronger focus on power relationships and discourses that impact adaptiveness of communities, in particular in development contexts.

The particular challenge of adaptive modes of governing dynamic ecosystems and their challenges for human societies has been addressed by Huitema et al. (2009) who stress the need for collaboration and participation on regional and related polycentric governance levels. Thus, power and potential conflicts can create imbalances and reduce ecosystem-related effects, social fairness, and political legitimacy of adaptive governance arrangements. Also, with a focus on water governance, Pahl-Wostl (2009) refers to the dynamics between knowledge and power through hierarchies and formalised institutions. She develops a conceptual framework for analysing adaptive capacity and transformation of governance drawing heavily on the social learning literature. Her particular focus is on informal networks that develop knowledge and novel practices and interact with power networks as well as with policy cycles in the established regulatory frameworks. Through this interaction transformative change with substantial changes in practices and policies can become possible. However, this dynamic is no one-way automatism, but can be suddenly halted or reversed through various instances such as new actors entering the scene, conflicts emerging, and other policy issues dominating public discourses.

With a focus on the local and community level of governance, Berkes and Ross (2013) advance the conceptual discussion around the resilience concept and apply it to community-level processes that are in large part challenged by climate adaptation needs. In their notion of 'community resilience', issues of power and conflict are only reflected at the margins of the concept. They are particularly relevant in the discussions around 'leadership', 'engaged leadership', and 'agency'. Berkes and Ross (2013: 17) openly acknowledge this gap, when stating that 'one relative silence in the community resilience literature is the relevance of power relationships'. Also, Williams (2011) is indicative of this gap in the adaptive management literature as being oblivious to power issues and persistent conflicts between actors in the perspective on adaptive natural resource management.

This gap is in part addressed in Armitage et al. (2011) within their empirical study of the Canadian Arctic region and the co-production of knowledge and adaptive management there. Following on from Armitage et al. (2009: 93) who call for a view on 'power differentials and the status of marginal groups in many rural, resource-dependent regions', they argue for a 'sensitivity for power dynamics' (Armitage et al., 2011: 1003) in knowledge-driven participatory processes in particularly challenged communities.

A more comprehensive focus on power and the political nature of adaptation can be found in a more recent and not yet much-cited contribution by Eriksen et al. (2015). The authors bring together knowledge and social theory based notions of authority understood as 'a concept used . . . to capture how the operation of power, both in terms of "power over" and the "power to act" results in social differentiation' (Eriksen et al., 2015: 525). In this sense, they conceptualise knowledge as legitimisation, reinforcement, or challenge to authority and subjectivities such as gender roles, social hierarchies, or cultural traditions. They conclude that these interactions need to be analysed and understood in the specific decision-making contexts in relation to adaptation to climate change.

With their influential 'Adaptive Capacity Wheel' as an analytical tool, Gupta et al. (2010) seek to bring together issues of power, knowledge, and other more technical factors relevant for adaptation. In doing so, power and conflicts are being addressed under the notion of authority that largely focuses on formalised power. It thus reflects the need for formal authority combined with other factors such as learning, room for change, or financial resources for adaptation measures and policies. However, the focus of this framework is predominantly to identify potentials and gaps in adaptive capacities vis-à-vis climate change. While some discussion on the concept relates to the internal relationships between these factors and the overall aggregation of the factors in a given case of application is still an issue of debate.

Likewise, equity implications of adaptive governance processes have been tackled only at the margins, constituting a still under-researched field in earth system governance. As numerous authors concede (Adger, 2001; Adger et al., 2006; Biermann et al., 2009), distributive implications and equity aspects play a significant role within adaptation processes. However, most conceptual and empirical contributions focus on functional aspects such as resilience, the technical and overall adaptive capacity of countries, and vulnerable areas such as islands or cities. Only a few of the most-cited papers address related issues of equity, distribution, and poverty. One of these exceptions is Douglas et al. (2008), which focuses empirically on the implications of climate change for the urban poor in African cities. Also, the compilation by Mearns and Norton (2010) highlights the repercussions of adaptiveness in the field of climate change vis-à-vis poor people, women, migrants, farmers in marginal rural areas, and others. In two more recent and less-cited case studies from India and Ecuador in the Global South, Chu et al.

(2016) scrutinise the dynamics of stakeholder participation processes in city adaptation planning. They find that equity issues and social issues immediately come to the fore in these processes that may take different routes in the further implementation of the adaptation policies. These could range from problem-centred practical measures to more formal institutional approaches to include climate adaptation into larger decision-making structures more formally. It thus remains a pivotal research perspective to further analyse adaptiveness in governance processes with a perspective on the social implications. It thus seems worth considering what the first ESG Science Plan claimed: 'We should therefore ask of adaptiveness: For whom and who benefits?' (Biermann et al., 2009: 46).

2.4.2 Which Governance Processes Foster Adaptiveness?

Referring to the governance of adaptiveness, the 2008 ESG Science Plan calls for a better understanding of 'the very criteria, scope and procedures of how power is allocated and decisions are being taken in a particular society or in the global community' (Biermann et al., 2009: 48). Also, the timing is of interest considering discrepancies between the timing of environmental change and electoral cycles, for example. Another key focus was on social learning processes at different scales and how transformative change towards adaptiveness can be promoted at different levels of governance.

In the most-cited publications related to this field, authors address some of the research gaps in the governance of adaptiveness, but acknowledge remaining knowledge deficits in particular in the understanding of transformative change and the institutionalisation of adaptiveness in political structures and decision-making processes. In doing so, Pahl-Wostl (2009) conceptualises adaptation through different levels of learning processes in adaptation governance with a particular interest in transformative change as triple-loop learning that changes the entire governance regime (e.g. by turning over paradigms or by creating new or substantially revised regimes). In doing so, she emphasises the knowledge and networking dimension of adaptation processes that are likely to also change formal institutions and policies. Learning is also seen as a crucial element of adaptive processes by Armitage et al. (2009) who see learning as a political process requiring conducive environments and a careful empirical research design to be assessed properly. The notion of transformative adaptation processes has been taken up and developed further by O'Brien (2012). She concludes that transformation is the most challenging strategy in the face of ongoing environmental change, in particular in the field of climate change. However, neither the research communities nor the societal and policy practice seem to be ready for this kind of approach. In a more recent publication, Termeer et al. (2017:

571) come to a similar conclusion when stating that 'governing transformational change thus requires transformation of the governance systems themselves'. However, there seems to be little empirical evidence for such structural change in the field of climate adaptation governance. Taking this thinking seriously, one would need to concede that adaptation may not be enough, but needs to be combined with mitigation and transformation of the entire economic and related governance systems towards more sustainable structures and behaviours.

Integrating governance research and adaptive management approaches is the key objective of the paper by Huitema et al. (2009). It explicitly discusses governance approaches regarding their feasibility for adaptive management of water resources. These include polycentric governance with effective decision-making at different nodes and levels, public participation as a means to integrate knowledge and advance legitimacy, experimentation as a methodological tool for testing hypotheses and novel practices, and a bioregional perspective that aligns ecosystem requirements with governance structures such as water basins. The paper sees advantages and disadvantages in all four approaches and proposes to consider them all with their profiles in concrete policy applications.

Addressing calls by Hinkel (2011) to apply specific indicators for analysing adaptive capacity and by Engle (2011) to focus on institutional aspects and governance when assessing adaptive capacity, Gupta et al. (2010) propose a helpful tool for the analysis of adaptive capacities of institutions. It includes categories of learning as well as fairness, leadership, and resources, among others, in the analysis of how well-prepared formal institutions in a specific field or level are regarding upcoming challenges of climate adaptation.

With their focus on experiments as a mode of governance in cities, Bulkeley and Castán-Broto (2013), building on Hoffman (2011), introduced a novel type of governance process to address climate change. By developing new rules, and new communities crossing conventional jurisdictions, cities were observed to find new ways of approaching the numerous challenges of climate change mitigation and adaptation. Examples with a focus on socio-technical innovations include living laboratories, niche innovations, and eco-city initiatives. Many of them involve hitherto unknown collaborations of different actors with private actors as well as grassroot movements playing central roles alongside local government actors. However, whether these experiments manage to initiate substantial and broader transitions beyond niche developments, remains a crucial question for future research.

Similarly addressing local level governance approaches, Measham et al. (2011) analyse the role of climate change adaptation in municipal planning processes as a means of addressing the adaptation challenge by established governance approaches, namely city planning. In doing so, they find a need to further look into barriers of such processes including leadership issues, larger institutional contexts, and competing planning agendas.

Focusing on larger regional dimensions such as a large river delta, the 'Dynamic Adaptive Policy Pathways' by Haasnoot et al. (2013) provide an approach to planning under consideration of substantial vulnerabilities and uncertainties. It identifies sequences of promising actions in a dynamic and adaptive plan in their case for the Dutch delta of the river Rhine. It guides a way for adaptation planning that has been applied to the case of flood protection of the Netherlands and other large infrastructure projects (Lawrence & Haasnoot, 2017).

2.4.3 What Attributes of Governance Systems Enhance Capacities to Adapt?

Related to the question on governance processes, the 2008 ESG Science Plan also seeks to better understand specific attributes of governance systems at various levels and whether and how they propel adaptiveness. In particular, participation, multilayered institutions, and knowledge-based deliberative governance approaches have been hypothesised to support adaptiveness in governance processes (Biermann et al., 2009). From the bulk of the reviewed papers it can be concluded that most of these factors have been found to be supportive for adaptation processes. For instance, in his programmatic paper, Ahern (2011) identifies a set of conditions under which cities and local governments can become more resilient and 'safe to fail' (i.e. less vulnerable vis-à-vis major stresses). These include multifunctional design and planning of cities such as green streets or floodplain parks, redundant modularised systems to be able to compensate failures of one (infrastructure) system, and biologically and socially diverse structures like permeable pavements and urban tree canopies. In general, planning and design should be error- and learning-friendly and allow for failures in the face of uncertain futures. This, however, requires a thorough and regular monitoring and evaluation to be able to adapt and change plans in case of need.

Arguing in a similar direction, Williams (2011) circled in knowledge from monitoring and feedback mechanisms as essential for adaptive management of natural resources. In line with several other papers (e.g. Brugnach et al., 2008; Crona & Parker, 2012; Voss & Bornemann, 2011), Berkes and Ross (2013) highlight the role of knowledge and learning in adaptation processes that involve change in socio-ecological systems due to stressors such as climate impacts, changing biodiversity, or ecosystem services at large. Also, in their often-cited paper on adaptive capacity of the highly vulnerable European forest sector, Lindner et al. (2010) call for more research and systematic knowledge on the vulnerability and adaptive capacities of forest systems as a basis for adaptive governance in the field. Thereby, they again refer to knowledge and learning capacities as an essential precondition for the adaptive governance systems. Likewise, Biesbroek et al. (2010) state in their study of national adaptation policies in Europe that broad information and public awareness raising is essential if public support and individual behavioural change is to be achieved.

In their more recent review of literature on the governance of adaptation, Huitema et al. (2016) add a specific twist to this debate on knowledge. Their lesson is that framing and the crossing between different problem framings are key for successfully addressing climate adaptation issues. In particular, when different social groups and their bodies of knowledge including related framings come together in participatory processes, this integration and crossing of framings and related bodies of knowledge is essential. However, participation in climate adaptation governance does not automatically lead towards advancing anticipatory or precautionary action, as Hegger and Dieperink (2014) find in their analysis of regional projects in the Netherlands. Thus, it seems to depend on the way participation is done, how information is provided and communicated, and who participates with what interests. This is supported by a recent meta-study on participation and learning in environmental governance indicating that 'neither non-state actor participation, nor stakeholder diversity mattered significantly for any of the studied learning variables; . . . findings highlight the importance of using methods for structuring communication and knowledge-exchange and the role of professional facilitation – as opposed to simply giving participants opportunities for open exchange' (Newig et al., 2019: 224–5). It is thus not only the number or diversity of stakeholders represented in the participatory processes that facilitates strong environmental regulations including climate adaptation measures. Based on the same data, Jager et al. (2019) conclude that participation formats with stronger decision-making roles of participants are more effective, including collaborative negotiations, round tables, councils, or steering groups. The 'how' thus seems to be more important than 'who' participates. Future research is called upon to disentangle these relationships further.

2.4.4 How, When, and Why Does Adaptiveness Influence Earth System Governance?

When looking at what the discussion about the governance of adaptiveness in the years between 2008 and 2018 has contributed to the larger debate and developments of earth system governance at large, one major strand needs to be flagged. Addressing the negative question as to why adaptiveness is not taking place, the literature brought together examples of gaps, omissions, and barriers in addressing adaptation challenges. This literature suggests the need to first study the negative factors keeping actors from actively implementing policies or adaptation measures before analysing positive pathways. Drawing on Urwin and Jordan (2008), Amundsen et al. (2010) analyse local municipalities' adaptation policies and related barriers in Norway. In their programmatic paper, Eisenack et al. (2014) call for more systematic research on barriers and ways to overcome them. In doing so, this literature contributed an important change of perspectives in earth system governance research by zooming in on failures and those factors that hinder progress or advancements in environmental governance. While this perspective potentially also provides new insights in other fields of study described in the ESG Science Plans, it essentially also needs to be advanced with respect to the specific challenges of this approach. In particular, the major drawback of this approach is the large number of potential barriers vis-à-vis an overseeable number of potential positive factors in the study of success cases and positive examples. Thus, the analyses of barriers need to be more systematic, addressing causal mechanisms (e.g. based on theoretically supported hypotheses) (Biesbroek et al., 2013).

Links to other themes and research topics of the earth system governance community can also be found in the multiple sectors that have been studied from an adaptiveness perspective. Many of them overlap with other research interests in the field. Specific governance arenas tackled in the most-cited papers in the period 2009–2018 include the fishing sector (Berkes, 2012), urban areas (Chu et al., 2016; Kabisch et al., 2016; Pelling & Manuel-Navarrete, 2011) and urban ecosystems (Cook et al., 2012), as well as coastal socio-ecological systems (Cohen et al., 2012; McCay et al., 2014). Others look at water catchments and their management in general (Ison et al., 2011) with a novel approach to iterative stakeholder involvement to bring in different bodies of knowledge into decision-making contexts. In their paper on wildlife management, Allen et al. (2011) advance the notion of adaptive management in this field linking adaptiveness studies to issues of biodiversity and nature conservation as examined by Maron et al. (2012). Also, forestry governance is a related key sector for adaptiveness research (Lindner et al., 2010).

2.5 Policy Relevance and Conclusions

In conclusion, we utilise the analytical questions (the 'Utrecht Questions') adopted in this book to examine the literature included here. The first analytical question asks, 'What are the conceptual frames used and what is the basis of the statements/ knowledge presented?' We find that adaptiveness has been taken up most in the literature related to medicine and psychology and behavioural science. The strategic choice of examining the literature one decade after the ESG Science Plan 2009 shows that the uptake of 'adaptiveness' in the new Science Plan is understood and used mostly as an umbrella concept, and rarely as a single concept itself.

The second analytical question asks, 'How generalisable is what you say/found, how confident can we be, and what are the knowledge gaps?' We acknowledge that generalisability is built on quantitative analysis through Scopus, but only secondary research, not primary study. Most of the papers are more local/case study-based, rather than larger comparisons or global assessments. There are studies that propose indicators, etc., but these are in the minority.

The next analytical question asks, 'What is the policy/practical relevance and how much is it grounded in practical evidence?' Many of the papers reviewed in this chapter build on empirical evidence from case studies or from a few meta-studies. They find quite a few practical insights and could give policymakers and practitioners advice. For instance, participation has been found to help learning, but not so much practical outcomes in the short term. However, if it is done well with strong roles of the stakeholders and supportive moderation techniques, impacts on practical change can be substantial.

Then, the analytical question asks, 'What are the new challenges and remaining gaps that are relevant to inform future development of the earth system governance framework? We find that new issues emerging such as transformations and scaling up are key in this as well as in other analytical themes of the 2009 ESG Science Plan. Also, more systematic research on barriers and hampering factors, blocking or limiting policy innovation and change is called for.

In the ESG Science Plan of 2018, issues of reflexivity and social justice gained more prominence. It therefore links adaptiveness and reflexivity in one analytical perspective (ESG, 2018). Coming from the understanding of reflexivity as the 'ability of actors and institutions to critically reflect on their own performance ... and to reshape their goals, practices and values accordingly' (ESG, 2018: 68), this analytical lens calls for the study of more reactive responses with more proactive reflections of values and orientations.

Finally, the last analytical question asks, 'What questions will we need answers to in five years and why?' We find from our review that disasters will constitute a growing threat for many people with strengthened scholarly and societal interest in adaptiveness and potential governance measures.

The chapter finds that 'adaptiveness' has hardly been taken up as a term, but rather as related concepts. The political nature and the conflicts of adaptiveness recognise that responses to massive changes in the ecological systems substantially impact on political relations and power structures on different governance levels. The learning processes in adaptation governance have a particular interest in transformative change as triple-loop learning. The 2008 ESG Science Plan also seeks to better understand specific attributes of governance systems at various levels and whether and how they propel adaptiveness.

Annex

Table 2.2. *Most-cited and most-relevant papers from 2008 to 2018*

No.	Author	Title	Source, Year	Citations
1.	Lindner, M., Maroschek, M., Netherer, S. et al.	Climate change impacts, adaptive capacity, and vulnerability of European forest ecosystems	*Forest Ecology and Management*, 25(4), 698–709; 2010	944
2.	Pahl-Wostl, C.	A conceptual framework for analysing adaptive capacity and multi-level learning processes in resource governance regimes	*Global Environmental Change*, 19(3), 354–5; 2009	867
3.	Hallegatte, S., Green, C., Nicholls, R.J., & Corfee-Morlot, J.	Future flood losses in major coastal cities	*Nature Climate Change*, 3(9), 802–6; 2013	617
4.	Hirabayashi, Y., Mahendran, R., Koirala, S. et al.	Global flood risk under climate change	*Nature Climate Change*, 3(9), 816–21; 2013	570
5.	Armitage, D., Marschke, M., & Plummer, R.	Adaptive co-management and the paradox of learning	*Global Environmental Change*, 18(1), 86–98; 2009	517
6.	Tittensor, D.P., Walpole, M., Hill, S.L.L. et al.	A mid-term analysis of progress toward international biodiversity targets	*Science*, 346(6206), 241–4; 2014	441
7.	Hinkel, J.	Indicators of vulnerability and adaptive capacity: towards a clarification of the science-policy interface	*Global Environmental Change*, 21(1), 198–208; 2011	430
8.	Berrang-Ford, L., Ford, J.D., & Patterson, J.	Are we adapting to climate change?	*Global Environmental Change*, 21(1), 25–33; 2011	415

Table 2.2. (*cont.*)

No.	Author	Title	Source, Year	Citations
9.	Huitema, D., Mostert, E., Egas, W. et al.	Adaptive water governance: Assessing the institutional prescriptions of adaptive (co-) management from a governance perspective and defining a research agenda	*Ecology and Society*, 14(1); 2009	414
10.	Haasnoot, M., Kwakkel, J.H., Walker, W.E., & Ter Maat, J.	Dynamic adaptive policy pathways: a method for crafting robust decisions for a deeply uncertain world	*Global Environmental Change*, 23(2), 485–98; 2013	413
11.	Berkes, F. & Ross, H.	Community resilience: toward an integrated approach	*Society and Natural Resources*, 26(1), 5–20; 2013	403
12.	Engle, N.L.	Adaptive capacity and its assessment	*Global Environmental Change*, 21(2), 647–56; 2011	400
13.	Lindenmayer, D.B. & Likens, G.E.	Adaptive monitoring: a new paradigm for long-term research and monitoring	*Trends in Ecology and Evolution*, 24(9), 482–6; 2009	379
14.	O'Brien, K.	Global environmental change II: from adaptation to deliberate transformation	*Progress in Human Geography*, 36(5), 667–76; 2012	355
15.	Bulkeley, H. & Castán Broto, V.	Government by experiment? Global cities and the governing of climate change	*Transactions of the Institute of British Geographers*, 38(3), 361–75; 2013	347
16.	Wise, R.M., Fazey, I., Stafford Smith, M. et al.	Reconceptualising adaptation to climate change as part of pathways of change and response	*Global Environmental Change*, 28, 325–36; 2014	340
17.	Gupta, J., Termeer, C., Klostermann, J. et al.	The Adaptive Capacity Wheel: a method to assess the inherent characteristics of institutions to enable the adaptive capacity of society	*Environmental Science and Policy*, 13(6), 459–71; 2010	340

Table 2.2. (*cont.*)

No.	Author	Title	Source, Year	Citations
18.	Measham, T.G., Preston, B.L., Smith, T.F. et al.	Adapting to climate change through local municipal planning: barriers and challenges	*Mitigation and Adaptation Strategies for Global Change*, 16(8), 889–909; 2011	338
19.	Armitage, D., Berkes, F., Dale, A., Kocho-Schellenberg, E., & Patton, E.	Co-management and co-production of knowledge: learning to adapt in Canada's Arctic	*Global Environmental Change*, 21(3), 995–1004; 2011	301
20.	Biesbroek, G.R., Swart, R.J., Carter, T.R. et al.	Europe adapts to climate change: comparing national adaptation strategies	*Global Environmental Change*, 20(3), 440–50; 2010	298
21.	Ahern, J.	From fail-safe to safe-to-fail: sustainability and resilience in the new urban world	*Landscape and Urban Planning*, 100(4), 341–3; 2011	286
22.	Urwin, K. & Jordan, A.	Does public policy support or undermine climate change adaptation? Exploring policy interplay across different scales of governance	*Global Environmental Change*, 18(1), 180–91; 2008	281
23.	Klerkx, L., Aarts, N., & Leeuwis, C.	Adaptive management in agricultural innovation systems: the interactions between innovation networks and their environment	*Agricultural Systems*, 103(6), 390–400; 2010	273
24.	Pelling, M., High, C., Dearing, J., & Smith, D.	Shadow spaces for social learning: a relational understanding of adaptive capacity to climate change within organisations	*Environment and Planning A*, 40(4), 876–84; 2008	271
25.	Williams, B.K.	Adaptive management of natural resources: framework and issues	*Journal of Environmental Management*, 92(5), 1346–53; 2011	267
26.	Alexander, D.E.	Resilience and disaster risk reduction: an etymological journey	*Natural Hazards and Earth System Sciences*, 13(11), 2707–16; 2013	260

Table 2.2. (*cont.*)

No.	Author	Title	Source, Year	Citations
27.	Birkmann, J., Cardona, O.D., Carreno, M.L. et al.	Framing vulnerability, risk and societal responses: the MOVE framework	*Natural Hazards*, 67(2), 193–211; 2013	255
28.	Maron, M., Hobbs, R.J., Moilanem, A. et al.	Faustian bargains? Restoration realities in the context of biodiversity offset policies	*Biological Conservation*, 155, 141–8; 2012	245
29.	Gonzalez, P., Neilson, R.P., Lenihan, J.M., & Drapek, R.J.	Global patterns in the vulnerability of ecosystems to vegetation shifts due to climate change	*Global Ecology and Biogeography*, 19(6), 755–68; 2010	245
30.	Douglas, I., Alam, K., Maghenda, M. et al.	Unjust waters: climate change, flooding and the urban poor in Africa	*Environment and Urbanization*, 20(1), 187–205; 2008	243
31.	Ochoa, L.F., Dent, C.J., & Harrison, G.P.	Distribution network capacity assessment: variable DG and active networks	*IEEE Transactions on Power Systems*, 25(1), 5332248, 87–95; 2010	242
32.	Park, S.E., Marshall, N.A., Jakku, E. et al.	Information adaptation responses to climate change through theories of transformation	*Global Environmental Change*, 22(1), 115–26; 2012	239
33.	Cannon, T. & Müller-Mahn, D.	Vulnerability, resilience and development discourses in context of climate change	*Natural Hazards*, 55(3), 621–35; 2010	231
34.	Masten, A.S. & Obradovic, J.	Disaster preparation and recovery: lessons from research on resilience in human development	*Ecology and Society*, 13 (1), 9; 2008	230
35.	Amundsen, H., Berglund, F., & Westkogh, H.	Overcoming barriers to climate change adaptation: a question of multilevel governance?	*Environment and Planning C: Government and Policy*, 28(2), 276–89; 2010	226

References

Adger, W.N. (2001). Scales of governance and environmental justice for adaptation and mitigation of climate change. *Journal of International Development*, 13, 921–31.

Adger, W.N., Paavola, J., Huq, S., & Mace, M.J. (eds.). (2006). *Fairness in Adaptation to Climate Change*. Cambridge, MA: MIT Press.

Ahern, J. (2011). From fail-safe to safe-to-fail: sustainability and resilience in the new urban world. *Landscape and Urban Planning*, 100(4), 341–3.

Alexander, D.E. (2013). Resilience and disaster risk reduction: an etymological journey. *Natural Hazards and Earth System Sciences*, 13(11), 2707–16.

Allen, C.R., Cumming, G.S., Garmestani, A.S., Taylor, P.D., & Walker, B.H. (2011). Managing for resilience. *Wildlife Biology*, 17(4), 337–49.

Amundsen, H., Berglund, F., & Westskog, H. (2010). Overcoming barriers to climate change adaptation: a question of multilevel governance? *Environment and Planning C: Government and Policy*, 28(2), 276–89. doi: http://doi.org/10.1068/c0941.

Armitage, D., Berkes, F., Dale, A., Kocho-Schellenberg, E., & Patton, E. (2011). Co-management and the co-production of knowledge: Learning to adapt in Canada's Arctic. *Global Environmental Change*, 21(3), 995–1004. doi: https://doi.org/10.1016/j.gloenvcha.2011.04.006.

Armitage, D., Plummer, R., Berkes, F. et al. (2009). Adaptive co-management for social-ecological complexity. *Frontiers in Ecology and Environment*, 7(2), 95–10.

Bakkalbasi, N., Bauer, K., Glover, J., & Wang, L. (2006). Three options for citation tracking: Google Scholar, Scopus and Web of Science. *Biomedical Digital Libraries*, 3.

Bar-Ilan, J. (2008). Which h-index? A comparison of WoS, Scopus and Google Scholar. *Scientometrics*, 74(2), 257–71.

Berkes, F. (2012). Implementing ecosystem-based management: evolution or revolution? *Fish and Fisheries*, 13(4), 465–76. doi: https://doi.org/10.1111/j.1467-2979.2011.00452.

Berkes, F. & Ross, H. (2013). Community resilience: toward an integrated approach. *Society & Natural Resources*, 26(1), 5–20. doi: https://doi.org/10.1080/08941920.2012.736605.

Berrang-Ford, L., Ford, J.D., & Patterson, J. (2011). Are we adapting to climate change? *Global Environmental Change*, 21(1), 25–33.

Biermann, F. (2007). 'Earth system governance' as a cross-cutting theme of global change research. *Global Environmental Change*, 17(3), 326–37.

Biermann, F., Betsill, M., Gupta, J. et al. (2009). *Earth System Governance: People, Places, and the Planet. Science Implementation Plan of the Earth System Governance Project*. Bonn: International Human Dimensions Programme on Global Environmental Change.

Biesbroek, G.R., Klostermann, J.E.M., Termeer, C.J.A.M., & Kabat, P. (2013). On the nature of barriers to climate change adaptation. *Regional Environmental Change*, 13(5), 1119–29. doi: http://doi.org/10.1007/s10113-013-0421-y.

Biesbroek, G.R., Swart, R., Carter, T.R. et al. (2010). Europe adapts to climate change: comparing national adaptation strategies. *Global Environmental Change*, 20(3), 440–50.

Birkmann, J., Cardona, O.D., Carreno, M.L. et al. (2013). Framing vulnerability, risk and societal responses: the MOVE framework. *Natural Hazards*, 67(2), 193–211.

Brereton, P., Kitchenham, B.A., Budgen, D., Turner, M., & Khalil, M. (2007). Lessons from applying the systematic literature review process within the software engineering domain. *Journal of Systems and Software*, 80(4), 571–83.

Brugnach, M., Dewulf, A., Pahl-Wostl, C., & Taillieu, T. (2008). Toward a relational concept of uncertainty: about knowing too little, knowing too differently, and accepting not to know. *Ecology and Society*, 13(2), 30.

Bulkeley, H. & Castán-Broto, V. (2013). Government by experiment? Global cities and the governing of climate change. *Transactions of the Institute of British Geographers*, 38(3), 361–75.

Burnham, J.F. (2006). Scopus database: a review. *Biomedical Digital Libraries*, 3(1), doi: https://doi.org/10.1186/1742-5581-3-1.

Cannon, T. & Müller-Mahn, D. (2010). Vulnerability, resilience and development discourses in context of climate change. *Natural Hazards*, 55(3), 621–35.

Chu, E., Anguelovski, I., & Carmin, J. (2016). Inclusive approaches to urban climate adaptation planning and implementation in the Global South. *Climate Policy*, 16(3), 372–92. doi: https://doi.org/10.1080/14693062.2015.1019822.

Cohen, P.J., Evans, L.S., & Mills, M. (2012). Social networks supporting governance of coastal ecosystems in Solomon Islands. *Conservation Letters*, 5(5), 376–86. doi: https://doi.org/10.1111/j.1755-263X.2012.00255.

Cook, E.M., Hall, S.J., & Larson, K.L. (2012). Residential landscapes as social-ecological systems: a synthesis of multi-scalar interactions between people and their home environment. *Urban Ecosystems*, 15(1), 19–52. doi: https://doi.org/10.1007/s11252-011-0197-0.

Crona, B.I. & Parker, J.N. (2012). Learning in support of governance: theories, methods, and a framework to assess how bridging organizations contribute to adaptive resource governance. *Ecology and Society*, 17(1), 32. doi: https://doi.org/10.5751/ES-04534-170132.

De Moya-Anegón, F., Chinchilla-Rodríguez, Z., Vargas-Quesada, B. et al. (2007). Coverage analysis of Scopus: a journal metric approach. *Scientometrics*, 73(1), 53–78.

Douglas, I., Alam, K., Maghenda, M. et al. (2008). Unjust waters: climate change, flooding and the urban poor in Africa. *Environment and Urbanization*, 20(1), 187–205.

Earth System Governance (ESG) Project. (2018). *Earth System Governance: Science and Implementation Plan of the Earth System Governance Project*. Utrecht: Earth System Governance.

Eggen, J.B. (1926). Is instinct an entity? *Journal of Abnormal and Social Psychology*, 21(1), 38.

Eisenack, K., Moser, S., Hoffmann, E. et al. (2014). Explaining and overcoming barriers to climate change adaptation. *Nature Climate Change*, 4(10), 867–72. doi: http://doi.org/10.1038/nclimate2350.

Engle, N.L. (2011). Adaptive capacity and its assessment. *Global Environmental Change*, 21(2), 647–56.

Eriksen, S.H., Nightingale, A.J., & Eakin, H. (2015). Reframing adaptation: the political nature of climate change adaptation. *Global Environmental Change*, 35, 523–33.

Falagas, M.E., Pitsouni, E.I., Malietzis, G.A., & Pappas, G. (2008). Comparison of PubMed, Scopus, Web of Science, and Google Scholar: strengths and weaknesses. *FASEB Journal*, 22(2), 338–42.

Gonzalez, P., Neilson, R.P., Lenihan, J.M., & Drapek, R.J. (2010). Global patterns in the vulnerability of ecosystems to vegetation shifts due to climate change. *Global Ecology and Biogeography*, 19(6), 755–68.

Gupta, J., Termeer, C., Klostermann, J. et al. (2010). The Adaptive Capacity Wheel: a method to assess the inherent characteristics of institutions to enable the adaptive capacity of society. *Environmental Science & Policy*, 13(6), 459–71.

Haasnoot, M., Kwakkel, J.H., Walker, W.E., & Ter Maat, J. (2013). Dynamic adaptive policy pathways: a method for crafting robust decisions for a deeply uncertain world. *Global Environmental Change*, 23(2), 485–98.

Hallegatte, S., Green, C., Nicholls, R.J., & Corfee-Morlot, J. (2013). Future flood losses in major coastal cities. *Nature Climate Change*, 3(9), 802.

Hegger, D. & Dieperink, C. (2014). Toward successful joint knowledge production for climate change adaptation: lessons from six regional projects in the Netherlands. *Ecology and Society*, 19(2), 34.

Hinkel, J. (2011). 'Indicators of vulnerability and adaptive capacity': towards a clarification of the science–policy interface. *Global Environmental Change*, 21(1), 198–208.

Hirabayashi, Y., Mahendran, R., Koirala, S. et al. (2013). Global flood risk under climate change. *Nature Climate Change*, 3(9), 816–21.

Hoffman, M.J. (2011). *Climate Governance at the Crossroads: Experimenting with a Global Response after Kyoto*. Oxford: Oxford University Press.

Huitema, D., Adger, W.N., Berkhout, F. et al. (2016). The governance of adaptation: choices, reasons, and effects. *Ecology and Society*, 21(3), 37.

Huitema, D., Mostert, E., Egas, W. et al. (2009). Adaptive water governance: assessing the institutional prescriptions of adaptive (co-) management from a governance perspective and defining a research agenda. *Ecology and Society*, 14(1), 26.

Ison, R., Collins, K., Colvin, J. et al. (2011). Sustainable catchment managing in a climate changing world: new integrative modalities for connecting policy makers, scientists and other stakeholders. *Water Resources Management*, 25(15), 3977–92.

Jager, N.W., Newig, J., Challies, E., & Kochskämper, E. (2019). Pathways to implementation: evidence on how participation in environmental governance impacts on environmental outcomes. *Journal of Public Administration Research and Theory*, 2019, 1–17. doi: http://doi.org/10.1093/jopart/muz034.

Kabisch, N., Frantzeskaki, N., Pauleit, S. et al. (2016). Nature-based solutions to climate change mitigation and adaptation in urban areas: perspectives on indicators, knowledge gaps, barriers, and opportunities for action. *Ecology and Society*, 21(2), 39.

Klerkx, L., Aarts, N., & Leeuwis, C. (2010). Adaptive management in agricultural innovation systems: the interactions between innovation networks and their environment. *Agricultural Systems*, 103(6), 390–400.

Kulkarni, A.V., Aziz, B., Shams, I., & Busse, J.W. (2009). Comparisons of citations in web of science, Scopus, and Google Scholar for articles published in general medical journals. *JAMA – Journal of the American Medical Association*, 302(10), 1092–6.

Lawrence, J. & Haasnoot, M. (2017). What it took to catalyse uptake of dynamic adaptive pathways planning to address climate change uncertainty. *Environmental Science & Policy*, 68, 47–57.

Leydesdorff, L., De Moya-Anegón, F., & Guerrero-Bote, V.P. (2010). Journal maps on the basis of Scopus data: a comparison with the journal citation reports of the ISI. *Journal of the American Society for Information Science and Technology*, 61(2), 352–69.

Lindenmayer, D.B. & Likens, G.E. (2009). Adaptive monitoring: a new paradigm for long-term research and monitoring. *Trends in Ecology and Evolution*, 24(9), 482–6.

Lindner, M., Maroschek, M., Netherer, S. et al. (2010). Climate change impacts, adaptive capacity, and vulnerability of European forest ecosystems. *Forest Ecology and Management*, 259(4), 698–709.

McCay, B.J., Micheli, F., Ponce-Díaz, G. et al. (2014). Cooperatives, concessions, and co-management on the Pacific coast of Mexico. *Marine Policy*, 44, 49–59.

Maron, M., Hobbs, R.J., Moilanen, A. et al. (2012). Faustian bargains? Restoration realities in the context of biodiversity offset policies. *Biological Conservation*, 155, 141–8. doi: https://doi.org/10.1016/j.biocon.2012.06.003.

Masten, A.S. & Obradovic, J. (2008). Disaster preparation and recovery: lessons from research on resilience in human development. *Ecology and Society*, 13(1), 9.

Mearns, R. & Norton, A. (eds.) (2010). *The Social Dimensions of Climate Change: Equity and Vulnerability in a Warming World*. Washington, DC: World Bank Group.

Measham, T.G., Preston, B.L., Smith, T. et al. (2011). Adapting to climate change through local municipal planning: barriers and challenges. *Mitigation and Adaptation Strategies for Global Change*, 16(8), 889–909.

Newig, J., Jager, N.W., Kochskämper, E., & Challies, E. (2019). Learning in participatory environmental governance – its antecedents and effects: findings from a case survey meta-analysis. *Journal of Environmental Policy & Planning*, 21(3), 213–27. doi: http://doi.org/10.1080/1523908X.2019.1623663.

O'Brien, K. (2012). Global environmental change II: from adaptation to deliberate transformation. *Progress in Human Geography*, 36(5), 667–76.

Ochoa, L.F., Dent, C.J., & Harrison, G.P. (2010). Distribution network capacity assessment: variable DG and active networks. *IEEE Transactions on Power Systems*, 25(1), 87–95.

Pahl-Wostl, C. (2009). A conceptual framework for analysing adaptive capacity and multi-level learning processes in resource governance regimes. *Global Environmental Change*, 19(3), 354–65.

Park, S.E., Marshall, N.A., Jakku, E. et al. (2012). Information adaptation responses to climate change through theories of transformation. *Global Environmental Change*, 22(1), 115–26.

Pelling, M., High, C., Dearing, J., & Smith, D. (2008). Shadow spaces for social learning: A relational understanding of adaptive capacity to climate change within organisations. *Environment and Planning A*, 40(4), 876–84.

Pelling, M. & Manuel-Navarrete, D. (2011). From resilience to transformation: the adaptive cycle in two Mexican urban centers. *Ecology and Society*, 16(2), 11.

Robinson, P. & Lowe, J. (2015). Literature reviews vs systematic reviews. *Australian and New Zealand Journal of Public Health*, 39(2), 103.

Termeer, C.J.A.M., Dewulf, A., & Biesbroek, G.R. (2017). Transformational change: governance interventions for climate change adaptation from a continuous change perspective. *Journal of Environmental Planning and Management*, 60(4), 558–76. doi: https://doi.org/10.1080/09640568.2016.1168288.

Tittensor, D.P., Walpole, M., Hill, S.L.L. et al. (2014). A mid-term analysis of progress toward international biodiversity targets. *Science*, 346(6206), 241–4.

Urwin, K. & Jordan, A. (2008). Does public policy support or undermine climate change adaptation? Exploring policy interplay across different scales of governance. *Global Environmental Change*, 18(1), 180–91. doi: https://doi.org/10.1016/j.gloenvcha.2007.08.002.

Voss, J.-P. & Bornemann, B. (2011). The politics of reflexive governance: challenges for designing adaptive management and transition management. *Ecology and Society*, 16(2), 9.

Williams, B.K. (2011). Adaptive management of natural resources: framework and issues. *Journal of Environmental Management*, 92(5), 1346–53.

Wise, R.M., Fazey, I., Stafford Smith, M. et al. (2014). Reconceptualising adaptation to climate change as part of pathways of change and response. *Global Environmental Change*, 28, 325–36.

Wollenberg, E., Edmunds, D., & Buck, L. (2000). Using scenarios to make decisions about the future: anticipatory learning for the adaptive co-management of community forests. *Landscape and Urban Planning*, 47(1–2), 65–77.

Xiao, Y. & Watson, M. (2019). Guidance on conducting a systematic literature review. *Journal of Planning Education and Research*, 39(1), 93–112.

3

Climate Change Adaptive Capacity Assessments

Conceptual Approaches and Operational Process

ANNIE MONTPETIT, FRÉDÉRIK DOYON, AND GUY CHIASSON*

3.1 Introduction

Climate change adaptive capacity is a term that has boomed in the scientific literature. After the creation of the United Nations Framework Convention on Climate Change (UNFCCC), which emphasised both mitigation and adaptation as strategies to deal with the adverse effects of climate change, academic research started to take into consideration human and social aspects related to climate change. Adaptation then slowly became a central topic in climate change research. With its statement on the responsibility of developed countries to assist developing ones in meeting the costs of adaptation to climate change, the UNFCCC contributed to adding a political necessity to the academic assessment of adaptation (Hinkel, 2011). As a result, adaptive capacity took a greater place on the climate research agenda, enabling a greater input from social sciences in adaptation assessment and, more specifically, the inclusion of non-climatic dimensions as factors influencing the ability to adapt to climate change (Ford et al., 2013).

The study of climate change adaptive capacity has crossed several disciplines and draws from other related concepts such as sustainability (Den Otter & Beckley, 2002; Scoones, 1998), community capacity (Beckley et al., 2008; Beckley et al., 2002), or social resilience (Berkes & Ross, 2013; Kelly et al., 2015). Those works have made significant contributions to investigate the social, cultural, and economic dimensions of adaptation and change. Despite this rich legacy, the conceptual and operational field of climate change adaptive capacity can be confusing for researchers and practitioners wanting to assess the concept. Indeed, the literature on the theoretical and conceptual dimensions of adaptive capacity established multiple definitions of adaptive capacity that are often vague (Hinkel,

* We are grateful for the funding received by the Social Sciences and Humanities Research Council of Canada (SSHRC), Mitacs Accelerate Fellowship programme, Institut des territoires (IDT), Centre de recherche sur le développement des territoires (CRDT), and Centre d'étude sur la forêt (CEF) to support this research.

2011). This lack of clarity makes the assessment of climate change adaptive capacity a difficult task to accomplish, especially when combined with the two following methodological challenges: (1) the latent nature of adaptive capacity, meaning that researchers and practitioners often only succeed to measure it after its mobilisation within a system (Lockwood et al., 2015; Whitney et al., 2017); and (2) the relative absence of empirical examples exploring adaptive capacity actions, or measures to improve adaptive capacity, in periods that might be representative of a future warmer climate (Hill, 2012). Consequently, the transition from theory to practice remains difficult (Miller et al., 2010).

Given those challenges, one can reasonably question the relevance of assessing adaptive capacity. However, the concept's importance is clearly revealed by looking at its political implications. Indeed, adaptive capacity assessments focus on aspects influenced by public policies. By understanding the inherent dimensions of adaptive capacity, it is possible to highlight the governance processes and actions that have the potential to improve the ability to adapt to change (Whitney et al., 2017). Adaptive capacity is also a core concept of adaptiveness, the central term of this book. Consequently, it holds the potential to describe and understand societal changes made in anticipation or in response to environmental challenges.

In light of its central position in enabling adaptation (Hill & Engle, 2013; Smit & Wandel, 2006), adaptive capacity is an under-researched topic within the sustainability and global change communities, which stresses the need to further reflect on its operational design. Furthermore, keeping in mind the importance of the assessment of adaptive capacity on the policy agenda and on the development of adaptation strategies, the importance of crafting an 'appropriate' operational process is crucial. Therefore, the guiding questions of this chapter are: How can we assess a system's adaptive capacity to climate change and what are the steps required to successfully conduct this assessment process? This chapter builds on the results from a literature review identifying key articles covering the concepts of adaptive capacity. Going beyond the operational endeavour inherent to this study, this chapter also focuses on the attributes of governance systems that enhance the capacities needed to adapt.

This chapter contributes to the operational field of research on adaptive capacity in three ways. First, by presenting a three-step operational process (Figure 3.1), it strives to support the assessment of adaptive capacity in a diversity of contexts. Second, it provides guidance on how to build an operational definition of adaptive capacity coherent with the research questions and objectives at stake. Indeed, since it is not a concept that can be directly measured, adaptive capacity needs to be translated into an operational definition that will highlight the dimensions to assess. Attributes of governance systems that enhance capacities to adapt are revealed in this

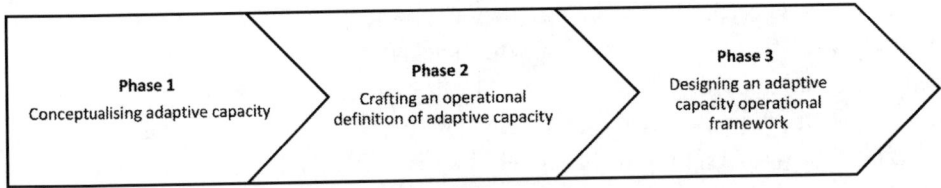

Figure 3.1 Three-step adaptive capacity operational process

second step. Third, this chapter seeks to demonstrate how an operational framework of climate change adaptive capacity that integrates multiple epistemic, spatial, and temporal dimensions can be developed. By using the suggested steps, it is possible to discuss the importance of adopting a reflective attitude with regards to climate change adaptive capacity assessments. In conclusion, this chapter argues that normative dimensions and policy considerations are paramount elements in guiding the design of adaptive capacity assessments.

3.2 Step One: Conceptualising Adaptive Capacity

Two broad approaches, namely the development and resilience studies, are used as a baseline to understand the multiple views from which to conceptualise adaptive capacity. Understanding them leads the way towards making reflexive choices in crafting an operational definition of adaptive capacity.

3.2.1 Contributions from Development Studies

Development studies have mostly focused on the vulnerability of human populations to risk and natural hazards. The concept of vulnerability is thus central and takes its roots from the studies on risk, constructivism, human ecology, and political economy (Janssen et al., 2006; Miller et al., 2010). Research objectives of studies adopting a vulnerability perspective are usually to identify the countries and regions where resources needed to adapt are lacking (Hinkel, 2011). Marino (2015) explains that the concept of vulnerability can be situated on a continuum starting from an exclusive focus on environmental and biophysical variables and moving towards perspectives centred on social variables.

An operational definition of adaptive capacity under this perspective focuses on the determinants and attributes that are assessed at a given scale (spatial, temporal) for a given social group (individuals, households, communities, regions, countries, etc.). Social science theories and models facilitated their identification and understanding. Without considering vulnerability solely as an effect of the social conditions characterising a system, a development perspective to vulnerability nevertheless implies that the inherent social dimensions of adaptive capacity, combined with the effect of environmental conditions (exposition and sensitivity) are having an impact on the overall vulnerability of a system. Thus, adaptive capacity can be perceived as the 'ability or capacity of a system to modify or change its characteristics or behaviour so as to cope better with existing or anticipated external stresses' (Adger et al., 2005: 34). This definition distinguishes coping capacity and adaptive capacity: the first is perceived as a short-term ability whereas the second refers to an ability to pursue long-term adaptation strategies (Kofinas et al., 2013; Smit & Wandel, 2006). Therefore, adaptive capacity depends on the close and intertwined relation between hazards and timescales (Brooks et al., 2005). In sum, this conceptual approach is often tied to an epistemic static vision of adaptive capacity, meaning that adaption is assessed at a specific spatial and temporal scale.

3.2.2 Contributions from Resilience Studies

Resilience is a concept that has been widely used in ecology and conceptualised according to many paradigms (Folke, 2006). The paradigm of the resilience of social-ecological systems (SES) puts forward the idea that a clear distinction between social and ecological systems is arbitrary, considering the strong interaction between the two (Berkes & Folke, 1998). In this type of analysis, the focus is on dynamic processes and circular loops that can lead to the understanding and solving of environmental problems. The stability of SES dynamics emerges from the complementarity of three attributes: resilience, transformability, and adaptability (Walker et al., 2004; Walker et al., 2006). Within an SES approach, adaptive capacity is tied to the concept of adaptability, which corresponds essentially to the collective capacity of human actors to influence (by managing) the resilience of a system (Walker et al., 2004).

Theoretical contributions that influenced this approach include the studies on community resilience (Berkes & Ross, 2013; Kelly et al., 2015), community-based management (Del Mar Delgado-Serrano et al., 2015), and social resilience (Adger, 2000). The latter is closely related to the concept of adaptive capacity to the extent that it can be perceived as a process leading to adaptive capacity or a synonym of it (Brown & Westaway, 2011; Maclean et al., 2014). Cuthill et al. (2008: 146) define social resilience as 'the way in which individuals, communities and societies adapt, transform, and potentially become stronger when faced with environmental, social, economic or political challenges'. Social resilience therefore focuses on the attributes of the social aspects of resilience that direct management efforts towards building on existing strengths rather than redressing deficits (Maclean et al., 2014). The overall idea is that the knowledge of the properties of social resilience can assist managers and resource users in designing policies supporting a sustainable use of natural resources.

From this conceptualisation, the operational definition of adaptive capacity resides in the identification of key properties or attributes needed to make systems cope or adapt to changes. In essence, adaptive capacity is related to management factors and processes (Keskitalo et al., 2011). Building on the idea that managed ecological systems are dynamic and unpredictable, adaptive resource management and adaptive governance translate the organisational and social requirements that are considered as essential for developing a sound socio-ecological management (Keskitalo, 2013). Brunner et al. (2005) perceive adaptive governance as a way of solving problems created by top-down command and control decision-making, while Gunderson et al. (1995) perceive it as a vector for the integration of science, policy, and decision-making. The concept of adaptive management recognises the complexity of ecological and social systems and aims at reconciling multiple interest uses (Williams & Brown, 2014). Therefore, diversity in the structure and governance system appears to be a key property and is captured by the concepts of co-management and adaptive-co-management (Armitage et al., 2008; Plummer et al., 2013).

This focus on sustainability, adaptation, and management requires a deep understanding of the complexity of the different systems involved (social, biophysical, economic, etc.) and their interactions (Cumming et al., 2013). Studies adopting this angle contributed to demonstrate that the oversimplification of human–nature relations and one-size-fits-all recommendations have produced mismanagement and failures (Wyborn & Bixler, 2013). Given this complexity, multiple frameworks are available and indeed necessary for understanding different aspects of SES (Poteete et al., 2010), including its adaptability. The variety of frameworks available for the study of SES also reflects the variety of disciplines and research fields – including sustainability science, landscape ecology, ecological economics, geography, resource economics, and resilience thinking – which all contribute different and valuable perspectives on social-ecological interactions and outcomes (Hinkel et al., 2014). This is well illustrated with the social-ecological framework (McGinnis & Ostrom, 2014; Ostrom, 2007, 2009) proposed to analyse the sustainability of SES, which integrate the management and governance attributes of resilience. In sum, the resilience perspective is strongly tied to a dynamic (or process) epistemic vision of adaptive capacity that can also closely relate to an action dimension.

3.2.3 Trends in Adaptive Capacity Conceptualisation

Tracing out the epistemic and theoretical differences among those two conceptual approaches revealed that each of them brings a singular lens from which to perceive adaptive capacity. Nevertheless, all conceptual approaches of climate change adaptive capacity have in common that they are seeking to understand the social dimensions – either attributes, characteristics, or interactions – that allow for human systems to adapt (or not) in the face of change. They all use theories – stemming from different disciplines from the social and natural sciences – to explain why particular dimensions may foster adaptive capacity in the face of climate change. Reviewing the adaptive capacity literature also revealed four general trends.

First, while looking at the theoretical influence of the two approaches, the contribution of social science theories, concepts, and frameworks is prominent. Even for the resilience approach that emerged from the study of natural systems, the conceptualisation of adaptive capacity involves an understanding of social processes. With adaptation taking a greater place on the climate change research agenda, there was a shift from an almost exclusive focus on climate and life science dimensions towards one that is more inclusive of social and human aspects of climate change (Simonet, 2015). This paradigmatic transformation explains why climate change is a research topic that mobilises many disciplines of climate, social, and human sciences. Similarly, there is a close link between the conceptual approaches of adaptive capacity and sustainability science. Indeed, the objective of climate change adaptation is, ultimately, to maintain or improve the well-being of populations (Magnan, 2009) and to ensure intergenerational equality (Spiller, 2016).

Second, the scale (temporal, social, spatial) of analysis is also of considerable importance in the operational definition of adaptive capacity, regardless of the approach. Indeed, adaptive capacity is inherently scale dependent (Cote & Nightingale, 2012). Keeping in mind the relevance of adaptive capacity assessments for policymaking, it is therefore very important to give proper considerations on the targeted scale of analysis and to justify the choices made when operationalising the concept. It is also essential to clearly understand the adaptation problem at stake (adaptation to what) and to identify the people that are concerned with this situation (adaptation for whom). Importantly, the targeted temporal scale matters since the indicators will unveil responses over fast and slow temporal scales (Whitney et al., 2017). For instance, if an adaptive capacity assessment is carried out at a local scale – targeting communities as a system of interest – the way communities' boundaries are defined will influence the outcome of the results (Paveglio et al., 2016). Rather than favouring one scale over another in the assessment of adaptive capacity, it is more important to bear in mind that this choice is related to its normativity, another intrinsic characteristic of all conceptualisation approaches of adaptive capacity.

The normative dimension of adaptive capacity assessments corresponds to the third trend. We believe that all approaches, including social-ecological resilience, imply a certain degree of normativity. Indeed, the normative dimension was even more evident with elements from the resilience approach such as the adaptability and transformability concepts (Walker et al., 2006). The idea of assessing the 'desirability' of certain systems and the inherent roles of culture and power in operationalising adaptive capacity makes the treatment of adaptive capacity under a single epistemology a challenge (Cote & Nightingale, 2012). For all approaches, choosing a temporal, spatial, or social scale of analysis over another also implies explicit normative decisions that need clarification. As such, the passage from descriptive to prescriptive domains, especially in matters involving governance and policy recommendations, is a risky exercise if the normative dimensions of adaptive capacity are not recognised.

The fourth trend relates to the polysemy of adaptive capacity. Looking at the operational perspectives of each approach, several meanings can be derived from the concept of adaptive capacity. The polysemic character of adaptive capacity also partly explains why the notion is still vaguely defined and not well understood. Indeed, adaptation refers to being adapted at a particular time period (a state), to a dynamic adaptation (a process), which takes places at multiple spatial and temporal scales, and to adaptation actions (Engle, 2011; Magnan, 2009; Simonet, 2009). Those three meanings reflect the various research communities and theoretical influences from which adaptive capacity was operationalised, the two most prominent ones being centred on the concepts of vulnerability and resilience. It appears that the mobilisation on the topic of climate change and other issues connecting human societies with nature created distinct research communities, with their own polysemous concepts and theories. As such, the vulnerability and resilience research communities – albeit characterised by conceptual similarities – traditionally evolved in separate ways (Engle, 2011; Janssen et al., 2006; Miller et al., 2010; Nelson et al., 2007; Turner et al., 2003). The epistemic differences of resilience and vulnerability (Miller et al., 2010) take their roots from two co-existing perspectives: an anthropocentric and constructed vision of reality, focused on achieving policy objectives (vulnerability) and an ecocentric and positivist vision of reality, focused on maintaining processes and dynamics (resilience). Nevertheless, the common thread linking these two research communities is the concept of adaptive capacity, which partially explains its polysemic character.

3.3 Step Two: Crafting an Operational Definition of Adaptive Capacity

An operational definition translates the concept into something measurable and constitutes the basis from which to draw the operational framework (Hinkel, 2011). This subsection provides two general considerations to support the crafting of an operational definition of adaptive capacity.

Table 3.1. *Adaptive capacity attributes related to each conceptual approach of adaptive capacity*

Conceptual approach	Attributes	Sources
Development studies	Technology; resources; infrastructures; institutions; information; human, social, financial, and natural capital; poverty, health status; economic situation; governance	Adger et al., 2007; Brooks et al., 2005; Smit & Pilifosova, 2001; Yohe & Tol, 2002
Resilience studies	Novelty; diversity; organisation of human capital; trust; cross-scale communication, redundancy; variety; learning capacity; social networks; governance; social learning; agency; self-organisation; distribution of power; rules for collective action; informal rules; social networks; trust; awareness of climate change; efficiency and flexibility of institutions; learning; communication; knowledge; maintaining economic growth; protecting property or land; exploiting new opportunities	Adger et al., 2005; Berkes & Ross, 2013; Berkes & Turner, 2006; Bromley, 2012; Glaas et al., 2010; Johnston & Williamson, 2007; Keskitalo & Kulyasova, 2009; Lebel et al., 2006; Pahl-Wostl, 2008; Spiller, 2016; Thiel et al., 2015; Walker et al., 2006; Williams & Brown, 2014

The first consideration pertains to the action-driven nature of adaptive capacity assessments. Based on the assumption that certain characteristics of systems will facilitate the ability to adapt to climate change, understanding those attributes is a relevant goal for adaptive capacity assessments. Smit and Wandel (2006: 287) define those attributes as 'the forces that influence the ability of the system to adapt'. By knowing the characteristics that enhance or reduce their capacity to adapt as well as the social processes and historical context in which those attributes are embedded, governance systems can design relevant adaptation actions and strategies. Furthermore, they can take an active role in achieving adaptation outcomes (Beckley et al., 2008). Therefore, defining the general factors that determine adaptive capacity has been a major interest within the climate adaptation literature (Keskitalo, 2013; Keskitalo et al., 2011) and the basis from which to operationalise the concept. Table 3.1 presents an overview of different attributes identified in the literature has having the potential to foster capacities to adapt. Theories such as the architecture of entitlements (Adger & Kelly, 1999) or the capitals approach (Chen et al., 2015; Tinch et al., 2015) influenced this operationalisation. Building on those scientific contributions, the attributes influencing adaptive capacity include a variety of system characteristics and are based on a synthesis of many case studies.

The second consideration is highly connected with the first one and relates to the normative dimension of adaptive capacity. Indeed, as presented in the previous section, an adaptive capacity assessment is necessarily normative and scale dependent (Adger, 2003; Cote & Nightingale, 2012; Whitney et al., 2017). Therefore, understanding the norms, perceptions, and processes that influenced the state of a governance system is a relevant goal of adaptive capacity assessments.

We argue that since the existing definitions of adaptive capacity do not provide much guidance for assessing it, operational frameworks and methodologies must be developed according to the specific research or policy questions at stake. Thus, the crafting of an operational definition and framework depends on normative decisions that have to be taken prior to the adaptive capacity assessment.

3.4 Step Three: Designing the Operational Framework of Adaptive Capacity

Assessments of adaptive capacity stemming from the two broad conceptual approaches presented in the first step of the operational design process have used a range of methods and approaches (Lockwood et al., 2015), including theory-driven approaches (Brown, 2009), indicator-based approaches (Williges et al., 2017), secondary data sources (Brooks et al., 2005), community-based approaches (Warrick et al., 2017), and modelling (Levin et al., 2013; Schlüter et al., 2014).

Based on the trends observed from undertaking the literature review on adaptive capacity, the third step puts forward an operational framework to assess climate change adaptive capacity. Table 3.2 presents an overview of the epistemic, theoretical, and methodological dimensions of adaptive capacity for each of the three operations suggested in the operational framework. It is important to underline that this overview is an attempt to operationalise a polysemic concept. In that sense, other suggestions are more than welcome. This framework encompasses multiple epistemic viewpoints and could very well be implemented for a variety of cases. It is also important to bear in mind that the dimensions and categories highlighted in this framework don't have fixed frontiers. Indeed, those categories and dimensions were designed as a way to organise adaptive capacity assessments and provide guidance on how to operationalise a polysemic concept.

3.4.1 Characterising Adaptive Capacity

Engle (2011: 653) defines the process of characterising adaptive capacity as 'an attempt to assess adaptive capacity based on predetermined system attributes,

Table 3.2. *Overview of the different dimensions included in the proposed operational framework of adaptive capacity*

Dimension	Characterising adaptive capacity	Understanding adaptive capacity	Measuring adaptive capacity
Epistemic	Static	Dynamic Action-based	Static Dynamic Action-based
Theoretical	Vulnerability	Resilience	Vulnerability Resilience
Methodological	Top-down Quantitative methods	Bottom-up Qualitative methods	Top-down and bottom-up Mixed methods

mechanisms or indicators that are purported in the literature to increase adaptive capacity'. Therefore, characterising adaptive capacity aims at describing the available resources, characteristics, and properties of a system (Williamson & Isaac, 2012). This method is relevant to address the static dimension of adaptive capacity and thus to assess it at a particular timescale.

Given the impossibility of directly measuring the generic determinants and attributes identified in Table 3.1, proxies and indicators are used to characterise them. When focusing on the static dimension of adaptive capacity assessments, profile indicators – those that are used for discovering 'how things came to be that way or what needs to happen for things to be different' (Beckley et al., 2002: 631) – are appropriate. Empirical examples of generic determinants and indicators include a methodological application to assess the potential contributions of adaptation options in tackling flood vulnerability in the Netherlands (Yohe & Tol, 2002), an assessment of community capacity of Canadian rural communities affected by the impacts of climate change (Wall & Marzall, 2006), and case studies of community-based adaptation to climate change in the Pacific island regions (Warrick et al., 2017).

The overall objective of this first operation is to draw portraits of systems without attempting to establish causal explanations. In addition, descriptions of adaptive capacity include assessments of how adaptive capacity characteristics differ among systems, or how they are distributed. It is thus a descriptive-oriented perspective.

3.4.2 Understanding Adaptive Capacity

The rationale behind this operation is to enlighten the processes that foster adaptive capacity. This assessment is aligned with the dynamic and action-oriented epistemic dimensions of adaptive capacity. Therefore, starting from the profiles drawn while characterising adaptive capacity, the second operation aims at understanding how the properties and attributes of systems are mobilised. The literature on social resilience provides meaningful insights about the specific determinants and attributes that contribute to the understanding of adaptive capacity dynamics at different spatial and temporal scales (see Table 3.1).

Key questions raised in this assessment relate to resource mobilisation, institutions, governance processes, and values (Williamson & Isaac, 2012). How are resources mobilised to implement adaptation measures? What are the institutions and governance processes through which systems use their adaptation resources? How are those structures and mechanisms influenced by particular beliefs and values? Those questions are framed around the management and decision-making levels, which are important components of the social-ecological resilience perspective. Thus, empirical examples on adaptive governance (Hill, 2012; Risvoll et al., 2014), institutional adaptation (Naess et al., 2005), and adaptive co-management (Trimble & Berkes, 2015) are relevant to understand how those adaptive capacity processes were identified.

Starting from the premise that the overemphasis on governance structures has limits (Cote & Nightingale, 2012), another important component to include with this assessment is the understanding of the historical and social factors in which institutions and governance mechanisms are framed. Situating adaptive capacity analysis around power, knowledge, and values allows to address equity questions such as adaptive capacity to what and for whom, as well as about the desired adaptive capacity outcomes. From an empirical standpoint, three studies focusing on processes occurring at the community level are worth mentioning. First, Lyon and Parkins (2013) identified distinctive interactions between culture and agency over time and were able to demonstrate the role of culture in community adaptive responses. Second, Morzillo et al. (2015) looked at the interactions between drivers of change and place-based characteristics while analysing trajectories of change from US rural communities. They pointed out at the available stock of resources, connectivity, and social adaptability as variables related to development patterns. Third, using two case studies from Canadian forest-dependent communities, Lyon (2014) describes how place itself (not its emotional dimension) acts as a system to inform adaptation processes.

The resilience of the SES concept and the social-ecological framework described in the first step have been used to study adaptive governance and the integration of local knowledge in management of SES (Blanco & Fedreheim, 2011; Risvoll et al., 2014), to analyse the robustness of forest communities to disturbance (Fleischman et al., 2010), or in the context of adaptive co-management of small-scale fisheries (Armitage et al., 2008; Trimble & Berkes, 2015) by using participatory approaches and case studies. In addition, studies using scenario planning and modelling (Levin et al., 2013; Schlüter et al., 2014) had as a general objective to support decision-making and planning of SES.

Therefore, the main objective behind understanding adaptive capacity is to clarify the processes related to the decision-making structure and management rules of the system as well as its values and beliefs.

3.4.3 Measuring Adaptive Capacity

Measuring adaptive capacity is an operation that was described by Engle (2011: 653) as 'an attempt to directly assess the amount of adaptive capacity within a system at a given time so as to understand what factors determine this capacity based on the response to a recent event'. Measuring adaptive capacity is a challenging task with regards to the latent nature of the concept. Accordingly, proxy events or case histories can provide insights into a system's capacity to cope with and adapt to climate change (Hill, 2012; Keskitalo et al., 2011; Williamson & Isaac, 2012). For instance, a proxy event describing how a particular community has coped with and adapted to a past disturbance (flooding, fire, drought) can help to identify the forces that were mobilised to adapt as well as the actions that can be taken to improve adaptability. This approach allows assessing adaptive capacity at times when the system's structures are challenged (Folke et al., 2005).

However, Hill (2012) warns against the short cut of establishing a causal link between a specific outcome and a governance approach when it comes to the use of proxy events. Despite this concern, some key questions can be asked to shed light on the outcomes triggered by a proxy event: What could be observed? Which impacts did the event yield on the natural ecosystem? How was adaptation characterised? Who was involved in the adaptation process? Was there any institutional change following the event? Were there any new collaborative mechanisms created? Was any climate change knowledge developed? Were there any changes in the people's values or beliefs? By opening up the range of outcomes assessed in a manner that combines the evaluation of the impacts of institutional designs together with the nested political and social processes that influence the production of these designs (Cote & Nightingale, 2012), it is possible to assess adaptive capacity within the structural and relational components (Beckley et al., 2008).

The rationale behind measuring is to mobilise the different epistemic dimensions, theoretical contributions, and temporal scales of adaptive capacity. Consequently, assessments of outcomes are analysed together with the profile and process indicators identified in the first two steps. The overall objective behind measuring adaptive capacity is to provide a coherent narrative of adaptation to climate change that can serve as a baseline from which to design relevant adaptation strategies.

3.5 Conclusions

Assessing adaptive capacity is of key importance in a context of climate change. However, there is a variety of conceptualisations for adaptive capacity stemming from various theoretical contributions and empirical traditions. This chapter presented the development and resilience studies perspectives. The rationale behind this overview was not to praise or criticise any of them. Rather, this review proves that every conceptualisation serves different purposes and allows different adaptation questions to be answered. Furthermore, the crafting of an operational definition in the design of adaptive capacity assessments is also essential to foster a strong interdisciplinary dialogue. Indeed, the conceptual development of adaptive capacity is not characterised by a linear trajectory. On the contrary, different research traditions and disciplines – focusing on climate change research and the collective actions to reduce its related risks – merged to provide insights on the meaningful dimensions to include in an operational definition of adaptive capacity. For instance, bridging contributions between both the resilience and vulnerability research communities put forward the relevance of operationalising adaptive capacity by tackling a combination of system characteristics, adaptive capacity attributes, social processes, or collective actions. We perceive this dialogue as an essential way to understand human–environmental relations, to design innovative solutions that will help tackle climate-induced problems, and to contribute to the future development of the earth system governance framework.

This chapter argues that those views and definitions as well as the various developed frameworks to assess them should not be regarded as a problem. On the contrary, researchers should be aware that adopting a certain operational definition of adaptive capacity is a reflexive choice that influences its assessment. As such, it appears that conceptual choices are best guided by clear research questions and objectives. The suggested operational design process is thus an attempt to organise the different steps leading to the crafting of an operational definition and framework of adaptive capacity. Given the diversity of possible methodological options that could be used for assessing adaptive capacity, the three-step design process provides a series of elements to consider in order to be transparent about the operational choices made. The operational assessment framework presented in the third step intends to foster the understanding of adaptive capacity attributes, their relations, and how they are mobilised in an adaptation situation.

Insights presented in this chapter are the results of a literature review focusing on theoretical and conceptual reflections on adaptive capacity, resilience, and vulnerability, as well as empirical examples that mobilised and assessed those concepts. Rather than trying to provide a single operational definition that could be generalisable to multiple contexts, we embrace the conceptual diversity and highlight that it constitutes a rich heritage from which to base adaptive capacity assessments. Adaptive capacity holds the power to provide important insights on the decision-making structures, values, social relations, and actions that foster adaptation in a climate change context. This review on the topic of adaptive capacity led to a novel way of designing the operationalisation of climate change adaptive capacity. Transparency and reflectivity in the choices made to craft an operational definition of adaptive capacity not only contribute to enrich the literature on adaptive capacity assessments but are also capital with respect to the development of a fruitful science–policy interface. As a result, adopting a transparent and reflective attitude is a strategy that should yield promising results.

Building knowledge in the field of climate change adaptive capacity requires research that is sensitive to particular context but at the same time intertwined with global, national, or regional patterns of information. This situation opens the door to more debates and ideas on the topic of adaptive capacity operationalisation. The operational assessment framework presented in this chapter stresses the relevance of methodological plurality, while highlighting the key role of normative dimensions and policy considerations. The crucial role of policy considerations is emphasised by looking at the temporal dimension of adaptation. Indeed, policy outcomes sometimes imply choosing between quick-response mechanisms and adaptation strategies that will yield results in the long term: 'The combination of uncertainty, a dynamic knowledge base, a mixture of global, regional, national and local socioeconomic forces, and potentially great harm makes the adaptability-versus-stability dilemma particularly challenging in the case of drastic earth system transformations' (Biermann, 2014: 181). Finding the appropriate balance between flexible but yet robust adaptive responses remains a constant challenge for policymakers. Indeed, tackling this well-known paradox is key for governance systems that strive to be well prepared in the long term but also able to respond to rapid transformation occurring at different scales.

Additional empirical studies supported by innovative operational frameworks are definitely needed to enrich the operational field of climate change adaptive capacity. Similarly, empirical insights related to the suggested three-step design process and operational assessment framework are essential in order to understand the contribution and limits related to a design embracing multiple epistemic, conceptual, and methodological viewpoints. Questions that researchers should answer within a short time period should aim at identifying the operational design requirements that demonstrate successful bridging between adaptive capacity assessments and adaptation actions as well as providing further empirical evidence on the variety of attributes of governance systems and their potential to enhance capacities to adapt.

References

Adger, W.N. (2000). Social and ecological resilience: are they related? *Progress in Human Geography*, 24(3), 347–64.
  (2003). Social capital, collective action, and adaptation to climate change. *Economic Geography*, 79, 387–404.
Adger, W.N., Agrawala, S., Mirza, M.Q. et al. (2007). Assessment of adaptation practices, options, constraints and capacity. In. L. Parry, O.F. Canziani, J.P. Palutikof et al., eds., *Climate Change 2007: Impacts, Adaptation and Vulnerability: Contribution of Working Group II to the Fourth Assessment Report of the Intergovernmental Panel on Climate Change*. Cambridge, UK: Cambridge University Press, 717–43.
Adger, W.N., Arnell, N.W., & Tompkins, E.L. (2005). Successful adaptation to climate change across scales. *Global Environmental Change*, 15, 77–86.
Adger, W.N. & Kelly, P.M. (1999). Social vulnerability to climate change and the architecture of entitlements. *Mitigation and Adaptation Strategies for Global Change*, 4, 253–66.
Armitage, D., Marschke, M., & Plummer, R. (2008). Adaptive co-management and the paradox of learning. *Global Environmental Change*, 18, 86–98.
Beckley, T.M., Martz, D., Nadeau, S., Wall, E., & Reimer, B. (2008). Multiple capacities, multiple outcomes: delving deeper into the meaning of community capacity. *Journal of Rural and Community Development*, 3, 56–75.
Beckley, T., Parkins, J., & Stedman, R. (2002). Indicators of forest-dependent community sustainability: the evolution of research. *Forestry Chronicle*, 78, 626–36.
Berkes, F. & Folke, C. (1998). *Linking Social and Ecological Systems for Resilience and Sustainability*. Cambridge, UK: Cambridge University Press.
Berkes, F. & Ross, H. (2013). Community resilience: toward an integrated approach. *Society & Natural Resources*, 26, 5–20.
Berkes, F. & Turner, N.J. (2006). Knowledge, learning and the evolution of conservation practice for social-ecological system resilience. *Human Ecology*, 34(4), 479.
Biermann, F. (2014). *Earth System Governance: World Politics in the Anthropocene*. Cambridge, MA: MIT Press.
Blanco, E. & Fedreheim, G.E. (2011). *National Parks in Norway as Socio-Ecological System: Wildlife, Conflict in Use, and Community-Based Management*. 13th IASC International Conference, 10–14 January 2011. Hyderabad: Sustaining Commons: Sustaining our Future.
Bromley, D.W. (2012). Environmental governance as stochastic belief updating: crafting rules to live by. *Ecology and Society*, 17(3), 14.
Brooks, N., Adger, W.N., & Kelly, P.M. (2005). The determinants of vulnerability and adaptive capacity at the national level and the implications for adaptation. *Global Environmental Change*, 15, 151–63.
Brown, H.C.P. (2009). Climate change and Ontario forests: prospects for building institutional adaptive capacity. *Mitigation and Adaptation Strategies for Global Change*, 14, 513–36.
Brown, K. & Westaway, E. (2011). Agency, capacity, and resilience to environmental change: lessons from human development, well-being, and disasters. *Annual Review of Environment and Resources*, 36, 321–42.
Brunner, R.D., Steelman, T.A., Coe-Juell, L. et al. (2005). *Adaptive Governance: Integrating Science, Policy, and Decision Making*. New York: Columbia University Press.
Chen, M., Sun, F., Berry, P. et al. (2015). Integrated assessment of China's adaptive capacity to climate change with a capital approach. *Climatic Change*, 128, 367–80.

Cote, M. & Nightingale, A.J. (2012). Resilience thinking meets social theory: situating social change in socio-ecological systems (SES) research. *Progress in Human Geography*, 36, 475–89.

Cumming, G.S., Olsson, P., Chapin, F., & Holling, C. (2013). Resilience, experimentation, and scale mismatches in social-ecological landscapes. *Landscape Ecology*, 28, 1139–50.

Cuthill, M., Ross, H., Maclean, K. et al. (2008). Reporting social outcomes of development: an analysis of diverse approaches. *International Journal of Interdisciplinary Social Sciences*, 3, 145–57.

Del Mar Delgado-Serrano, M., Escalante, R., & Basurto, S. (2015). Is the community-based management of natural resources inherently linked to resilience? An analysis of the Santiago Comaltepec community (Mexico). *Ager: Revista de Estudios sobre Despoblacion y Desarrollo Rural*, 2015(18), 91–114.

Den Otter, M.A. & Beckley, T.M. (2002). *'This Is Paradise': Community Sustainability Indicators for the Western Newfoundland Model Forest*. Fredericton: Canadian Forest Centre, Atlantic Forestry Centre.

Engle, N.L. (2011). Adaptive capacity and its assessment. *Global Environmental Change*, 21, 647–56.

Fleischman, F.D., Boenning, K., Garcia-Lopez, G.A. et al. (2010). Disturbance, response, and persistence in self-organized forested communities: analysis of robustness and resilience in five communities in southern Indiana. *Ecology and Society*, 15(4), 9.

Folke, C. (2006). Resilience: the emergence of a perspective for social-ecological systems analyses. *Global Environmental Change*, 16, 253–67.

Folke, C., Hahn, T., Olsson, P., & Norberg, J. (2005). Adaptive governance of social-ecological systems. *Annual Review of Environment and Resources*, 30, 441–73.

Ford, J.D., Berrang-Ford, L., Lesnikowski, A., Barrera, M., & Heymann, S.J. (2013). How to track adaptation to climate change: a typology of approaches for national-level application. *Ecology and Society*, 18(3), 40.

Glaas, E., Jonsson, A., Mattias, H., & Andersson-Sköld, Y. (2010). Managing climate change vulnerabilities: formal institutions and knowledge use as determinants of adaptive capacity at the local level in Sweden. *Local Environment*, 15(6), 525–39.

Gunderson, L., Holling, C.S., & Light, S.S. (1995). *Barriers and Bridges to Renewal of Ecosystems and Institutions*. New York: Columbia University Press.

Hill, M. (2012). *Climate Change and Water Governance: Adaptive Capacity in Chile and Switzerland*. Dordrecht: Springer Science & Business Media.

Hill, M. & Engle, N.L. (2013). Adaptive capacity: tensions across scales. *Environmental Policy and Governance*, 23, 177–92.

Hinkel, J. (2011). Indicators of vulnerability and adaptive capacity: towards a clarification of the science-policy interface. *Global Environmental Change*, 21(1), 198–208.

Hinkel, J., Bots, P.W.G., & Schlüter, M. (2014). Enhancing the Ostrom social-ecological system framework through formalization. *Ecology and Society*, 19(3), 51.

Janssen, M., Schoon, M.L., Ke, W., & Boerner, K. (2006). Scholarly networks on resilience, vulnerability and adaptation within the human dimensions of global environmental change. *Global Environmental Change*, 16, 240–52.

Johnston, M. & Williamson, T. (2007). A framework for assessing climate change vulnerability of the Canadian forest sector. *Forestry Chronicle*, 83(3), 358–61.

Kelly, C., Ferrara, A., Wilson, G.A. et al. (2015). Community resilience and land degradation in forest and shrubland socio-ecological systems: evidence from Gorgoglione, Basilicata, Italy. *Land Use Policy*, 46, 11–20.

Keskitalo, C. (2013). Understanding adaptive capacity in forest governance: editorial. *Ecology and Society*, 18(4), 45.

Keskitalo, C., Klenk, N., Bullock, R., Smith, A.L., & Bazely, D.R. (2011). Preparing for and responding to disturbance: examples from the forest sector in Sweden and Canada. *Forests*, 2, 505–24.

Keskitalo, E.C.H. & Kulyasova, A.A. (2009). The role of governance in community adaptation to climate change. *Polar Research*, 28(1), 60–70.

Kofinas, G., Clark, D., Hovelsrud, G.K. et al. (2013). Adaptive and transformative capacity. In Arctic Council, *Arctic Resilience Interim Report*. Stockholm: Stockholm Environment Institute and Stockholm Resilience Centre, 75–93.

Lebel, L., Anderies, J.M., Campbell, B. et al. (2006). Governance and the capacity to manage resilience in regional social-ecological systems. *Ecology and Society*, 11(1), 19.

Levin, S., Xepapadeas, T., Crépin, A.-S. et al. (2013). Social-ecological systems as complex adaptive systems: modeling and policy implications. *Environment and Development Economics*, 18, 111–32.

Lockwood, M., Raymond, C.M., Oczkowski, E., & Morrison, M. (2015). Measuring the dimensions of adaptive capacity: a psychometric approach. *Ecology and Society*, 20(1), 37.

Lyon, C. (2014). Place systems and social resilience: a framework for understanding place in social adaptation, resilience, and transformation. *Society & Natural Resources*, 27, 1009–23.

Lyon, C. & Parkins, J.R. (2013). Toward a social theory of resilience: social systems, cultural systems, and collective action in transitioning forest-based communities. *Rural Sociology*, 78, 528–49.

McGinnis, M.D. & Ostrom, E. (2014). Social-ecological system framework: initial changes and continuing challenges. *Ecology and Society*, 19(2), 30.

Maclean, K. Cuthill, M., & Ross, H. (2014). Six attributes of social resilience. *Journal of Environmental Planning and Management*, 57, 144–56.

Magnan, A. (2009). Proposition d'une trame de recherche pour appréhender la capacité d'adaptation au changement climatique. *VertigO*, 9, 3. doi: https://doi.org/10.4000/vertigo.9189.

Marino, E. (2015). *Fierce Climate, Sacred Ground: An Ethnography of Climate Change in Shishmaref*. Alaska: University of Alaska Press.

Miller, F., Osbahr, H., Boyd, E. et al. (2010). Resilience and vulnerability: complementary or conflicting concepts. *Ecology and Society*, 15(3), 11.

Morzillo, A.T., Colocusis, C.R., Munroe, D.K. et al. (2015). 'Communities in the middle': interactions between drivers of change and place-based characteristics in rural forest-based communities. *Journal of Rural Studies*, 42, 79–90.

Naess, L.O., Bang, G., Eriksen, S., & Vevatne, J. (2005). Institutional adaptation to climate change: flood responses at the municipal level in Norway. *Global Environmental Change*, 15, 125–38.

Nelson, D.R., Adger, W.N., & Brown, K. (2007). Adaptation to environmental change: contributions of a resilience framework. *Annual Review of Environment and Resources*, 32, 395–419.

Ostrom, E. (2007). A diagnostic approach for going beyond panaceas. *Proceedings of the National Academy of Sciences of the United States of America*, 104, 15181–7.

 (2009). A general framework for analyzing sustainability of social-ecological systems. *Science*, 325, 419–22.

Pahl-Wostl, C. (2008). Requirements for adaptive water management. In C. Pahl-Wostl, P. Kabat, & J. Möltgen, eds., *Adaptive and Integrated Water Management.* Berlin: Springer, 1–22.

Paveglio, T., Carroll, M.S., & Boyd, A.D. (2016). Re-conceptualizing community in risk research. *Journal of Risk Research*, 20, 931–51.

Plummer, R., Armitage, D.R., & De Loë, R.C. (2013). Adaptive co-management and its relationship to environmental governance. *Ecology and Society*, 18(1), 21.

Poteete, A.R., Janssen, M.A., & Ostrom, E. (2010). *Working Together: Collective Action, the Commons, and Multiple Methods in Practice.* Princeton, NJ: Princeton University Press.

Risvoll, C., Fedreheim, G.E., Sandberg, A., & Burnsilver, S. (2014). Does pastoralists' participation in the management of national parks in northern Norway contribute to adaptive governance? *Ecology and Society*, 19(2), 71.

Schlüter, M., Hinkel, J., Bots, P.W., & Arlinghaus, R. (2014). Application of the SES framework for model-based analysis of the dynamics of social-ecological systems. *Ecology and Society*, 19(1), 36.

Scoones, I. (1998). *Sustainable Rural Livelihoods: A Framework for Analysis.* Brighton: Institute for Development Studies.

Simonet, G. (2009). Le concept d'adaptation: polysémie interdisciplinaire et implication pour les changements climatiques. *Natures Sciences Sociétés*, 17, 392–401.

(2015). Une brève histoire de l'adaptation: l'évolution conceptuelle au fil des rapports du GIEC (1990–2014). *Natures Sciences Sociétés*, 23, S52–64.

Smit, B. & Pilifosova, O. (2001). Adaptation to climate change in the context of sustainable development and equity. In. L. Parry, O.F. Canziani, J.P. Palutikof et al., eds., *Climate Change 2007: Impacts, Adaptation and Vulnerability: Contribution of Working Group II to the Fourth Assessment Report of the Intergovernmental Panel on Climate Change.* Cambridge, UK: Cambridge University Press, 877–913.

Smit, B. & Wandel, J. (2006). Adaptation, adaptive capacity and vulnerability. *Global Environmental Change*, 16, 282–92.

Spiller, M. (2016). Adaptive capacity indicators to assess sustainability of urban water systems: current application. *Science of the Total Environment*, 569, 751–61.

Thiel, A., Adamseged, M.E., & Baake, C. (2015). Evaluating an instrument for institutional crafting: how Ostrom's social-ecological systems framework is applied. *Environmental Science & Policy*, 53, 152–64.

Tinch, R., Jäger, J., Omann, I. et al. (2015). Applying a capitals framework to measuring coping and adaptive capacity in integrated assessment models. *Climatic Change*, 128, 323–37.

Trimble, M. & Berkes, F. (2015). Towards adaptive co-management of small-scale fisheries in Uruguay and Brazil: lessons from using Ostrom's design principles. *Maritime Studies*, 14, 14.

Turner, B.L., Kasperson, R.E., Matson, P.A. et al. (2003). A framework for vulnerability analysis in sustainability science. *Proceedings of the National Academy of Sciences of the United States of America*, 100, 8074–9.

Walker, B., Gunderson, L., Kinzig, G. et al. (2006). A handful of heuristics and some propositions for understanding resilience in social-ecological systems. *Ecology and Society*, 11(1), 13.

Walker, B., Holling, C.S., Carpenter, S.R., & Kinzig, A. (2004). Resilience, adaptability and transformability in social-ecological systems. *Ecology and Society*, 9(2), 5.

Wall, E. & Marzall, K. (2006). Adaptive capacity for climate change in Canadian rural communities. *Local Environment*, 11, 373–97.

Warrick, O., Aalbersberg, W., Dumaru, P., Mcnaught, R., & Teperman, K. (2017). The 'Pacific adaptive capacity analysis framework': guiding the assessment of adaptive capacity in Pacific Island communities. *Regional Environmental Change*, 17, 1039–51.

Whitney, C.K., Bennett, N.J., Ban, N.C. et al. (2017). Adaptive capacity: from assessment to action in coastal social-ecological systems. *Ecology and Society*, 22(2), 22.

Williams, B.K. & Brown, E.D. (2014). Adaptive management: from more talk to real action. *Environmental Management*, 53, 465–79.

Williamson, T.B. & Isaac, K.J. (2012). *Adapting Sustainable Forest Management to Climate Change: An Overview of Approaches for Assessing Human Adaptive Capacity*. Ottawa: Canadian Council of Forest Ministers.

Williges, K., Mechler, R., Bowyer, P., & Balkovic, J. (2017). Towards an assessment of adaptive capacity of the European agricultural sector to droughts. *Climate Services*, 7, 47–63.

Wyborn, C. & Bixler, R.P. (2013). Collaboration and nested environmental governance: scale dependency, scale framing, and cross-scale interactions in collaborative conservation. *Journal of Environmental Management*, 123, 58–67.

Yohe, G. & Tol, R.S.J. (2002). Indicators for social and economic coping capacity: moving toward a working definition of adaptive capacity. *Global Environmental Change*, 12(1), 25–40.

4

Assessing the Adaptive Capacity of Collaborative Governance Institutions

PEDRO FIDELMAN

4.1 Introduction

The concepts of adaptive capacity and governance institutions are critical to the earth system governance focus on *adaptiveness*. Adaptive capacity refers to the preconditions that enable adaptation, including resources (e.g. social and physical elements) and the ability to mobilise these resources in anticipation or response to social-ecological change (Engle, 2011; Nelson et al., 2007). How societies respond and adapt to such change is influenced to a large extent by governance institutions (Gupta et al., 2010; Young, 2002). These institutions consist of 'formal and informal rules, rule-making systems, and actor networks at all levels of human society (from local to global) that are set up to steer societies towards preventing, mitigating, and adapting to global and local environmental change' (Biermann et al., 2009: 4).

Institutions have received sustained attention as primary determinants of adaptive capacity (Adger et al., 2005; Engle, 2011; Gupta et al., 2010; Mandryk et al., 2015; Nelson et al., 2007). Responding to contemporary and future social-ecological change will require institutions that facilitate the adaptive capacity of individuals, groups, and organisations (Adger et al., 2005; Agrawal, 2008; Engle, 2011; Nelson et al., 2007). This will involve responsive and flexible institutions that support the ability of social actors to respond through both planned and spontaneous processes (Gupta et al., 2010). Collaborative decision-making involving a range of social and political actors (e.g. government, resource users, and non-governmental organisations (NGOs)) should underpin these institutions (Carlsson & Berkes, 2005; Plummer & Armitage, 2007).

A key research issue for earth system governance is how to assess and compare adaptiveness (ESG, 2018). Several studies have attempted to assess adaptive capacity by drawing on selected institutional (and, more broadly, governance) attributes (e.g. Engle & Lemos, 2010; Fidelman, 2019; Fidelman et al., 2017; Gupta et al., 2010; Mandryk et al., 2015). Fidelman et al. (2017) propose an evaluative approach that provides specific insights into which institutions may influence adaptive capacity and how. The application of their approach to empirical studies helps shed light on the complex and interrelated nature of institutions in how they may enable (or otherwise) key attributes of adaptive capacity (Fidelman et al., 2017). Accordingly, it provides specific guidance on institutional design and governance interventions that may be required to enhance such capacity. The aims of this chapter are to review the evaluative approach in question and distil lessons from its application to case studies on coastal resources management and marine conservation. The chapter draws on recent work by this author published in the peer-reviewed literature (i.e. Fidelman, 2019; Fidelman et al., 2017). It underscores the role of contextual factors and power relations in shaping the nexus between institutions and adaptive capacity and, therefore, the need to consider such a role in future adaptive capacity assessments.

The next section reproduces the evaluative approach proposed in Fidelman et al. (2017). It is followed by a description of the case studies. The subsequent two sections summarise key lessons from the application of the evaluative approach and addresses their implications for earth system governance, respectively.

4.2 An Evaluative Approach to Adaptive Capacity

Assessments of adaptive capacity usually draw on predetermined attributes or indicators believed to be necessary to foster such capacity (Engle, 2011). In terms of governance institutions, these attributes correspond to 'the inherent characteristics of institutions that empower social actors to respond to short- and long-term impacts, either through planned measures or through allowing and encouraging creative responses from society both *ex ante* and *ex post*' (Gupta et al., 2010: 461). They can be grouped into six general categories (Gupta et al., 2010): the ability of institutions to (1) encourage the inclusion of various actors, perspectives, and solutions; (2) enable actors to learn and improve their institutions; (3) allow and motivate these actors to self-organise, design, and reform their institutions; (4) mobilise their leadership qualities; (5) mobilise resources for decision-making and implementation; and (6) support principles of fair governance, such as legitimacy, equity, responsiveness, and accountability. These attributes have been employed – as part of the 'Adaptive Capacity Wheel' (Gupta et al., 2010) – to examine adaptive capacity in different settings and sectors (e.g. water management, coastal protection, agriculture, regional planning, and climate vulnerability) (Bergsma et al., 2012; Grecksch, 2014; Grothmann et al., 2013; Gupta et al., 2016; Munaretto & Klostermann, 2011; van den Brink et al., 2014; van den Brink et al., 2011). They are conceptualised here as variety, learning capacity, autonomy, leadership, resources, and fair governance (Table 4.2).

Table 4.1. *Types of institutional rules*

Position rules specify the participants (who in turn have a combination of resources, perspectives, and preferences) and their roles in adaptation to social-ecological change

Boundary rules specify how participants can take part in adaptation efforts

Choice rules specify the actions participants can take as part of their roles

Aggregation rules specify decision-making procedures, including arrangements to aggregate the preferences of participants

Information rules specify the arrangements for information exchange between participants

Pay-off rules specify the incentives and disincentives, in terms of resources available to support decision-making and action

Scope rules specify the functional scope and geographic domain that can be affected by adaptation efforts

Drawing on the institutional analysis and development framework's concept of *action situation* (Ostrom, 2005), Fidelman et al. (2017) describe the links between institutions and the attributes of adaptive capacity. The action situation is the social space where actors interact, make decisions, and realise outcomes from their interactions (McGuinnis, 2011; Ostrom, 2011). Accordingly, it is the locus where individuals and/or organisations make decisions and implement actions in response to social-ecological change (Fidelman et al., 2017). Seven categories of institutional rules (Table 4.1; see Ostrom, 2011) affect the action situation: position, boundary, choice, aggregation, information, pay-off, and scope (Figure 4.1).

In affecting the action situation, these seven types of rules, therefore, affect the determinants of adaptive capacity (i.e. variety, learning capacity, autonomy, leadership, resources, and fair governance) that manifest in that situation. For example, by determining the participants in adaptation efforts, their actions, and potential outcomes, the position, boundary, choice, and scope rules, respectively, affect *variety* through inclusive participation, diversity of actions, and issues addressed. Likewise, aggregation and choice rules affect *autonomy* by determining participants' decision-making authority and their actions. Table 4.2 identifies the primary institutional rules relating to each of the adaptive capacity attributes.

4.3 Case Studies Background

The evaluative approach described in Table 4.2 has been applied in case studies on collaborative governance of coastal resources in Cambodia and Vietnam (Fidelman et al., 2017), and marine conservation in the Coral Triangle (Fidelman, 2019). Data for the case studies came from desktop reviews, interviews, and workshops with relevant stakeholders, including resource users, government officials, and NGO

Pedro Fidelman

Table 4.2. *Adaptive capacity attributes, indicators, and relevant institutional rules*

Attribute	Definition	Indicators	Relevant rule
Variety	The ability of institutions to include a variety of actors, perspectives, and solutions. Because social-ecological change is complex and unstructured (lacks agreement on values), embedding diverse interests and perspectives, responding and adapting to such change requires multiple perspectives and solutions. This includes the participation of relevant stakeholders across different sectors and levels of governance in problem framing and formulation of solutions	Inclusive participation of relevant actors Diversity of perspectives, and actions and issues addressed	Position, boundary, choice, scope
Learning capacity	Learning is critical for dealing with uncertainty, surprises, and variability that characterise social-ecological change. There is an ongoing need to revise existing knowledge and understanding to enable adaptation. Learning allows actors to reformulate knowledge and understanding based on experiences. Adaptive institutions are, therefore, those that enable social actors to continuously learn and experiment to improve their institutions	Activities and mechanisms that entail learning (meetings, joint decision-making, collaborative activities, monitoring, and evaluation, etc.)	Information, choice
Autonomy	The ability of social actors to autonomously review and adjust institutions in response to social-ecological change. Adaptive institutions allow and motivate actors to self-organise, design, and reform their institutions.	Authority to make and implement decisions Authority is not undermined by other actors/decision-making entities	Aggregation, choice, pay-off

Table 4.2. (*cont.*)

Attribute	Definition	Indicators	Relevant rule
	Authority (legitimate or accepted forms of power) for decision-making and implementation is key to autonomy, when it is supported (or at least not challenged) by other actors		
Leadership	Leadership may be regarded as a driver for change when it points to (a) direction(s) and motivates others to follow, facilitate access to resources, and bridge and build partnerships. Institutions supporting adaptive capacity are those that can mobilise leadership qualities of actors in the process of (re)designing institutions	Ability of actors to direct and motivate others to follow, gain access to resources, and bridge and build partnerships	Position, boundary, choice
Resources	Resources are critical in generating incentives and reducing transaction costs for actors to engage in collective action. Therefore, adaptive institutions have the capacity to mobilise resources (human, financial, technical) for making and implementing decisions (e.g. adaptation measures)	Human, financial and technical resources	Pay-off
Fair governance	Fair governance includes institutions that are accepted and supported by their constituents (legitimacy), considered to be fair (equity), responsive (responsiveness), and/or accountable to actors (accountability)	Legitimacy, equity, responsiveness, accountability	Boundary, choice, aggregation, information

Source: Fidelman et al. (2017), Gupta et al. (2010), and Termeer et al. (2011).

Pedro Fidelman

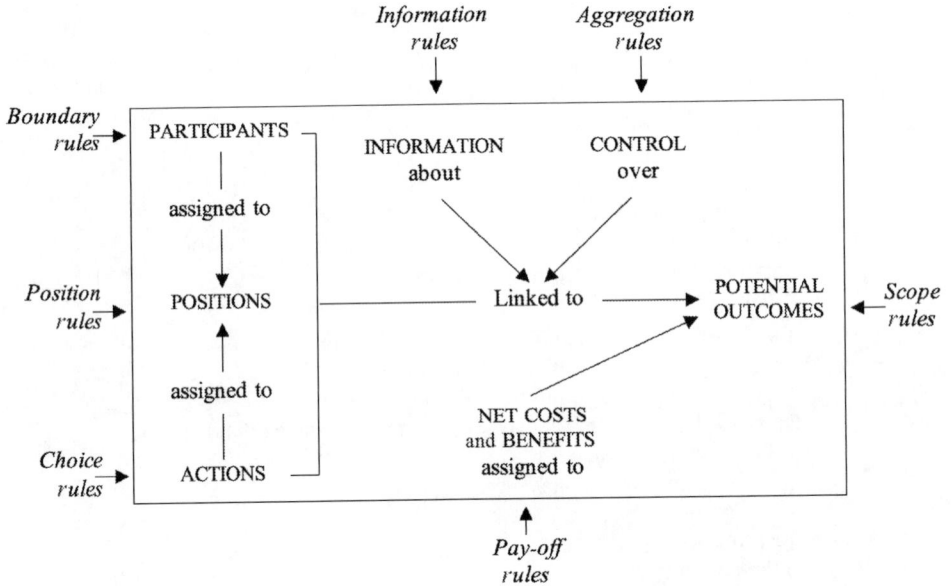

Figure 4.1 The influence of institutional rules on the action situation.
Source: Ostrom (2011)

representatives (for details, see Fidelman et al., 2017). The case studies are summarised, as follows:

Peam Krasaop Wildlife Sanctuary (PKWS) is located in the Koh Kong province, southwest Cambodia. The PKWS contains approximately 24,000 hectares of mangroves (Marschke & Nong, 2003) and is home to 10,000 people who live across three administrative districts, containing 6 communes and 15 villages. For most of these people, mangroves and associated resources provide income generation and livelihood. However, since the early 1990s, coastal resources have significantly declined as a result of population growth, clearing of mangroves for aquaculture and charcoal production, destructive fishing practices (e.g. cyanide fishing), and illegal fishing (Marschke, 2012; Marschke & Nong, 2003). In response to resource decline, in the late 1990s, a collaborative governance initiative known as Participatory Management of Mangrove Resources, led by the Ministry of Environment, facilitated the establishment of village management committees comprising members of the community and resource users (Participatory Management of Coastal Resources Project, 2008). These committees with the support of provincial and national authorities had responsibility for resource management at the local level.

The **Tam Giang Lagoon (TGL)** is located in Thua Thien Hue Province, Central Vietnam. It covers an area of approximately 22,000 hectares and stretches approximately 70 km along the coast (Tuyen et al., 2010). The lagoon's aquatic resources are directly or indirectly important for 300,000 people living in 33 communes and towns, and 326 villages across the lagoon area (Tuyen, 2002; Tuyen et al., 2010). A rapid resource-use intensification over the past 15 years or so led to the decline in fish catch and restricted access to the lagoon (Tuyen, 2002). In addition, these problems were exacerbated by agricultural development and urbanisation (Tuyen et al., 2010). Collaborative governance (i.e. co-management) was initially adopted at the district level to complement the existing centralised, top-down management approach. Fundamental elements of co-management in the TGL include fishing associations (i.e. a type of social-professional organisation with responsibility for resource management at the local level) (Tuyen et al., 2010).

The **Coral Triangle Initiative (CTI)** is an intergovernmental agreement between Malaysia, the Philippines, Indonesia, Timor Leste, Papua New Guinea, and the Solomon Islands. Formally adopted in 2009, it aims to address critical issues in the Coral Triangle (e.g. overfishing, unsustainable fishing practices, land-based sources of marine pollution, coastal habitat conversion, and climate change) and pursue a more sustainable use of the region's resources. A regional plan of action is a core component of the CTI; it comprises a legally non-binding document containing goals and actions over a period of 10–15 years. The Regional Plan of Action focuses primarily on (a) designating and effectively managing priority seascapes, (b) applying an ecosystem approach to fisheries management and other marine resources, (c) establishing and effectively managing marine protected areas, (d) adopting climate change adaptation measures, and (e) improving the status of threatened species. The regional plan provides an overarching framework for the national plans of action developed by each Coral Triangle country with support from NGOs and other stakeholders. Like other large-scale marine governance efforts, the CTI features institutions for coordinating actions among stakeholders to address resource use and management across jurisdictions.

The case studies consist of collaborative governance institutions in the context of resource management and conservation. These institutions define the participation of a range of actors, such as international donor agencies, researchers, government officials, and resource users (boundary rules) who are regarded as partners (position rules) and focus on a range of mechanisms (e.g. awareness raising, capacity building, and conflict resolution [choice rules]). Responsibility for resources management and conservation is shared among relevant such actors (aggregation rules). Decision-making and implementation focus on multiple aspects, such as protection, conservation, allocation, and livelihoods within a given geographical area (scope rules). The participation of both state and non-state actors entails consideration of both technical and non-technical knowledge (information rules). Collaborative governance is supported by resources shared by the actors involved (pay-off rules). Specific institutional arrangements characterising each of the case studies and their influence on the six dimensions of adaptive capacity are examined in detail in Fidelman et al. (2017) and Fidelman (2019).

4.4 Lessons from the Application of the Evaluative Approach

Critical insights from the analysis of the case studies include the role of institutions, contextual factors, and power relations in shaping adaptive capacity. These are discussed in the following subsections.

4.4.1 Institutions Can Both Enable and Disable Adaptive Capacity

Institutions have supported to varying degrees the six dimensions of adaptive capacity (i.e. variety, learning capacity, autonomy, leadership, resources, and fair governance; see Fidelman, 2019; Fidelman et al., 2017), creating both enabling and disabling conditions (Table 4.3).

In the PKWS and TGL, institutions enabled actors to self-organise; learn and improve resource management; mobilise leadership, resources, and authority; and make progress towards improved governance (Fidelman et al., 2017). Similarly, for the Coral Triangle, institutions enabled multiple stakeholders to collaborate to address pressing issues affecting the area; mobilise resources, leadership, and authority; and contribute to improved regional governance (Fidelman, 2019). On the other hand, top-down approaches to governance and power asymmetry and conflicting interests among the actors comprised instances where building and mobilisation of adaptive capacity can be constrained (Fidelman, 2019; Fidelman et al., 2017).

Institutions can inherently both expand and/or limit human decision-making and action (Ostrom, 2005) and, therefore, enable and/or constrain adaptation (Eakin et al., 2014; Engle & Lemos, 2010). This is compounded by their interconnected nature, interacting in a configurational manner rather than independently. Further, one type of institutional rule can, through its direct impact on one of the components of the action situation, affect other components of that situation (Ostrom & Crawford, 2005). For example, position and boundary rules affect *variety*, which has significant implications for other dimensions of adaptive capacity, particularly learning, autonomy, resources, and fair governance through its effects on information and aggregation rules. In the TGL, fishers perceived the fishing associations as a bridge for information from district and provincial authorities (*learning capacity*); links with commune authorities provided opportunity for engagement in addressing threats to the lagoon resources and

Table 4.3. *Examples of enabling and disabling conditions of adaptive capacity*

Dimension	Enabling conditions	Disabling conditions
Variety	Engagement of state and non-state actors from various sectors and multiple levels of governance Involvement of diverse knowledge and expertise	Conflicts and tensions between actors resulting from diverse perspectives, interests, and authority
Learning capacity	Decision-making and management activities with potential to entail learning through interaction and information exchange (e.g. training workshops, discussion forums, joint implementation, regular meetings)	Limited resources for activities entailing learning, conflict and tensions between actors, power imbalance, weak leadership
Autonomy	Policies and legislation supporting collaborative decision-making and action	Limited decision-making and implementation authority Partial support from higher-level authorities
Leadership	Engagement and commitment of local and external leaders	Leadership qualities eroded by limited resources, self-interest, power imbalance, conflicts and tensions between actors
Resources	Ability of actors to mobilise external and internal resources (financial, technical, and human)	Limited, inconsistent resources, overdependence on external support
Fair governance	Decentralisation of decision-making, devolution of authority, allocation of property rights	Tensions and conflicts, power imbalance, partial support from high-level authorities, limited resources, inconsistent policy implementation

Source: Fidelman et al. (2017: 109).

dispute resolution strategies (*autonomy*); and, through their membership in these associations, greater involvement in decisions regarding resource use and management was made possible (*fair governance*).

The configurational nature and interconnectedness of institutional rules may also determine the interdependent nature of the six dimensions of adaptive capacity, as these dimensions can reinforce and/or constrain each other (Gupta et al., 2010). For example, external financial and technical resources were critical to support learning activities in the cases studied (*resources* have supported *learning capacity*). In the PKWS and TGL cases, such activities aimed to enhance the ability of villagers, fishermen, government authorities, and technical staff to participate in collaborative governance (*learning* has reinforced *variety*). *Resources* also helped mobilise *leadership* by, for example, reducing the transaction costs of participation. *Leadership*, in turn, proved critical to mobilise further external technical *resources* and authority (*autonomy*). Later, policies and legislation formalised and provided legitimacy and legal authority for local actors to take part in collaborative governance (*autonomy* has supported *governance* and *variety*). Conversely, limited *resources* and *autonomy* have constrained *leadership* qualities of local actors; and inconsistent policy implementation and law enforcement have undermined local authority in some instances (*governance* has constrained *autonomy*).

4.4.2 Contextual Factors Matter

Engle (2011) argues that adaptive capacity is context-specific and may be influenced by dynamic variables. Further, the context in which collaborative governance takes place is remarkably complex, and therefore can both enable and constrain governance efforts (Fidelman, 2019; Fidelman et al., 2012; Fidelman et al., 2017).

In terms of the institutional analysis and development framework, institutional rules interact with other contextual factors in affecting the action situation (i.e. the locus where adaptive capacity emerges and is mobilised). These contextual factors comprise the *characteristics of the biophysical environment* and *attributes of the community* of individuals involved (Ostrom, 2005). The cases studied feature heterogeneous and complex factors. In the Coral Triangle, for example, marine species attributes (e.g. mobility, spatial and temporal patchiness, and distinctive markings) vary across resources. Similarly, political, economic, and cultural attributes are remarkably diverse both between and within Coral Triangle countries. These include population size, composition and growth, language, religion, gross domestic product, and political and legal systems. In this case, contextual factors create diverse (and very often challenging) situations that governance institutions must address (Fidelman et al., 2012).

Enabling adaptive capacity will, therefore, require context-dependent strategies – which is consistent with the argument against panaceas (i.e. universal solutions) for social-ecological problems (Ostrom, 2007; Ostrom & Cox, 2010). For example, in the PKWS and TGL, reinforcing existing enabling conditions will involve – in addition to changing institutional rules to provide adequate financial and technical resources (*pay-off rules*), authority (*choice rules*) and conflict resolution mechanisms (*aggregation rules*) – providing alternative livelihoods, alleviating poverty, reducing inequality, and building human and social capital. In the CTI context, strategies aiming to enhance adaptive capacity will require attention to how power relations influence the relationship between institutions and adaptive capacity, as discussed in the next section.

4.4.3 *Power Relations as a Constraining Factor*

Power relations are a critical factor underpinning institutional constraints to adaptive capacity. In the CTI, such relations enabled international NGOs to ensure that institutional design served their interests. The ability of international NGOs to access legal authority, public opinion, information, supporters, financial resources, and skilful leadership gave them disproportionate influence in relation to other stakeholders. They used such ability to help establish the CTI and shape its development (Rosen & Olsson, 2013). This includes influencing *variety* in terms of inclusive (or otherwise) participation in decision-making. The limited representation of relevant stakeholders, in turn, affected the diversity of perspectives and issues addressed. Power relations also affected *learning capacity*, given the ability of international NGOs to access and distribute information and make their knowledge common ground (von Heland et al., 2014). This, in turn, contributed to the strong focus on ecological aspects of marine governance underpinning the CTI. While international NGOs provided important *leadership*, including the mobilisation of human, technical, and financial *resources*, such influence may have limited the sense of ownership of national stakeholders (WorldFish Centre/USAID, 2010) and raised questions about *fair governance* in terms of equity, legitimacy, and accountability.

Power relations are inherently embedded in governance institutions (Nightingale, 2017), which may explain the constrains to adaptive capacity highlighted earlier in the chapter. On one hand, institutions affect power distribution, which, in turn, determine who is involved in adaptation efforts and in which manner. On the other hand, power distribution directly affects institutional design and reform (Clement, 2012; Kashwan, 2016; Nightingale, 2017). In this context, addressing power asymmetry in collaborative governance would involve, to some extent, reviewing those institutional rules that may contribute to creating and reinforcing such asymmetry (e.g. choice rules, which limit or expand actors' actions, and aggregation rules, which limit or expand decision-making of these actors as they interact). In this case, institutional change should aim at enhancing the capacity of relevant actors to participate in decision-making. Such capacity would be further enhanced by changes in pay-off rules aiming at providing adequate resources to those actors. In addition, changes in prevailing discourses that legitimate institutions would also be needed (Clement, 2010). Finally, institutional change aiming at enhancing adaptive capacity (e.g. changing position and boundary rules to increase the variety of interests represented in collaborative governance) needs to pay attention to how the different interests mediate power relations. This includes understanding struggles over authority and the desire of actors for social and political recognition (Nightingale, 2017). This is particularly important if one assumes that power relations underscore the different social, economic, and political contexts.

4.5 Implications for Earth System Governance

This chapter makes contributions to key issues identified in the Earth System Governance (ESG) Science and Implementation Plan (ESG, 2018). First, it presents an evaluative approach that links governance institutions to attributes believed to support societies in responding to social-ecological change. The application of such an approach to empirical studies demonstrates how adaptiveness can be assessed and compared in a systematic fashion. Second, the analysis of empirical studies sheds light on how different political, economic, and social factors enable or constrain adaptiveness. Third, by investigating the complex and interrelated nature of governance institutions and interdependence of adaptive capacity attributes, the chapter offers insights into the kinds of governance qualities that are more conducive to adaptiveness. Lastly, the chapter addresses the influence of power relations in mediating the nexus between institutions and adaptive capacity; ultimately, underscoring the role of such relations in adaptiveness – a key, nonetheless, under-researched topic in earth system governance (ESG, 2018).

Despite the contributions just outlined, important knowledge gaps persist. For example, future studies seeking to investigate how contextual factors interact with governance institutions to affect adaptive capacity would benefit assessments of such capacity. In addition, enhancing the capacity of society to adapt to social-ecological change will require, in addition to reforming institutions, considering power relations that shape and are shaped by governance institutions (Nightingale, 2017). Future studies seeking to incorporate the notion of power in institutional analysis would further expand the scope of adaptive capacity assessments. Developing an institutional analysis framework that enables mapping specific institutional rules that shape, and are shaped by, power would be particularly beneficial. The approach articulated in this chapter may provide a promising starting point.

References

Adger, N.W., Arnell, N.W., & Tompkins, E.L. (2005). Successful adaptation to climate change across scales. *Global Environmental Change*, 15, 77–86.
Agrawal, A. (2008). *The Role of Local Institutions in Livelihoods Adaptation to Climate Change*. Ann Arbor: University of Michigan.
Bergsma, E., Gupta, J., & Jong, P. (2012). Does individual responsibility increase the adaptive capacity of society? The case of local water management in the Netherlands. *Resources, Conservation and Recycling*, 64, 13–22.
Biermann, F., Betsill, M.M., Gupta, J. et al. (2009). *Earth System Governance: People, Places, and the Planet. Science Implementation Plan of the Earth System Governance Project*. Bonn: International Human Dimensions Programme on Global Environmental Change.
Carlsson, L. & Berkes, F. (2005). Co-management: concepts and methodological implications. *Journal of Environmental Management*, 75, 65–76.

Clement, F. (2010). Analysing decentralised natural resource governance: proposition for a 'politicised' institutional analysis and development framework. *Policy Sciences*, 43, 129–56.

   (2012). For critical social-ecological system studies: integrating power and discourses to move beyond the right institutional fit. *Environmental Conservation*, 40, 1–4.

Eakin, H.C., Lemos, M.C., & Nelson, D.R. (2014). Differentiating capacities as a means to sustainable climate change adaptation. *Global Environmental Change*, 27, 1–8.

Earth System Governance (ESG) Project (2018). *Earth System Governance: Science and Implementation Plan of the Earth System Governance Project*. Utrecht: Earth System Governance Project.

Engle, N.L. (2011). Adaptive capacity and its assessment. *Global Environmental Change*, 21, 647–56.

Engle, N.L. & Lemos, M.C. (2010). Unpacking governance: building adaptive capacity to climate change of river basins in Brazil. *Global Environmental Change*, 20, 4–13.

Fidelman, P. (2019). Climate change in the Coral Triangle: enabling institutional adaptive capacity. In P. Harris, ed., *Ocean Governance and Climate Change: Politics and Policy for Threatened Seas*. Cambridge, UK: Cambridge University Press, 274–89.

Fidelman, P., Evans, L., Fabinyi, M. et al. (2012). Governing large-scale marine commons: contextual challenges in the Coral Triangle. *Marine Policy*, 36, 42–53.

Fidelman, P., Truong van, T., Nong, K., & Nursey-Bray, M. (2017). The institutions–adaptive capacity nexus: insights from coastal resources co-management in Cambodia and Vietnam. *Environmental Science & Policy*, 76, 103–12.

Grecksch, K. (2014). Adaptive capacity and regional water governance in north-western Germany. *Water Policy*, 15, 794–815.

Grothmann, T., Grecksch, K., Winges, M., & Siebenhüner, B. (2013). Assessing institutional capacities to adapt to climate change: integrating psychological dimensions in the Adaptive Capacity Wheel. *Natural Hazards and Earth System Sciences*, 13, 3369–84.

Gupta, J., Bergsma, E., Termeer, C. et al. (2016). The adaptive capacity of institutions in the spatial planning, water, agriculture and nature sectors in the Netherlands. *Mitigation and Adaptation Strategies for Climate Change*, 21, 883–903.

Gupta, J., Termeer, C., Klotermann, J. et al. (2010). The Adaptive Capacity Wheel: a method to assess the inherent characteristics of institutions to enable the adaptive capacity of society. *Environmental Science & Policy*, 13, 459–71.

Kashwan, P. (2016). Integrating power in institutional analysis: a micro-foundation perspective. *Journal of Theoretical Politics*, 28, 5–26.

Mcguinnis, M. (2011). An introduction to IAD and the language of the Ostrom workshop: a simple guide to a complex framework. *Policy Studies Journal*, 39, 169–83.

Mandryk, M., Reidsma, P., Kartikasari, K., van Ittersum, M., & Arts, B. (2015). Institutional constraints for adaptive capacity to climate change in Flevoland's agriculture. *Environmental Science & Policy*, 48, 148–62.

Marschke, M. (2012). *Life, Fish and Mangroves: Resource Governance in Coastal Cambodia*. Ottawa: University of Ottawa Press.

Marschke, M. & Nong, K. (2003). Adaptive co-management: lessons from coastal Cambodia. *Canadian Journal of Development Studies/Revue Canadienne d'études du Développement*, 24, 369–83.

Munaretto, S. & Klostermann, J. (2011). Assessing adaptive capacity of institutions to climate change: a comparative case study of the Dutch Wadden Sea and the Venice Lagoon *Climate Law*, 2, 219–50.

Nelson, D.R., Adger, N.W., & Brown, K. (2007). Adaptation to environmental change: contributions of a resilience framework. *Annual Review of Environment and Resources*, 32, 395–419.

Nightingale, A. (2017). Power and politics in climate change adaptation efforts: struggles over authority and recognition in the context of political instability. *Geoforum*, 84, 11–20.

Ostrom, E. (2005). *Understanding Institutional Diversity*. Princeton, NJ: Princeton University Press.

   (2007). A diagnostic approach for going beyond panaceas. *Proceedings of the National Academy of Science*, 104, 15181–7.

   (2011). Background on the institutional analysis and development framework. *Policy Studies Journal*, 39, 7–27.

Ostrom, E. & Cox, M. (2010). Moving beyond panaceas: a multi-tiered diagnostic approach for social-ecological analysis. *Environmental Conservation*, 37, 451–63.

Ostrom, E. & Crawford, S. (2005). Classifying rules. In E. Ostrom, ed., *Understanding Institutional Diversity*. Princeton, NJ: Princeton University Press, 186–215.

Plummer, R. & Armitage, D. (2007). Crossing boundaries, crossing scales: the evolution of environment and resource co-management. *Geography Compass*, 1, 834–49.

Rosen, F. & Olsson, P. (2013). Institutional entrepreneurs, global networks, and the emergence of international institutions for ecosystem-based management: the Coral Triangle Initiative. *Marine Policy*, 38, 195–204.

Termeer, C., Biesbroek, R., & van den Brink, M. (2011). Institutions for adaptation to climate change: comparing national adaptation strategies in Europe. *European Political Science*, 1, 1–13.

Participatory Management of Coastal Resources Project. (2008). *Learning for Change: Ten Years of Experience on Community-Based Coastal Resource Management and Livelihood Improvement in Koh Kong, Cambodia*. Phnom Penh: Ministry of Environment.

Worldfish Centre/USAID. (2010). *The US Coral Triangle Initiative (CTI) Support Program: Midterm Program Performance Evaluation Report*. Penang: WorldFish Center (WorldFish) and United States Agency for International Development (USAID).

Tuyen, T.V. (2002). Dynamics of property rights in the Tam Giang Lagoon. In V.J. Brezeski & G.F. Newkirk, eds., *Lessons in Resource Management from the Tam Giang Lagoon*. Halifax: CoRR, CIDA, and IDRC, 39–52.

Tuyen, T.V., Armitage, D., & Marschke, M. (2010). Livelihoods and co-management in the Tam Giang lagoon, Vietnam. *Ocean & Coastal Management*, 53, 327–35.

van den Brink, M., Meijerink, S., Termeer, C., & Gupta, J. (2014). Climate-proof planning for flood-prone areas: assessing adaptive capacity of planning institutions in the Netherlands. *Regional Environmental Change*, 14, 981–95.

van den Brink, M., Termeer, C., & Meijerink, S. (2011). Are Dutch water safety institutions prepared for climate change? *Journal of Water and Climate Change*, 2, 272–87.

von Heland, F., Crona, B., & Fidelman, P. (2014). Mediating science and action across multiple boundaries in the Coral Triangle. *Global Environmental Change*, 29, 53–64.

Young, O.R. (2002). *The Institutional Dimensions of Global Environmental Change: Fit, Interplay and Scale*. Cambridge, MA: MIT Press.

5

The Marine Debris Nexus

Plastic, Climate Change, Biodiversity, and Human Health

PETER STOETT AND JOANNA VINCE

5.1 Introduction

Efforts to establish global environmental governance related to marine debris, including revamping the United Nations Convention on the Law of the Sea (UNCLOS), establishing new marine 'areas beyond national jurisdiction' (ABNJ) regimes (De Santo, 2018), and promulgating a global treaty committing states to reduce plastic usage and waste, are proliferating as we face the stark reality that plastic presence in marine ecosystems presents a variety of increasing threats at the ecosystem level. The observational science is incontrovertible, and policy has been playing catch-up for well over two decades now. Collective adaptation to this crisis will be essential, but the challenge is compounded because the problem cannot be treated in conceptual isolation. Can utilising the widespread concern over plastic abundance as a means to further promote the fight against climate change, biodiversity loss, and threats to human health be seen as an adaptive measure with compounded co-benefits? Would this be a way to enhance the adaptive capacity of concerned governments, and through a process of social learning, educate decision makers and the public about the other crises intertwined in this nexus?

International attention on the plastics issue has never been as strong as it is presently (2021), and a recent flourish of counter-plastic debris policy, mostly focused on curtailing or banning the use of single-use products, is welcome (Xanthos & Walker, 2017).[1] Yet the theme is habitually treated in isolation, as if plastic – and, by extension, the political and cultural narratives shaping related discourse – floats above the other problems it encounters, exacerbates, and deepens. The hard fact is that the fisheries crisis, ocean acidification, rising sea

---

[1] This refers to products, such as plastic bags, water bottles, straws, etc. that are intended primarily for single use; they may in fact be re-used several times (others, such as tea bags and cigarette butts, are more strictly viewed as single-use products). Most policy initiatives have focused on banning or charging for plastic bags, straws, and cutlery, which is vital but merely scrapes the surface of the global plastics addiction, though efforts to ban (or voluntary commitments related to) microbeads and microfibres are also gaining traction.

levels, the spread of invasive species, and increased plastic volume and density are not isolated phenomena, nor do they have single causes. Co-beneficial policy interventions to what are intimately linked collective action problems are possible.

This chapter asserts that the scientific, policy, and even cultural narratives centred on plastic have reached a point of maturity that should animate serious thinking about its links to other major planetary problems of our age; and this in turn demands an understanding of the eco-justice implications of this confluence. The global threat from the 'marine debris nexus' is of the first order and will have a deleterious impact on the quality of life of future generations.[2] This nexus is made up of the marine plastic debris problem and the threats posed by climate change to marine ecosystems, and their combined impact on biodiversity and human health. This evokes *obligations ergo omnes*. If the plastic debris issue is exacerbating threats to environmental and human security on a global level, we can assert that a global imperative based on the four most widely accepted tenets of international environmental law has arisen. These tenets include the precautionary principle, common but differentiated responsibilities, intergenerational equity, and the common heritage of humankind. Perhaps this is the framing necessary to evoke a concerted effort on reducing plastic waste and thereby encouraging progressive polices affecting other aspects of the marine debris nexus; or, perhaps it is simply asking too much at this time, and the piecemeal policy development we are currently witnessing is more likely to curtail the marine plastic deluge. The aim of this chapter, therefore, is to provide a contextual overview of marine plastic pollution and to identify the knowledge gaps with regards to earth system governance; it then explores future concerns on the marine horizon.

5.2 Contextual Overview

Marine plastic pollution can be subdivided into three basic categories: (1) *macroplastics*, including debris such as fishing nets, large pieces of Styrofoam, and parcels that have been lost or discarded from cargo ships; (2) *microplastics*, which comprise particles under 5 mm in diameter that remain when plastic objects, including plastic nurdles (which are used in various production processes), enter the sea and phytodegrade; and (3) *nanoplastics*, the end state of microplastic degradation (Koelmans et al., 2015), which are invisible to the naked eye and, because they are so small (1,000 times smaller than an algal cell), are more likely than microplastics to pass through biological membranes. All of these categories of plastics are regrettable intrusions on natural ecosystems, but the latter are

---

[2] The issue impacts intergenerational justice from both an egalitarian and sufficiency perspective (Gosseries & Meyer, 2009; Page, 2006).

particularly worrisome for those concerned with environmental change, leading some scientists to call for the inclusion of plastics in the planetary boundaries calculus (Villarrubia-Gómez et al., 2018).

Synthetic polymers can be manufactured from fossil fuels or biomass. The complete biodegradation of plastic occurs when none of the original polymer remains, a result of microbial action breaking plastic down into carbon dioxide, methane and water (UNEP, 2016). Most plastic in circulation today is a petroleum and natural gas by-product and photodegrades into tiny particles that can both release toxic chemicals and absorb persistent organic pollutants and hydrophobic chemicals (Stoett, 2019). Easily mistaken for food, this material enters the marine and terrestrial food chains (Provencher et al., 2015) and has been found in organisms living in the deep sea (Taylor et al., 2016) and identified in every type of marine habitat (Ivar do Sul & Costa, 2014). Remote Arctic sea ice has been found to contain high concentrations of microplastics, and the extent to which melting ice will release various anthropogenic particulates back into the ocean and atmosphere is not yet fully known (Obbard et al., 2014). A 2014 study found that microplastic fibres were 'up to four orders of magnitude more abundant (per unit volume) in deep sea sediments from the Atlantic Ocean, Mediterranean Sea and Indian Ocean than in contaminated sea-surface waters' (Woodall et al., 2014: 1; see also van Cauwenberghe et al., 2013).

A special section in volume 96 of *Marine Policy*, co-edited by the present authors, offers further scientific evidence of discovered microplastic density in the Pacific Ocean, off the coasts of both Costa Rica and Japan, and at deeper levels than previously suspected (Chiba et al., 2018; Johnson et al., 2018). It is clear that there is widespread ecological vulnerability to this contaminant. Extricating this plastic is not feasible. And biologists have investigated 'life in the plastisphere', where entirely new microbial communities are evolving (Zettler et al., 2013). The link with human health concerns is most evident in terms of harbouring and transporting contaminants, including cholera and other water-borne disease and potentially dangerous invasive species, as well as ingestion by humans in drinking water and food, especially fish (WHO-CBD, 2015). Plastic debris also diminishes aquatic sunlight and oxygen levels, contributing to dead zones.

Shorelines are the most obvious repository of plastic debris, from fishing material to degraded plastic bottles. The discovery of five so-called garbage patches in the oceanic gyres, first in the North and South Pacific and then the North and South Atlantic and the Indian Ocean, rang early alarm bells (Kaiser, 2010; Moore et al., 2001; Titmus & Hyrenbach, 2011); they serve as conductor belts for masses of immeasurable subsurface microplastic. Early pelagic studies even indicated a higher abundance of microplastics than zooplankton (the building block of the marine food chain) in some areas (Moore et al., 2001), which is especially troubling given the important role zooplankton play in regulating climate (CIEL, 2019; O'Sullivan, 2019; Richardson, 2008). Debris also has a direct impact on wildlife health; for example, plastic bags look very similar to jellyfish and are often ingested by sea turtles leading to suffocation or starvation. The reduction in the number of sea turtles, in turn, exacerbates the growing problem of invasive jellyfish abundance (Schuyler et al., 2014; Wilcox et al., 2015). Plastic ingestion by coral reefs add to the threat climate change and ocean acidification poses to these precious biodiverse resources (Hall et al., 2015).

In general, increased water temperatures and acidification can accelerate the breakdown of macroplastic into micro and nanoplastic. Increased carbon levels in the oceans are already contributing to ocean acidification and other problems, but microzooplankton and zooplankton form the basis of the marine food chain, and their collapse would spell biological disaster, as well as the continued loss of potential medical discoveries in the coral reef zones. Ocean currents may shift due to climate change, delivering plastic to (increasingly rare) untainted areas, and sea level rise will claim more litter from shorelines with tidal activity and extreme weather events such as hurricanes and cyclones. A combination of shifting temperature zones and the use of plastic debris as vectors will exacerbate the problem of invasive species, including that of travelling microbes (Derraik, 2002). Warming waters will also release plastic and related toxic material (and potential pathogens dangerous to human health) captured in marine ice (CBD, 2012), and recent studies suggest plastic degradation contributes methane and ethylene to the atmosphere (Royer et al., 2018). In short, climate change and heavy microplastic pollution, both 'wicked problems' and with significant challenges to their governance (Landon-Lane, 2018) are working in tandem to lower marine ecosystem resilience, and in an endless positive feedback loop, this threatens biodiversity and thus human health (Stoett & Vince, 2019).

The plastics industry itself has been estimated to produce a 10 per cent contribution to total 'global warming potential' (STAP, 2011) – this is probably a low estimate that does not include the carbon footprint of the immense global recycling industry. Microplastics and nanoplastics can be ingested by zooplankton and microzooplankton, which can negatively impact algal feeding. This has the potential to increase algal blooms and disrupt zooplankton growth and fecundity (Cole et al., 2013). Phytoplankton use photosynthesis, creating oxygen and organic matter for other organisms to eat (Pomeroy, 1974). If organisms are ingesting microplastic, or their permeable membranes are absorbing nanoplastic, they are ingesting less organic carbon-based matter and thus the carbon-cycling function of ocean ecosystems may be compromised (Cole et al., 2016; Koelmans et al., 2015; O'Sullivan, 2019). This is admittedly speculative at this juncture, but the implications could be severe for the global carbon cycle because oceans act as sinks for at least half of anthropocentric carbon emissions (Stoett & Vince, 2019). This is a potential 'tipping point' or positive feedback loop that we cannot afford to ignore; reducing the plankton–plastic overlap is a strategic priority (Sherman & van Sebille, 2016).

Plastic debris originates from many sources. Nurdles used as pre-production pellets escape the product cycle at various stages and end up in oceans (Hammer et al., 2012; Ogata et al., 2009). Microbeads used in cosmetic cleansers and other personal products, including toothpaste, are too small to be stopped by waste water filtration systems. Three-quarters or more of litter in the ocean comes from land-based sources (Derraik, 2002; Hardesty et al., 2014; Jambeck et al., 2015). Regulation of the use of microbeads in cosmetic products has been timely; however, enforcement and implementation is slow (for example, the US Microbead-Free Waters Act was passed in 2015, yet the manufacture of products with microbeads was not prohibited until 2017 and retail sales were not prohibited until January 2018). Canada recently announced plans to ban single-use plastics by 2021 without giving any specific details as to what would be banned! A global database of cumulative plastics regulation is an obvious necessity for researchers at this stage.

Improved technology can be used in the plankton–plastic overlap and to reduce or remove plastic from the oceans. However, technological solutions present serious limitations. Pelagic vacuum cleaners (such as the crowd-sourced SeaVax), or trailing suction hopper dredging ships (such as the *Queen of the Netherlands*), can have a substantive impact. However, it would take a navy of such ships to affect significant change given the mass of plastic in oceans, lakes, and rivers. The call for regulatory efforts is thus quite loud. However, regulation is only one approach to managing macroplastic and microplastic marine debris. Economic/market and community-based efforts are also an integral part of the management, prevention, and mitigation of plastic pollution. Similar to climate change, this mixture of governance approaches is developed and implemented at the local, national, regional, and global levels, all at varying scales and degrees of success (Vince & Hardesty, 2016, 2018). In the United States in 2015, the California Assembly voted to prohibit the sale of microbeads in personal care products from 2020. California's actions with regard to marine debris are significant, and already the impact of the 'California effect' (Fredriksson and Millimet, 2002; Perkins & Neumayer, 2012). Other jurisdictions around the world have followed suit by introducing microbead bans (Rochman et al., 2015). However, by the time they are fully implemented, tons of microplastics will have entered the ocean. In Australia, microbead legislation has not been enacted and state and federal governments have only agreed to voluntary approaches. Rwanda's outright ban, Kenya's fines for those caught importing, making, or selling plastic bags, and the European Union's Single-Use Plastics Directive that bans single-use plastic items such as straws, plates, and cutlery by 2021 are promising, but resistance to such bans is also fierce in the United States and elsewhere (Parker, 2019).

Local community action has been growing in many regions (GhostNets Australia, 2015; Vince & Hardesty, 2016). Education (Derraik, 2002; Duckett & Repaci, 2015) and the use of 'citizen science' (Hidalgo-Ruz & Thiel, 2015; Jambeck & Johnsen, 2015) increases engagement with the community and changes the behaviour of those involved with the use and removal of plastics from the marine environment. Local communities and non-state actors are using social licence to bring about change where regulation is lagging (Cullen-Knox et al., 2016; Vince & Hardesty, 2016, 2018). While the larger non-governmental organisations (NGOs), such as Greenpeace, Worldwide Fund for Nature, and the International Union for Conservation of Nature, usually take a holistic approach to the problem of plastic debris, other NGOs are issue specific.

Legislative changes and the voluntarily driven consumer demand have had a number of positive impacts on industries and the use of microbeads. Major retailers such as Woolworths have introduced microbead bans (Browne, 2016). Johnson & Johnson, and Proctor & Gamble have all agreed to remove gradually polyethylene microbeads from their products (Abrams, 2015). According to a report by the Secretariat of the Convention on Biological Diversity and the Scientific and Technical Advisory Panel (GEF, 2012: 352) 'many companies now see packaging and plastics sustainability as part of broader corporate social responsibility, and negative brand image is becoming a major driving force which is being harnessed in the interests of improving packaging materials and technologies'. In 2011, industry plastics associations came together and developed a global Declaration for Solutions on Marine Litter (Marine Litter Solutions, 2017). The United Nations Environment Programme's (UNEP) *Guidelines on the Use of Market-Based Instruments to Address the Problem of Marine Litter* (UNEP, 2009) identify market-based instruments as taxes, charges, fees, fines, penalties, liability and compensation schemes, subsidies and incentives, and tradable permit schemes. There are several basic principles behind these instruments: the polluter pays principle, the user/beneficiary pays principle and the principle of full cost recovery. While market-based instruments have been used successfully to reduce macroplastic pollution (e.g. Cho, 2009; Hardesty et al., 2014), little progress has occurred with their application in the management of microplastics, just as their ultimate impact on climate change mitigation remains contested.

The direction of earth system governance over the last few decades has focused more on soft law or 'pledge and review' approaches (Burch et al., 2019). For instance, globally, the need to address the plastic problem is increasingly recognised with discussions on marine plastic pollution occurring at international assemblies such as the World Ocean Summit (2017), Group of Seven (G7) and

Group of 20 (G20) meetings. For the first time, a Ministerial Declaration 'Towards a Pollution Free Planet' was adopted by consensus by the United Nations Environment Assembly (UNEA) (2017). During the March 2019 UNEA meeting, four resolutions on the reduction of plastics and waste management were adopted. Resolution 6 called for a multi-stakeholder platform to be created within UNEP 'to take immediate action towards the long-term elimination, through a life-cycle approach, of discharges of litter and microplastics into the oceans' (UNEP, 2019: 12). Further effort has been made to implement these goals through the Oceans Conference held in June 2017, which resulted in the creation of the Communities of Ocean Action that included representation from governments, NGOs, and civil society groups (Haward, 2018). In December 2017, UNEA passed a non-binding resolution on marine litter and microplastics that encouraged member states to 'develop integrated and source-to-sea approaches to combat marine litter and microplastics from all sources' (resolution UNEP/EA.3/L.20: 2). Calls for a new legally binding international agreement have been made by a number of scholars (Chen, 2015; Mika et al., 2013; Raubenheimer & McIlgorm, 2017; Stoett, 2016; Vince & Hardesty, 2016), demonstrating the large gap in international law for specifically dealing with land-based plastic marine pollution.

UNCLOS Part XII (articles 192–237) is dedicated to the protection and preservation of the marine environment (see Chapter 2), and requires states to take all measures 'that are necessary to prevent, reduce and control pollution of the marine environment from any source, using for this purpose the best practicable means at their disposal and in accordance with their capabilities, and they shall endeavour to harmonize their policies in this connection' (UN General Assembly, 1982: art. 194(1)). Although UNCLOS sets out the responsibilities of states and necessary measures they need to undertake to minimise pollution, there are doubts that UNCLOS on its own can solve the plastics problem. While UNCLOS recognises that there are six different sources of marine pollution, including land-based pollution, it does not go into detail about the type of pollutants and technical rules (Palassis, 2011). States are directed to adopt their own laws and regulations dealing with marine pollution and to work with relevant international organisations. Lost fishing gear is still a major concern and only regional agreements deal explicitly with monitoring and loss avoidance (Gilman et al., 2016). While the shift from hard-law (such as UNCLOS) to soft-law approaches can be seen as 'a symptom of a general decline in multilateralism, the new approaches can also be seen as "all-hands-on-deck" and crowd-sourced models where both state and non-state actors contribute and can be held to account by their respective constituencies' (Burch et al., 2019: 2).

Despite considerable progress, there remains a global governance gap regarding marine debris. Linking it to the other problems facing the oceans, from biodiversity loss to climate change to human health, could provide a more concerted effort to integrate this problem into wider decision-making bodies and policy developments. That has yet to occur despite the wide embrace of the UNCLOS mandate and suggests that our institutions are better geared to tackle single-issue problems, lacking the political will and technical sophistication to apply legal frameworks to multiple-issue problems. We turn now to a largely conceptual discussion of the thematic question raised within this volume on earth system governance.

5.3 Conceptual Frames and Knowledge Gaps

There are several conceptual frames that have highlighted the marine debris issue. One is that of the broader 'oceans crisis': plastic is but part of the crisis, and not the most startling part (that, we would argue, must be the overfishing and climate crises). Another is that the plastics issue is a vivid expression of the Anthropocene, embodied in expressions such as the plastisphere. No doubt, archaeologists, geologists, and historians alike will be tempted to refer to ours as the plastic age. At the very least plastic pollution is seen as 'the dark side of a modern gift' (Hammer et al., 2012), a technological marvel that we were clearly not ready to manage properly in our pursuit of profit and comfort, so deeply engrained in modern life that even its temporary absence is almost unimaginable.

Where the plastic–climate–biodiversity–health nexus is most clear, however, is in the normative sphere. Ultimately, these are social justice issues where deleterious impacts are suffered by those who have typically contributed the least to the problems and are least able to escape them. The overlap between plastic pollution and climate change is just beginning to receive serious scientific investigation, but the political similarities are already quite striking. For example, both involve common but differentiated responsibilities. This is well known in the case of greenhouse gas emissions, where a minority of countries are effectively responsible for the majority of pollution. In the plastic context, according to one estimate, '20 countries, out of a total of 192 coastlines, are responsible for 83% of the plastic debris put into the world's oceans' (Tibbetts, 2015: 91; note this figure predates the recent Chinese decision to stop recycling most Western plastic debris). Another study concluded that reducing waste by 50 per cent in the top 20 countries would result in a nearly 40 per cent decline in inputs of plastics to the oceans (Leonard, 2015). More pollution (carbon, methane, plastic) now comes from the Asia Pacific region than others, but historically both industrial emissions and plastic were largely European and American innovations. A painful discussion of the historical and contemporary *plastic footprint* of countries is due.

Environmental justice concerns permeate the plastic, climate change adaptation, and biodiversity conservation discourses for good reasons. Small island states, for example, are as disproportionately impacted by aquatic microplastics as they are by sea level rise, extreme weather events, invasive species, and related health threats (Costa & Barletta, 2015). This was acknowledged in the landmark 2011 Honolulu Commitment, in which parties 'recognised the need to address the special requirements of developing countries, in particular the Least Developed Countries and Small Island Developing States, and their need for financial and technical assistance, technology transfer, training and scientific cooperation to enhance their ability to prevent, reduce and manage marine debris' (UNEP, 2011: 1). Even with financial and technological assistance, implementing integrated policy approaches to deal with marine plastics will be difficult, as has been the case in the Pacific where oceans governance responses have been slow (Chasek, 2010; Vince et al., 2017).

Similarly, the marine plastic debris threat to biodiversity and human health has obvious environmental justice implications. Microplastic ingestion can harm fish populations and the coastal ecosystems (including reefs) on which coastal dwellers are dependent, especially in the southern hemisphere (Lamb et al., 2018). It is self-evident that people who live and work in 'plastic soup' rivers and coastal areas are not members of high- or middle-income groups. Much of this can be said about any environmental pressure today, of course; we are not claiming marine plastic presents a unique context in this regard. But our impression is that plastic has, arguably, been presented largely as an environmental contaminant with repercussions for the natural world without due respect paid to the social implications of living in a plastic world.

Issues subjected to international remediation can be framed in multiple, simultaneous ways (Stoett, 2010). Climate governance efforts need to take the plastic plague seriously because, as already discussed, plastic debris can disrupt the food chain and by implication the ocean ecosystem's ability to regulate climate, especially if serious tipping points on climate are approaching. Climate governance approaches assume that ecosystem resilience (and the reduction of vulnerability to change) is a positive factor, necessary for the success of both long- and short-term efforts to mitigate and adapt to climate change. Indeed, the ecosystem-based adaptation approach hinges on this assumption (IUCN, 2019). Plastic marine debris is a major threat to this resilience and could render many climate governance and biodiversity conservation efforts fruitless if it is not addressed, with downstream, deleterious impacts on human health.

There is little research on the governance of marine plastic debris (exceptions include Chen, 2015; Stoett & Vince, 2019; Vince & Hardesty, 2016, 2018; Vince et al., 2018) mainly due to the fragmented nature and soft-law approaches to this complex issue. Could the idea of a *nexus of problems* – in this case, plastic pollution, climate change, biodiversity, and threats to human health – be a strong animating conceptualisation to encourage strong policy development and the earth system governance agenda in general? Is there room within the already crowded agendas related to climate, biodiversity, and human health for plastic? Arguably, the issue has already permeated these discourses, but it would be premature to consider this anything but superficial in nature at this point. However, our optimism that the nexus approach could enhance adaptive capacity for governance is restrained by the fact that large knowledge gaps and unanswered questions remain.

The positive correlation between loss of marine biodiversity and reductions in marine ecosystem services has been known for quite some time (Worm et al., 2006). However, although plastic pollution has been observed for decades, awareness of microplastics is relatively new, dating back to the late 1990s. There was solid scientific evidence that plastic debris, even at the micro level, was an emerging problem in the Atlantic Ocean in the early 1970s (Carpenter et al., 1972; Colton et al., 1974), but it was not until the 1990s and early 2000s that a flood of research emerged finding microplastic abundance in the oceans (Ivar do Sul & Costa, 2014) and, still later, in freshwater systems (Eerkes-Medrano et al., 2015). An alarming European Commission (EC) report suggested that approximately 10 per cent of the global plastic manufactured each year, about 265 million tons, ends up in the oceans or other water systems (EC, 2011).

As the authors of an article in our recent special section of *Marine Policy* conclude:

A remaining question to be answered is if the concentration of plastic in the ocean, today or in the future, will reach levels above a critical threshold leading to global effects in vital Earth-system processes, thus granting the consideration of marine plastic pollution as a key component of the planetary boundary threat associated with chemical pollutants ... The irreversibility and global ubiquity of marine plastic pollution mean that two essential conditions for a planetary boundary threat are already met. The Earth system consequences of plastic pollution are still uncertain, but ... it is certain that marine plastic pollution is closely intertwined with global processes to a point that deserves careful management and prevention. (Villarrubia-Gómez et al., 2018: 213)

As Mendenhall (2018) points out, there are many knowledge gaps involved. The true long-term impact of plastic pollution ingestion on human health is still an unknown, for example, though there is emerging evidence it is harmful.

Beyond these broad, disturbing questions, there are informational gaps. Clear indicators are necessary for tracking progress. For example, the Convention for the Protection of the Marine Environment of the North-East Atlantic employs three indicators of marine plastic: seabed litter, beach litter, and ingestion by northern fulmar seabirds. The Joint Group of Experts on the Scientific Aspects of Marine Environmental Protection and others are working on operational indicators. Such measurements should be integrated with climate models and assessments. More research is also needed on the behavioural economics of marine litter (Wyles, 2014). Incentive structures need to be constructed for both governmental policymaking and for consumer and producer behaviour to reduce plastic consumption as well as greenhouse gas emissions. As already mentioned, an easily accessible global database of legislated regulatory efforts and international commitments would be beneficial as well.

The governance arrangements that address marine plastic pollution on global, regional, and national levels are complex and multifaceted and require hard-to-achieve integrated responses. While global and regional governance can create a favourable context for national action, national level policy actions are central to policy implementation efforts. Policy solutions, however, require political support and leadership (Young et al., 2007), ideally of a bipartisan nature. The politics of 'two-level games' (Putnam, 1988) where international relations (on one level) and domestic politics (on the second level) are entangled is an important aspect of marine plastic pollution governance. National ocean policies are often subject to policy reversal or a change of focus when a new government is elected. While politics drives integrated policies on to national agendas it can also be the source of their failure. However, the political conditions as for how, and why, marine plastic pollution issues end up on or are left off the political agenda are an important knowledge gap.

Regardless, we would argue that, if a substantive new global accord or convention is reached, state parties should be required to submit National Plastic Strategies and Action Plans (NPSAPs). This is similar to the demand for National Biodiversity Strategies and Action Plans required for adherence to the Convention on Biological Diversity (CBD). Regular reporting and external monitoring are key elements. Some countries already have such plans in effect or under construction, so it would not be akin to a wholly new demand, though many countries have yet to seriously address this issue. Since 80 per cent of the plastic found in the marine environment comes from land-based sources and it is the jurisdictional responsibility of individual nation states, NPSAPs should be at the heart of global marine debris policy development.[3] An international convention will be hollow without them. Perhaps the most seminal success of the CBD and the United Nations Framework Convention on Climate Change (UNFCCC) has been the encouraged development of nationally appropriate strategies that require reporting to those respective mechanisms. While they are hardly devoid of the usual list of problems pertaining to international regulatory mechanisms with limited enforcement measures (chiefly, the problem of non-compliance), they do force

---

[3] A most welcome project would be the construction of hypothetical NPSAPs for a wide variety of countries in order to demonstrate the utility of this idea. CBD NPSAPs could be used as illustrative models.

governments to respond to the issue, providing a forum for public embarrassment in the absence of compliance. They can raise expectations about indicators and encourage the evolution of specific targets and goals. They can also encourage multilateral action to tackle the problems that escape the technical and governance capabilities of individual states. Most importantly, perhaps, they can provide an arena for strategic systems thinking about cross-sectoral collaboration that reflects the interconnected nature of the marine debris nexus under the rubric of global governance informed by the imperatives of environmental justice.

5.4 Future Concerns on the Marine Horizon

Developing nexus-oriented thinking is very difficult, because it demands considerable conceptual flexibility and forces policymakers to consider interactions and reciprocal relationships instead of straightforward linear relationships. The absence of an easy technological solution might be the most important factor spurring on legislative or policy development. Stimulating phytoplankton presence and activity by increasing nutrient availability in areas swamped by plastic waste is one such proposal that would, theoretically, also increase carbon dioxide (CO_2) uptake. Unfortunately, introducing iron or nitrogen into areas with especially high plastic density may cause as many problems as it solves. Stimulating plastic-bound bacteria to increase their nitrogen-fixing capacity is another idea that seems rather far-fetched to most scientists. In general, stimulating phytoplankton can lead to eutrophication and 'dead zones' with low oxygen content in which anaerobic bacteria thrive; their respiration produces nitrous oxide, a greenhouse gas about 265 times more potent than CO_2. Biodegradable plastics, meanwhile, do not offer a solution to the aquatic plastics problem. Most biodegradable plastic products do not decompose unless a temperature of 50°C is reached, which is (to put it mildly) highly undesirable in any aquatic context.

In five years, we will need to know what impact the emerging slate of pollution abatement policies has had; what further combined impact climate change and plastic pollution has had on the marine ecosystem food chain; and what impacts on marine biodiversity, human health, and the climate regulating function of marine ecosystems.

As societies move toward an aquaculture-based global protein regime, it is already a major source of plastic pollution (Austin, 2014; Mathalon & Hill, 2014). Studies have found that aquaculture was a major contributor of marine litter off the coasts of Chile, South Korea, Japan, Taiwan, and other areas (Chen et al., 2018; Hinojosa & Thiel, 2009).[4]

---

[4] Styrofoam is used liberally in aquaculture operations and it often breaks down and escapes fish pens. Some regulatory measures have been introduced to control this.

How plastic and climate change will continue to affect the polar regions will also be interesting to see and serves as another example of concern for multilateral governance on a global scale. Plastic has already been found in the Southern Ocean and polar regions (Masura et al., 2015). During the 42nd meeting of the Antarctic Treaty Consultative Parties, Resolution 5 Reducing Plastic Pollution in Antarctica and the Southern Ocean (2019) was adopted. It states that there is a 'current lack of plastics monitoring data to inform decision-making' and acknowledges that 'the majority of plastic found in Antarctica originates from outside of Antarctica' (Secretariat of the Antarctic Treaty, 2019: 417). It is anticipated that this issue will continue to grow in significance for the Antarctic Treaty parties. The solution to plastic pollution will require extensive coordination with other international organisations, states, and NGOs so that holistic solutions can reduce plastic pollution in the Antarctic region and in all the world's oceans (Vince & Hardesty, 2018). This is a good example of how a number of 'regime complexes' may need to be created in earth system governance to tackle plastic debris (Young, 2012).

Another future concern will be the rise of 3D printing, since 'using plastic "ink" will guarantee expanded use of polymeric feedstocks' (Moore, 2015: vii). Even the recycling industry, which is vital for reducing plastic pollution, comes with its own pollution and climate change issues, although exciting ideas for secondary uses of plastics, such as the construction of roads and sidewalks in the Netherlands and Indonesia, are appearing (Sulistiyono, 2017; Valentine, 2015). China's 2018 decision to cease taking all foreign trash imports has changed the landscape of the global recycling industry and it is at present unknown what the industry will look like in five years.

The most important question from an earth systems governance perspective remains: Have the sporadic efforts at global governance managed to induce policy shifts at the national and local level, and have they further integrated the themes forming the marine debris nexus in the thinking of policymakers? Or have national and community-level efforts to reduce single-use plastic been the only truly effective policy initiatives, failing to further provoke the public imagination towards due consideration of the many interactive linkages found in the marine debris nexus? Obviously it is too early to definitively answer this question at this time, but careful observations of both national and international policy developments will provide a living laboratory to test the hypothesis that widespread and serious threats will provoke adaptive responses at the collective level.

5.5 Conclusion

Converging international legal principles, actors, and governance mechanisms are involved in the marine debris nexus. Responses such as beach maintenance and coastal ecosystem conservation involve many government agencies and clients who are also engaged in climate change mitigation/adaptation, biodiversity conservation, and human health protection. The evolving legal framework for plastic waste reduction may provide helpful models for the climate regime, and vice versa: the Paris Agreement, with its limited and self-defined legal obligations, is a viable model for internationally monitored plastic pollution reduction. Though it is also a limited device, UNCLOS will undoubtedly play an organisational role in both of these policy objectives, and it could place emphasis on their continued convergence.

The relatively recent and fast-growing movement toward single-use plastic bans is welcome, but the broader task of welding the public imagination to the marine debris nexus – the confluence of plastic pollution, climate change, biodiversity loss, and human health threats – is far from realised. For a variety of reasons it is worth pursuing this cognitive shift, which also feeds into an environmental justice agenda: if some of the worst-case scenarios about the impact of the nexus prove true, the limits of earth system governance adaptation will be severely tested in the process.

References

Abrams, R. (2015). Fighting pollution from microbeads used in soaps and creams. *New York Times*, 22 May. Retrieved from www.nytimes.com/2015/05/23/business/energy-environment/california-takes-step-to-ban-microbeads-used-in-soaps-and-creams.html.

Austin, B. (2014). The aquaculture industry. *Microbiology Today*, 41(4), 166–9. Retrieved from www.microbiologysociety.org/publications/microbiology-today/pastissues.cfm/publication/water/article/7A993C5D-AE1E-4428-B8F391A1E9DBEFED.

Browne, R. (2016). Coles and Woolworths ban products containing plastic microbeads. *Sydney Morning Herald*, 8 January. Retrieved from www.smh.com.au/environment/coles-and-woolworths-ban-products-containing-microbeads-20160107-gm1mwm.html.

Burch, S., Gupta, A., Inoue, C.Y.A. et al. (2019). New directions in earth system governance research. *Earth System Governance*, 1(100006), 1–18.

Carpenter, E.J., Anderson, S.J., Harvey, G.R., Miklas, H.P., & Peck, B.B. (1972). Polystyrene spherules in coastal waters. *Science*, 178(4062), 749–50.

Center for International Environmental Law (CIEL). (2019). *Plastic and Climate: The Hidden Costs of a Plastic Planet*. Retrieved from www.ciel.org/wp-content/uploads/2019/05/Plastic-and-Climate-FINAL-2019.pdf.

Chasek, P.S. (2010). *Confronting Environmental Treaty Implementation Challenges in the Pacific Islands*. Pacific Islands Policy, No. 6. Honolulu: East-West Center.

Chen, C.-L. (2015). Regulation and management of marine litter. In M. Bergmann, L. Gutow, & M. Klages, eds., *Marine Anthropogenic Litter*. New York: Springer, 395–428.

Chen, C.-L., Kuo, P.H., Lee, T.C., & Liu, C.H. (2018). Snow lines on shorelines: solving Styrofoam buoy marine debris from oyster culture in Taiwan. *Ocean & Coastal Management*, 165, 346–55.

Chiba, S., Saito, H., Fletcher, R. et al. (2018). Human footprint in the abyss: 30-year records of deep-sea plastic debris. *Marine Policy*, 96, 204–12.

Cho, D.-O. (2009). The incentive program for fishermen to collect marine debris in Korea. *Marine Pollution Bulletin*, 58, 415–17.

Cole, M., Lindeque, P., Fileman, E. et al. (2013). Microplastic ingestion by zooplankton. *Environmental Science & Technology*, 47(12), 6646–55.

Cole, M., Lindeque, P., Fileman, E. et al. (2016). Microplastics alter the properties and sinking rates of zooplankton fecal pellets. *Environmental Science & Technology*, 50(6), 3239–46.

Colton, J., Knapp, F., & Burns, B. (1974). Plastic particles in surface waters of the Northwestern Atlantic. *Science*, 185(4150), 491–7.

Convention on Biological Diversity (CBD). (2012). *Impacts of Marine Debris on Biodiversity*. CBD Technical Series No. 67. Montreal: Secretariat of the Convention on Biological Diversity.

Costa, M.F. & Barletta, M. (2015). Microplastics in coastal and marine environments of the western tropical and sub-tropical Atlantic Ocean. *Environmental Science: Processes & Impacts*, 17(11), 1868–79.

Cullen-Knox, C., Eccleston, R., Haward, M., Lester, L., & Vince, J. (2016). Contemporary challenges in environmental governance: the rise of social licence. *Environmental Policy and Governance*, 27(1), 3–13.

Derraik, J. (2002). The pollution of the marine environment by plastic debris: a review. *Marine Pollution Bulletin*, 44(9), 842–52.

De Santo, E.M. (2018). Implementation challenges of area-based management tools (ABMTs) for biodiversity beyond national jurisdiction (BBNJ). *Marine Policy*, 97, 34–43.

Duckett, P.E. & Repaci, V. (2015). Marine plastic pollution: using community science to address a global problem. *Marine and Freshwater Research*, 66, 665–73.

Eerkes-Medrano, D., Thompson, R.C., & Aldridge, D.C. (2015). Microplastics in freshwater systems: a review of the emerging threats, identification of knowledge gaps and prioritisation of research needs. *Water Research*, 75, 63–82.

European Commission (EC). (2011). *Plastic Waste: Ecological and Human Health Impacts*. Brussels: EC Directorate-General.

Gilman, E., Chopin, F., Suuronen, P., & Kuemlangan, B. (2016). *Abandoned, Lost, and Discarded Gillnets and Trammel Nets: Methods to Estimate Ghost Fishing Mortality, and the Status of Regional Monitoring and Management*. FAO Fisheries and Aquaculture Technical Paper No. 600. Rome: Food and Agriculture Organization of the United Nations (FAO).

Fredriksson, P.G. & Millimet, D.L. (2002). Is there a 'California effect' in US environmental policy making? *Regional Science and Urban Economics*, 32(6), 737–64.

GEF – Secretariat of the Convention on Biological Diversity and the Scientific and Technical Advisory Panel. (2012). *Impacts of Marine Debris on Biodiversity: Current Status and Potential Solutions*. Technical Series No. 67. Montreal: Secretariat of the Convention on Biological Diversity.

GhostNets Australia. (2015). *GhostNets Australia*. Retrieved from www.ghost nets.com.au/.

Gosseries, A. and Meyer, L. (eds.) (2009). *Intergenerational Justice*. Oxford: Oxford University Press.

Hall, N.M., Berry, K.L.E., Rintoul, L., & Hoogenboom, M.O. (2015). Microplastic ingestion by scleractinian corals. *Marine Biology*, 162(3), 725–32.

Hammer, J., Kraak, M.H., & Parsons, J.R. (2012). Plastics in the marine environment: the dark side of a modern gift. *Reviews of Environmental Contamination and Toxicology*, 220, 1–44.

Hardesty, D., Wilcox, C., Lawson, T.J., van der Velde, T., & Lansdell, M. (2014). *Understanding the Effects of Marine Debris on Wildlife: Final Report to Earthwatch Australia*. Canberra: CSIRO.

Haward, M. (2018). Plastic pollution of the world's seas and oceans as a contemporary challenge in ocean governance. *Nature Communications*, 2018(9), 667.

Hidalgo-Ruz, V. & Thiel, M. (2015). The contribution of citizen scientists to the monitoring of marine litter. In M. Bergmann, L. Gutow, & M. Klages, eds., *Marine Anthropogenic Litter*. New York: Springer, 429–45.

Hinojosa, I.A. & Thiel, M. (2009). Floating marine debris in fjords, gulfs and channels of southern Chile. *Marine Pollution Bulletin*, 58(3), 341–50.

International Union for the Conservation of Nature (IUCN). (2019). *Ecosystem-Based Approaches to Climate Change Adaptation*. Retrieved from www.iucn.org/theme/ecosystem-management/our-work/ecosystem-based-approaches-climate-change-adaptation.

Ivar do Sul, J.A. & Costa, M.F. (2014). The present and future of microplastic pollution in the marine environment. *Environmental Pollution*, 185, 352–64.

Jambeck, J.R., Geyer, R., Wilcox, C. et al. (2015). Plastic waste inputs from land into the ocean. *Science*, 347(6223), 768–71.

Jambeck, J.R. & Johnsen, K.J. (2015). Citizen-based litter and marine debris data collection and mapping. *Computing in Science & Engineering*, 17(4), 20–6.

Johnson, D.E., Salazar, E.R., Gallagher, A. et al. (2018). Preventing plastics pervading an oceanic oasis: building the case for the Costa Rica Thermal Dome to become a World Heritage site in ABNJ. *Marine Policy*, 96, 235–42.

Kaiser, J. (2010). The dirt on ocean garbage patches. *Science*, 328(5985), 1506.

Koelmans, A., Besseling, E., & Shim, W.J. (2015). Nanoplastics in the aquatic environment: critical review. In M. Bergmann, L. Gutow, & M. Klages, eds., *Marine Anthropogenic Litter*. New York: Springer, 325–40.

Lamb, J.B., Willis, B.K., Fiorenza, E.A. et al. (2018). Plastic waste associated with disease on coral reefs. *Science*, 359(6374), 460–2.

Landon-Lane, M. (2018). Corporate social responsibility in marine plastic debris governance. *Marine Pollution Bulletin*, 127, 310–19.

Leonard, G. (2015). *Trashing the Ocean: New Study Provides First Estimate of How Much Plastic Flows into the Ocean*. Ocean Conservancy, 13 February. Retrieved from http://blog.oceanconservancy.org/2015/02/13/trashing-the-ocean-new-study-provides-first-estimate-of-how-much-plastic-flows-into-the-ocean/.

Marine Litter Solutions. (2017). *Joint Declaration*. Retrieved from: www.marinelittersolutions.com/who-we-are/joint-declaration.aspx.

Masura, J., Baker, J.E., Foster, G., Arthur, C., & Herring, C. (2015). *Laboratory Methods for the Analysis of Microplastics in the Marine Environment: Recommendations for Quantifying Synthetic Particles in Waters and Sediments*. NOAA Technical Memorandum NOS-OR&R No. 48 (National Ocean Service). Silver Spring, MD: National Oceanic and Atmospheric Administration (NOAA), Marine Debris Program.

Mathalon, A. & Hill, P. (2014). Microplastic fibers in the intertidal ecosystem surrounding Halifax Harbor, Nova Scotia. *Marine Pollution Bulletin*, 81(1), 69–79.

Mendenhall, E. (2018). Oceans of plastic: a research agenda to propel policy development. *Marine Policy*, 96, 291–8.

Mika, K., Leitner, L., Gold, M., Horowitz, C., & Herzog, M. (2013). Stemming the tide of plastic marine litter: a global action agenda. *Pritzker Policy Brief 5*. Retrieved from https://law.ucla.edu/centers/environmental-law/emmett-institute-on-climate-change-and-the-environment/publications/stemming-the-tide-of-plastic-marine-litter/.

Moore, C. (2015). Foreword. In M. Bergmann, L. Gutow, & M. Klages, eds., *Marine Anthropogenic Litter*. New York: Springer, vii–viii.

Moore, C.J., Moore S.L., Leecaster, M.K., & Weisberg, S.B. (2001). A comparison of plastic and plankton in the north Pacific central gyre. *Marine Pollution Bulletin*, 42(12), 1297–300.

Obbard, R.W., Sadri, S., Wong, Y.Q. et al. (2014). Global warming releases microplastic legacy frozen in Arctic Sea ice. *Earth's Future*, 2, 315–20.

Ogata, Y., Takada, H., Mizukawa, K. et al. (2009). International pellet watch: global monitoring of persistent organic pollutants (POPs) in coastal waters. 1. Initial phase data on PCBs, DDTs, and HCHs. *Marine Pollution Bulletin*, 58(10), 1437–46.

O'Sullivan, K. (2019). Plastic eaten by plankton may impair oceans' ability to trap CO2. *Irish Times*, 30 April. Retrieved from www.irishtimes.com/news/environment/plastic-eaten-by-plankton-may-impair-oceans-ability-to-trap-co2-1.3875434.

Palassis, S. (2011). Marine pollution and environmental law. In R. Baird & D. Rothwell, eds., *Australian Coastal and Marine Law*. Annandale, NSW: Federation Press, 228–63.

Parker, L. (2019). Plastic bag bans are spreading. But are they truly effective? *National Geographic*, 17 April. Retrieved from www.nationalgeographic.com/environment/2019/04/plastic-bag-bans-kenya-to-us-reduce-pollution/.

Perkins, R. & Neumayer, E. (2012). Does the 'California effect' operate across borders? Trading-and investing-up in automobile emission standards. *Journal of European Public Policy*, 19(2), 217–37.

Pomeroy, L.R. (1974). The ocean's food web, a changing paradigm. *BioScience*, 24(9), 499–504.

Provencher, J., Bond, A.L., & Mallory, M.L. (2015). Marine birds and plastic debris in Canada: a national synthesis, and a way forward. *Environmental Reviews*, 23(1), 1–13.

Putnam, R.D. (1988). Diplomacy and domestic politics: the logic of two-level games. *International Organization*, 42(3), 427–60.

Raubenheimer, K. & Mcilgorm, A. (2017). Is the Montreal Protocol a model that can help solve the global marine plastic debris problem? *Marine Policy*, 81, 322–9.

Richardson, A.J. (2008). In hot water: zooplankton and climate change. *ICES Journal of Marine Science*, 65(3), 279–95.

Rochman, C.M., Kross, S.M., Armstrong, J.B. et al. (2015). Scientific evidence supports a ban on microbeads. *Environmental Science & Technology*, 49(18), 10759–61.

Royer, S.-J., Ferrón, S., Wilson, S.T., & Karl, D.M. (2018). Production of methane and ethylene from plastic in the environment. *PloS One*, 13(8), e0200574.

Schuyler, Q.A., Wilcox, C., Townsend, K., Hardesty, B.D., & Marshall, N.J. (2014). Mistaken identity? Visual similarities of marine debris to natural prey items of sea turtles. *BMC Ecology*, 14, 1–7.

Scientific and Technical Advisory Panel (STAP). (2011). *Marine Debris as a Global Environmental Problem: Introducing a Solutions-Based Framework Focused on Plastic. A STAP Information Document*. Washington, DC: Global Environment Facility.

Secretariat of the Antarctic Treaty. (2019). *Final Report of the Forty-Second Antarctic Treaty Consultative Meeting, Volume I*. Antarctic Treaty Consultative, Prague, Czech Republic, 1–11 July. Retrieved from https://documents.ats.aq/ATCM42/fr/ATCM42_fr001_e.pdf.

Sherman, P. & van Sebille, E. (2016). Modeling marine surface microplastic transport to assess optimal removal locations. *Environmental Research Letters*, 2016(11), 1–6.

Stoett, P. (2010). Framing bioinvasion: biodiversity, climate change, security, trade, and global governance. *Global Governance: A Review of Multilateralism and International Organizations*, 16(1), 103–20.

Stoett, P. (2016). *People and Plastic: The Oceans Plastic Crisis, Global Governance, and Development Norms*. Annual Meeting of the Academic Council on the United Nations System, 18 June, Fordham University, New York.

(2019). *Global Ecopolitics: Crisis, Governance, and Justice*. Toronto: University of Toronto Press.

Stoett, P. & Vince, J. (2019). The plastic–climate nexus: linking science, policy, and justice. In P.G. Harris, ed., *Climate Change and Ocean Governance: Politics and Policy for Threatened Seas*. New York: Cambridge University Press, 345–61.

Sulistiyono, A.G. (2017). Indonesia works on plastic tar road project to reduce marine debris. *Jakarta Post*, 8 June. Retrieved from www.thejakartapost.com/news/2017/06/08/indonesia-works-on-plastic-tar-road-project-to-reduce-marine-debris.html.

Taylor, M.L., Gwinnett, C., Robinson, L.F., & Woodall, L.C. (2016). Plastic microfibre ingestion by deep-sea organisms. *Scientific Reports*, 6, 2016(33997), 1–9.

Tibbetts, J.H. (2015). Managing marine plastic pollution: policy initiatives to address wayward waste. *Environmental Health Perspectives*, 123(4), A90–3.

Titmus, A.J. & Hyrenbach, K.D. (2011). Habitat associations of floating debris and marine birds in the North-East Pacific Ocean at coarse and meso spatial scales. *Marine Pollution Bulletin*, 62(11), 2496–506.

United Nations Environment Programme (UNEP). (2009). *Guidelines on the Use of Market-Based Instruments to Address the Problem of Marine Litter*. Retrieved from http://minisites.ieep.eu/assets/477/Economic_Instruments_and_Marine_Litter.pdf.

(2011). *The Honolulu Commitment*. 5th International Marine Debris Conference, 20–5 March, Honolulu. Retrieved from https://5imdc.wordpress.com/about/commitment/.

(2016). *Biodegradable Plastics and Marine Litter: Misconceptions, Concerns and Impacts on Marine Environments*. New York: United Nations.

(2019). *Compilation of United Nations Environment Assembly Resolutions on Marine Litter and Microplastics*. Bangkok: United Nations Environment Programme (UNEP).

United Nations General Assembly. (1982). *Law of the Sea Convention (UNCLOS)*. Retrieved from www.un.org/depts/los/convention_agreements/texts/unclos/clos indx.htm.

Valentine, K. (2015). *Netherlands Company Introduces Plastic Roads That Are More Durable, Climate Friendly Than Asphalt*. Think Progress, 22 July. Retrieved from http://think progress.org/climate/2015/07/22/3682552/plastic-roads-netherlands/.

van Cauwenberghe, L., Vanreusel A., Mees J., & Janssen, C.R. (2013). Microplastic pollution in deep-sea sediments. *Environmental Pollution*, 182, 495–9.

Villarrubia-Gómez, P., Cornell, S.E., & Fabres, J. (2018). Marine plastic pollution as a planetary boundary threat: the drifting piece in the sustainability puzzle. *Marine Policy*, 96, 213–20.

Vince, J., Brierley, E., Stevenson, S., & Dunstan, P. (2017). Ocean governance in the South Pacific region: progress and plans for action. *Marine Policy*, 79, 40–5.

Vince, J. & Hardesty, B.D. (2016). Plastic pollution challenges in marine and coastal environments: from local to global governance. *Restoration Ecology*, 25(1), 123–8.

(2018). Governance solutions to the tragedy of the commons that marine plastics have become. *Frontiers in Marine Science*, 5(214), 1–10.

Vince, J., Hardesty, B.D., & Stoett, P. (2018). *Governance Solutions to the 'Tragedy' of Marine Plastics*. 6th International Conference on Marine Debris, 12–16 March, San Diego.

Wilcox, C., Mallos, N., Leonard, G., Rodriguez, A., & Hardesty, B. (2015). Estimating the consequences of marine litter on seabirds, turtles and marine mammals using expert elicitation. *Marine Policy*, 65, 107–14.

Woodall, L.C., Sanchez-Vidal, A., Canals, M. et al. (2014). The deep sea is a major sink for microplastic debris. *Royal Society Open Science*, 4(1). Retrieved from http://rsos .royalsocietypublishing.org/content/1/4/140317.

World Health Organization and Secretariat of the Convention on Biological Diversity (WHO-CBD). (2015). *Connecting Global Priorities: Biodiversity and Human Health*. Montreal: CBD Secretariat.

Worm, B., Barbier, E.B., Beaumont, N. et al. (2006). Impacts of biodiversity loss on ocean ecosystem services. *Science*, 314(5800), 787–90.

Wyles, K.J., Pahl, S., & Thompson, R.C. (2014). Perceived risks and benefits of recreational visits to the marine environment: integrating impacts on the environment and impacts on the visitor. *Ocean and Coastal Management*, 88, 53–63.

Xanthos, D. & Walker, T.R. (2017). International policies to reduce plastic marine pollution from single-use plastics (plastic bags and microbeads): a review. *Marine Pollution Bulletin*, 118(1–2), 17–26.

Young, O.R. (2012). Building an international regime complex for the Arctic: current status and next steps. *Polar Journal*, 2(2), 391–407.

Young, O.R., Osherenko, G., Ekstrom, J. et al. (2007). Solving the crisis in ocean governance: place-based management of marine ecosystems. *Environment: Science and Policy for Sustainable Development*, 49(4), 20–32.

Zettler, E., Mincer, T., & Amaral-Zettler, L. (2013). Life in the plastisphere: microbial communities on plastic marine debris. *Environmental Science and Technology*, 47(13), 7137–46.

6

Synergies and Trade-Offs between Climate Change Adaptation and Mitigation across Multiple Scales of Governance

ASIM ZIA

6.1 Introduction

The climate change policy mediated by the United Nations Framework Convention on Climate Change (UNFCCC) and adopted by member countries tends to split into two approaches: mitigation (cutting emissions or 'soaking up' carbon pollution) and adaptation (coping with climate change) (Biesbroek et al., 2009; Zia, 2013). This holds true across sectors from forest management and agriculture to energy, transportation, and city planning (see Landauer et al., 2015 for a systematic review); and it makes allocating scarce resources for sustainable and resilient community development much harder (Ingalls & Dwyer, 2016; Zia et al., 2011). When governments divide policies between mitigation and adaptation, and then add on existing bilateral and multilateral development funds, precious resources get wasted as they trickle down to local communities. 'Mitigation is a global problem but adaptation a local issue' is a statement often repeated like a mantra in the annual UNFCCC Conference of the Parties (COP) meetings. It is literally true. But, in practice, splitting efforts along those lines often works at cross-purposes (e.g. see Beymer-Faris & Bassett, 2012; Locatelli et al., 2015; Martens et al., 2009). Figure 6.1, for example, shows cross-scale interactions between the causes and consequences of global climate change as mediated by policy regimes and human behaviours. While human-induced climate at global spatial scale changes relatively slowly (decadal to century timescales), land-use land-cover change (LULCC) (e.g. forest to agriculture or urban land use) changes relatively faster (hourly to annual timescales). Cascading-up interactions from LULCC to climate change (shown as loops (a), (e), and (f) in Figure 6.1) interact against cascading-down interactions from climate change to LULCC. This chapter uses a social-ecological systems (SES) approach (e.g. see Ostrom, 2009) to unravel the complexity induced by both mitigation and adaptation to climate change policies from global to local spatial scales and vice versa.

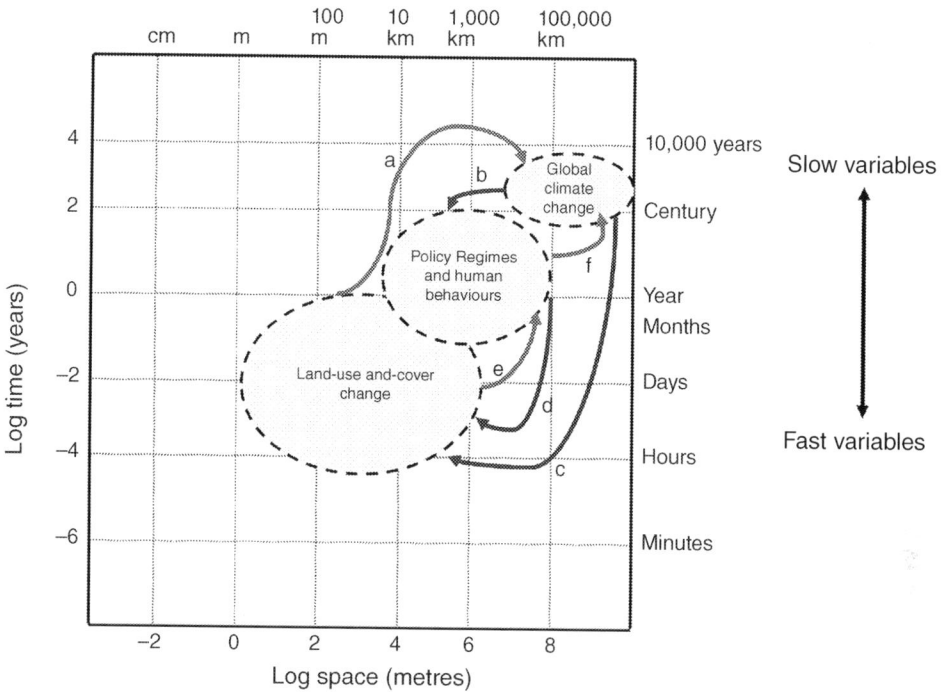

Figure 6.1 Cross-scale interactions in SES

For example, biofuel plantations may meet global mitigation goals, but if they replace temperate and tropical forests used by indigenous communities, those communities struggle to adapt to food and water security challenges that would have been better met by conserving old-growth forests (e.g. see Hirsch et al., 2011). Similarly, mega hydropower dams meet mitigation goals but moving communities from familiar environments undermines their capacity to adapt to climate change (e.g. see Berga, 2016; Mata & Budhooram, 2007). Conversely, adaptation projects may strengthen roads and bridges facing increasing flood risks, but more roads and bridges also increase greenhouse gas (GHG) emissions, undermining mitigation targets (Schulz et al., 2017).

To catalyse action for both mitigation and adaptation, improved understanding of synergies and trade-offs induced by differential policy and governance interventions in earth system dynamics is needed at multiple scales – local to national, regional, and global (e.g. see Jarvis et al., 2011; Locatelli et al., 2015; Shaw et al., 2014; Thornton & Comberti, 2017; Viguié & Hallegatte, 2012; Wollenberg et al., 2013; Zia & Kauffman, 2018). This chapter uses an SES analytical approach and a novel interdisciplinary integrative framework embedded within the SES approach (described in Section 6.2), to analyse the synergies and trade-offs induced by three specific UNFCCC Kyoto/Paris policy mechanisms

aimed at mitigation and/or adaptation to global climate change: Reduced
Emissions from Deforestation and Forest Degradation (REDD+) (Section 6.3)
and Clean Development Mechanism (CDM) vs Adaptation Fund (AF) (Section
6.4). Through this SES approach to analysis of REDD+, CDM, and AF policy
mechanisms, evidence from published studies is utilised to assess the synergies
and trade-offs on mitigation vs adaptation impact of these specific policies.
Further, this evidence is used to develop an argument that the SES approach may
provide a scalable, replicable, and integrative analytical approach to analyse the
synergies and trade-offs of different policy mechanisms ensuing from Paris Treaty
and other global to local climate policy and governance actions. Knowledge gaps
in this context are discussed. Section 6.5 concludes with a discussion of the policy/
practical relevance of the proposed SES approach to navigate synergies and trade-
offs and future research directions for earth system governance.

6.2 The SES Approach

Ostrom (2009) argued that understanding of the processes that lead to
improvements in or deterioration of natural resources is limited because scientific
disciplines use different concepts and languages to describe and explain complex
SES. While pitching an interdisciplinary SES approach, Ostrom (2009)
hypothesised that in a complex SES, subsystems such as a resource system (e.g.
global atmosphere, tropical forests), resource units (e.g. food, water, energy), users
(e.g. human population), and governance systems (e.g. the United Nations (UN),
nation states, regional governments) are relatively separable but interact to produce
outcomes at the SES level, which in turn feedback to affect these subsystems and
their components. Figure 6.2, for example, shows an SES approach to characterise
the subsystem components of global climate mitigation and adaptation policies
(discussed in this chapter) that interact with the 'resource users' spread across
forestry, agriculture, housing, energy, and water 'resource systems'. The
'governance systems' constrain the behaviours of resource users but are in turn
effected by endogenous evolution of the social norms and leadership within and
across resource users. In major action arenas (e.g. UN deliberative bodies),
governance network actors design collective action policies to induce behavioural
change among the resource users for addressing environmental problems. The
socio-environmental 'outcomes', as described in Figure 6.2, in turn induce a
continuous stream of feedbacks on resource units, users, resource systems, and
governance systems.

Within this SES framework, the Stockholm Resilience Alliance (SRA) has
developed a theory of adaptive governance for analysing the social, institutional,
economic, and ecological foundations of multilevel governance modes that are

Social, economic, and political settings
(economic development, population, state stability, government policies, market incentives)

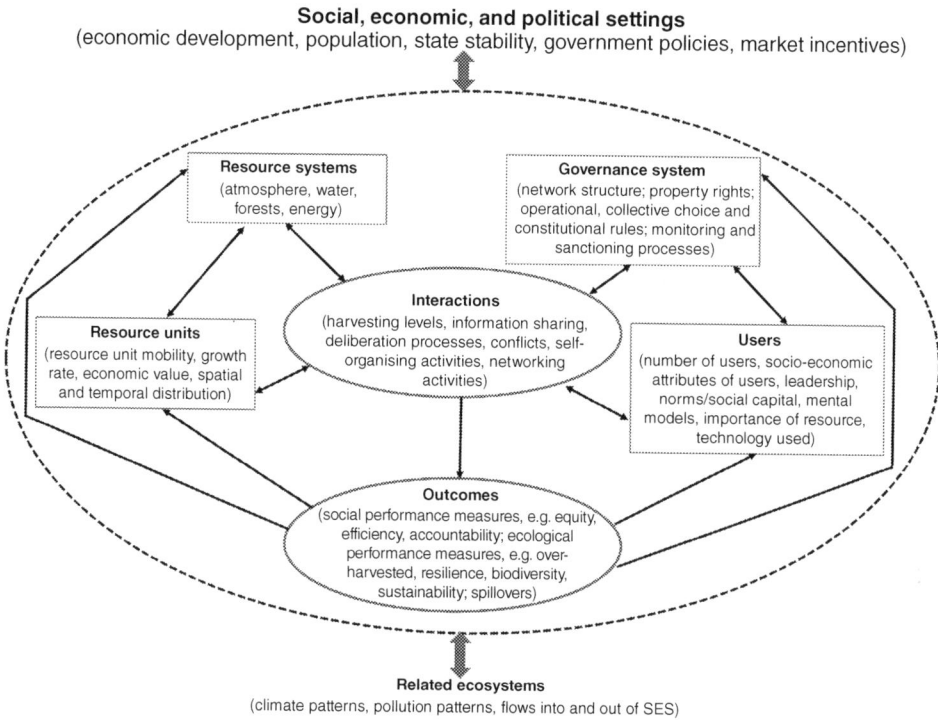

Figure 6.2 The core subsystems in a framework for analysing SES.
Source: Adapted from Ostrom (2009)

successful in building resilience for the vast challenges posed by global change. Folke et al. (2005) laid out theoretical foundations for a deeper study of adaptive governance of SES. Folke et al. (2005) argued that adaptive governance systems often self-organise as social networks with teams and actor groups that draw on various knowledge systems and experiences for the development of a common understanding and policies, in particular during periods of abrupt change (crisis) in SES. Further, Folke et al. (2005: 441) concluded that 'the emergence of "bridging organizations" seem to lower the costs of collaboration and conflict resolution, and enabling legislation and governmental policies can support self-organization while framing creativity for adaptive co-management efforts'. In this context, the SRA laid out two grand challenges for the study of adaptive governance: 'What are the important multiscale processes in SES governance that lead to more or less resilient outcomes on the ground? What are the trade-offs between management priorities and SES for long-term sustainable futures and how do these play out over different scales?' (SRA, 2020: 1).

In this theoretical context, the United Nations University Institute for the Advanced Study of Sustainability (UNU-IAS) is contributing towards more applied research on adaptive governance. For UNU-IAS, a key characteristic of adaptive governance is collaborative, flexible, and learning-based issue management across different scales. UNU-IAS considers Dietz et al. (2003), Folke et al. (2005), Gunderson and Holling (2002), and Olsson et al. (2006) as key theoretical contributions towards establishing adaptive governance as a research field. Brunner et al. (2005), drawing on five case studies from the American West, explored how to expedite a transition toward adaptive governance and break the deadlock in natural resource policymaking. Unlike scientific management, which relies on science as the foundation for policies made through a central bureaucratic authority, Brunner et al. (2005) argue that adaptive governance integrates various types of knowledge and organisations. Adaptive governance relies on open decision-making processes recognising multiple interests, community-based initiatives, and an integrative science in addition to traditional science. Brunner and Lynch (2010) apply an adaptive governance framework to investigate global climate change problematics. Scholz and Stiftel (2010) apply an adaptive governance framework to study water governance issues across multiple spatial and temporal scales.

Adaptive management literature can also be considered part of the adaptive governance framework, notwithstanding theoretical differences between governance and management. Norton (2005), for example, has argued that we need adaptive management to solve wicked environmental policy and governance problems. In adaptive management, the environmental policy decisions are modelled at two interactive levels. At the level of action, descriptive analysis is undertaken to ascertain the current state of the world, such as existing environments, institutions, and policies, and the outcomes ensuing from current policies/decisions. At the meta-level of reflection, normative analysis is employed to determine the socially desirable values by which outcomes of (current and future) policy actions are measured.

At the meta-level of reflection, the planners and policy designers compare the outcomes measured at the level of action with the outcomes that are deemed normatively desirable within the space–time horizon of environmental policy decisions. At this level, meta-decision choice problems are resolved through iterative experimentation and active collaboration/participation between expert and lay decision makers. The normative analysis at the meta-level of reflection results in policy prescriptions/recommendations that aim at getting 'there' from 'here' given all the uncertainty, ignorance, and incomplete information.

To advance the assessment of synergies and trade-offs among different policy and governance designs within the broader SES approach, an integrative framework (Hirsch et al., 2013), as shown in Figure 6.3, was developed and applied in three mid-scale tropical countries. This integrative framework enables

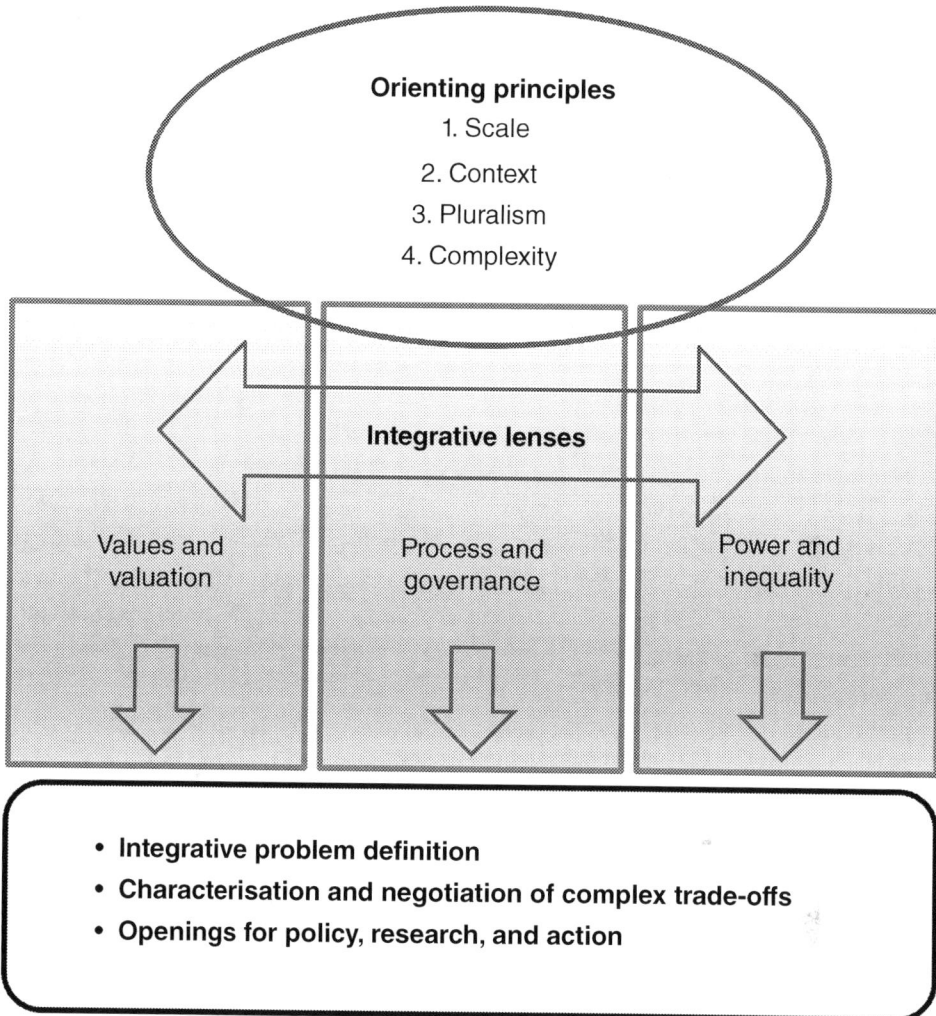

Figure 6.3 Integrative framework.
Source: Adapted from Hirsch et al. (2013: 104)

interdisciplinary assessment of trade-offs from *valuation*, *process*, and *power* perspectives. To develop a more robust notion of trade-offs embedded in sustainable development, McShane et al. (2010) articulated a set of orienting principles that set the stage for the integrative framework to navigate trade-offs in complex SES (shown in Figure 6.3). These guiding principles were derived from the foundational assumption that 'a focus on trade-offs allows multiple actors to recognize the hard choices involved in conservation and development, the outcomes of which will change the diversity, functioning, and services provided by ecosystems and the range of opportunities available to people over space and time'

(McShane et al., 2011: 969). Four principles for negotiating hard choices and trade-offs concerned scale, context, pluralism, and complexity. Principle 1 on scale states that 'successful negotiation of trade-offs will come only with reasonable attention to political, social, economic, and ecological dynamics at multiple spatial and temporal scales, and are critically dependent on interactions across these scales' (Hirsch et al., 2013: 106; as shown in Figures 6.1 and 6.2). Further, in some cases, dynamics operating at one scale may prevent or constrain successful negotiation of trade-offs at another. Principle 2 on context states that there are no panaceas or one-size-fits-all solutions (Ostrom, 2007), nor are there necessary solutions with long-term staying power. Principle 3 on pluralism states that trade-offs are experienced and understood from a variety of legitimate perspectives; and each perspective highlights certain trade-off dimensions and obscures others. Finally, principle 4 on complexity states that human and natural systems are inextricably linked, many important environmental issues will always involve uncertainty, and all models and analytical tools involve some form of simplification of complexity but none provide a comprehensive picture.

Later, Hirsch et al. (2013) advocated for an approach to understanding and navigating trade-offs that is sensitive to the various dimensions of trade-off problems. These dimensions include the losses and gains that occur (values and valuation dimension), the ways they are experienced and interpreted from different perspectives (process and governance dimension), and the power-laden dynamics within which problems are defined and solutions are developed (power and inequality dimension).

This integrative framework is organised according to three 'integrative lenses' that correspond to three distinct dimensions of perceiving how the world works in relation to illuminating and navigating complex trade-offs in conservation and development. The three lenses – values and valuation, process and governance, and power and inequality – are designed to make space for a multiplicity of perspectives and to simultaneously orient those perspectives around three sets of questions and concepts. From the values and valuation perspective, trade-offs consist of gains and losses that can be accounted for by various means and methods. In contrast, from the process and governance lens, trade-offs consist of active choice processes that can be more or less democratic, more or less transparent, and so on. Finally, from the power and inequality perspective, the trade-offs concept is a framing device that can be productively used to illustrate that there are winners and losers associated with different interventions. Yet, at the same time, it can also be used in problematic ways to obscure the political dimensions of complex problems by rendering them in 'objective' terms (Hirsch et al., 2013). The result is a more integrative process of problem definition that accounts for the multiplicity of issues identified, and for the diverse perspectives and beliefs underlying these issues. The integrative framework is intended to provide openings for further research and/or action that no single perspective could yield in isolation. This integrative framework within the broader SES approach underlies the analytical approach that is adopted in this chapter to assess the synergies and trade-offs that ensue from REDD+ (Section 6.3) and CDM and AF (Section 6.4) vis-à-vis mitigation and adaptation to global climate change.

6.3 REDD+: Synergies and Trade-Offs between Climate Change Mitigation and Adaptation

The recent evolution of the international climate policy mechanism that was initially known as 'Reduced Emissions from Deforestation' (RED), then 'Reduced Emissions from Deforestation and Forest Degradation' (REDD) and its variant REDD+, provides an example of both explicit and implicit synergies and trade-offs in mitigation and adaptation to global climate change that will ensue from the implementation of these programmes on the future trajectories of tropical SES (Pistorius, 2012; Zia & Kauffman, 2018). A deeper understanding of the REDD+ policy mechanism, which is a prominent component of the Paris Agreement, can shed light on how and why global governance on climate change, food security, and biodiversity loss has 'synergistically' converged around the international policy goal of conserving tropical forests. In general, REDD+ has been conceptualised as a 'win–win–win' policy mechanism for mitigating climate, protecting biodiversity, and conserving indigenous culture by institutionalising payments on carbon sequestration values of ecosystems services from global to local communities. Adaptation to climate change may also be added as a fourth 'win' as many field studies show that forest conservation is critical for building adaptive capacity in tropical countries. The Union of Concerned Scientists (UCS), for example, assert that REDD is an option that 'not only averts global warming's worst consequences but also generates enormous co-benefits for biodiversity conservation and sustainable development' (Boucher, 2008: 1). The UN-REDD Programme (2009) states that REDD policy is an effort to create a financial value for the carbon stored in forests, offering incentives for developing countries to reduce emissions from forested lands and invest in low-carbon paths to sustainable development. The UN-REDD Programme focuses on the multiple benefits that can be provided by REDD, specifically the ecosystem benefits. According to the UN-REDD Programme definition, multiple benefits of REDD, in addition to its contribution to climate mitigation, include forest conservation, which will protect biodiversity and provide ecosystem services. Despite these pronounced win–win–win policy goals, there is increasing evidence of valuation, governance, and distributional trade-offs across multiple scales induced by REDD+. For example,

McElwee et al. (2017) found that there continues to be a lack of coordination between mitigation and adaptation policies in Vietnam, particularly with regard to REDD+. Policies for forest-based climate mitigation at the national and subnational level, as well as site-based projects, have paid little attention to the adaptation needs of local communities, many of whom are already suffering from noticeable weather changes in their localities, and there is insufficient discussion of how REDD+ activities could facilitate increased resilience. While there were some implicit and coincidental adaptation benefits of some REDD+ activities, most studied projects and policies did not explicitly target their activities to focus on adaptation or resilience, and in at least one case, negative livelihood impacts that have increased household vulnerability to climate change were documented (McElwee et al., 2017). Similar challenges with respect to policy coherence and coordination in the Indonesian context have been discovered by Di Gregorio et al. (2017).

While emissions from tropical deforestation must be reduced to keep global temperatures from increasing more than 2°C by 2050 (mitigation role), global warming will contribute to the destruction of tropical forests over time and will negatively impact forest biodiversity (adaptation role). REDD+ projects can in theory also help preserve biodiversity, which in turn improves the resiliency of the forests. Although the idea behind the REDD+ policy mechanism may be simple (compensate developing countries for sustaining tropical forests), actors in the policy arena do not necessarily agree on how REDD+ policy should be designed, the costs and benefits of implementation, and whether REDD+ is the best approach to reduce emissions. Tropical deforestation is an inherently complex problem (e.g. see Weatherley-Singh & Gupta, 2015), and many efforts and policy approaches have failed so far. Any attempt to solve the deforestation problem generates unintended consequences that will undoubtedly impact the implementation of solutions in the future (Hirsch et al., 2011). Global deforestation and degradation are the result of an increasingly global economy; the demand for particular goods from developed countries has encouraged the conversion of tropical forests to other agricultural uses, including growing soybeans, raising cattle, and producing crops for new biofuel technologies (Parker et al., 2009). Weatherley-Singh and Gupta (2015) found that REDD+ interventions target some local direct, and some regional indirect, drivers of deforestation, but they are not yet tackling most indirect national and international drivers of deforestation, such as international trade and global commodity markets. Far from being a win–win, REDD+ policy is an intervention in a highly complex system, and inevitably involves trade-offs; therefore, it is important to question 'win–win–win' discourse.

In general, REDD+ payments are calculated by measuring an opportunity cost of foregoing deforestation that generates a variety of ecological valuation puzzles.

Opportunity cost of REDD+ is defined as the cost that will be incurred in retaining existing tropical forests. 'Retention means sacrificing the opportunities that would be gained by converting the forest to other uses, such as crops or pasture' (Boucher, 2008: 4). Opportunity cost is thus considered as the minimum amount that would need to be paid to keep the land in forest. The major thrust of economic analysis of REDD+ has been to calculate this opportunity cost ($), which is typically divided by carbon density of the forest (e.g. tons per hectare) to calculate the minimum cost of REDD+ that is expressed in units of money/area (e.g. $/hectare). The measurement of opportunity costs requires heroic assumptions, such as future prices of soybean or other crops that could have been grown on the deforested lands. It is due to these inherent uncertainties about future counter-factuals (i.e. future phase spaces) that different economic models come up with different opportunity costs for REDD+. Global models produce REDD+ cost curves that are typically higher than regional or local models (Boucher, 2008; Nabuurs et al., 2007). While this inconsistency is still being debated, this version of opportunity cost ignores other costs associated with implementation of REDD+ such as administration or capacity-building costs. There have been no reliable global studies that estimate administration or capacity-building costs. A subtler methodological problem in the calculation of REDD+ costs in terms of carbon abatement (e.g. $/tCO^2) includes concerns about the underlying assumptions as to whether a single buyer or a cartel is assumed to set the market price (typically area under the abatement curve), or a global carbon market price be used to determine the price of REDD+ payments. The uncertainties about the non-linear curvature of carbon abatement curves further complicates the calculation of REDD+ payments.

Notwithstanding difficult challenges and uncertainties in measuring carbon abatement curves and opportunity costs, the calculation of carbon densities poses even more daunting challenges (Ramankutty et al., 2007). It is due to these measurement problems that the overall contribution of REDD+ to global climate change GHG flux is still contested. According to the fourth assessment report from the Intergovernmental Panel on Climate Change (IPCC) (Nabuurs et al., 2007), tropical deforestation contributes about 20 per cent of global GHG emissions. There are, however, important methodological issues that underlie this 'narrative' of 20 per cent estimate. DeFries et al. (2002) and Achard et al. (2004) used remotely sensed tropical deforestation data to estimate carbon releases and found that Houghton (2003) had overestimated carbon emissions from land-cover change by up to a factor of two, mainly because of different estimates of the rates of tropical deforestation. The differences among these studies can be ascribed to modelling different geographic ranges and time periods, different types of land-cover changes, different assumptions about land-cover change, and different carbon cycle models/fluxes. There are considerable scientific uncertainties about quantification of several key elements for an accurate and complete analysis of carbon-density estimates in tropical forests. These include rates and dynamics of land-cover change, initial stock of carbon in vegetation and soils, mode of clearing and fate of cleared carbon, response of soils following land-cover change, influence of historical land-cover legacies, and the representation of processes in the models used to integrate all of these elements (Ramankutty et al., 2007). Differences in carbon-density calculations will inevitably affect the calculation of REDD+ payments, which can be potentially used by the developed countries to underestimate REDD+ payments or by the developing countries with tropical forests to overestimate the REDD+ payments.

Calculating a baseline upon which to compare subsequent activity is essential to valuing reductions in carbon emissions. Depending on the method of calculation used, data may not be available for all countries. Reference levels can either be based on historical or projected rates of deforestation in a particular country or region. Historical baselines aim to measure any reductions in deforestation below past trends. A variation on this approach is the historical adjusted baseline; this method incorporates factors that may impact the rate of deforestation in the future due to development pressures and adjusts the historical baseline accordingly. One caveat of the historical adjusted baseline is that it could actually provide financial incentives to countries that achieve a net increase in deforestation, as long as the rate of deforestation is below the adjusted baseline. Projected baselines require the most sophisticated data because the method relies on econometrics to assess the future rate of deforestation in a country or region based on the social and economic driving forces of deforestation. Again, the projected baseline approach is susceptible to allowing financial rewards to countries that actually contribute to a net gain in deforestation (Parker et al., 2009). To avoid these perverse incentives, negotiations during the Paris Agreement focused extensively on institutionalising measurement, reporting, and verification (MRV) procedures for REDD+ projects. Recent studies (e.g. Ochieng et al., 2018) have, however, found that the level of MRV institutionalisation across different countries varies significantly.

Another important REDD+ policy design problem is whether carbon (biodiversity) offsets or credits are issued at the national or the project level. On the one hand, national-based approaches are favourable because REDD+ efforts will be weakened unless incentives to convert forests to other land uses are eliminated. A national approach is also more conducive to establishing baselines and addressing leakage; however, project-based and/or community-based approaches may be appropriate if a country is not ready to implement a national REDD+ policy and take on the responsibilities of monitoring forest activity. Further, it has been empirically demonstrated through an analysis of the International Forestry Resources and Institutions (IFRI) database that community-based governance of forest commons is more effective in the long run than national-level governance approaches (Chhatre & Agarwal, 2009). On the other hand, a national-based approach to developing and implementing REDD+ policy is preferable to minimise the possibility of leakage within a country or across countries. It is argued that monitoring emissions reductions at a national level discourages leakage, or the displacement of deforestation and degradation activities, to other parts of the same country. But there is a trade-off here as national governments are generally in conflict on tenure-right issues with many local and indigenous communities. Community goals are not necessarily included in the codification procedures of REDD+ projects, as recently discovered by Milne et al. (2019) through ethnographic studies of REDD+ projects in South East Asia. In addition, there are significant disagreements even about the definition of local and indigenous communities in REDD+ negotiations, (e.g. see Gupta et al., 2016; Shankland & Hasenclever, 2011; Sunderlin et al., 2009). In addition to these definitional issues, there are significant power asymmetries and long-standing conflicts between indigenous communities and national governments; and the implementation of REDD+ projects by national governments could further exacerbate these conflicts depending upon who is defined as 'indigenous' by the national governments for transferring REDD+ benefits (e.g. see Larson et al., 2013). To manage such persistent conflicts, Gupta et al. (2016) proposed the enhanced institutionalised role of 'bridge organisations' – the voluntary, multi-stakeholder REDD+ partnership bringing together state and non-state (e.g. indigenous) actors from global to local scales. From an SES perspective, the role and function of bridging organisations is thus central to 'bridge' the fragmented forest governance across polycentric power centres (e.g. international trading firms to civil society actors) (see also Sunderlin et al., 2015 for challenges and opportunities with polycentric governance of REDD+).

REDD+ policy will undoubtedly require an exchange of resources among relevant actors, but the allocation of REDD+ policy benefits and burdens among actors is not determined at this time. A more thorough/complete review of the projected costs and benefits identifies some incommensurate puzzles in terms of the impacts that the international REDD+ policy mechanism may have on individual stakeholder groups, especially three target populations: developed countries, developing countries, and local and indigenous people. Developed countries are by and large expected to provide the bulk of the financing for any REDD+ mechanism that is put in place. Financing is the crux of the success for REDD+ project proposals; without monetary support, developing countries will not be able to effectively reduce emissions from land-use practices. Although the pressure to finance REDD+ projects could be seen as a burden on the developed countries, it is also a benefit to these actors because it is arguably less costly to pay for REDD+ projects in developing countries rather than invest significant financial capital to reduce fossil fuel-driven emissions from energy sectors through improving their own infrastructure and technology. The pressure for developed countries to finance REDD+ has also provided them with extreme bargaining power. Developing countries are dependent upon the developed world to support their actions; until concrete figures of anticipated financial compensation are provided, it is unreasonable for anyone to expect developing countries to implement REDD+ projects on a broad scale. The financing of REDD+ projects remains well below the expectations set during Paris Agreement negotiations, and even the financing of baseline MRV activities is leading to the emergence of cost traps for developing countries (Köhl et al., 2020).

Each developing country that chooses to participate and support REDD+ policy mechanisms will need to assess their institutional capacity for implementation and monitoring efforts. Other national land-use policies may need to be revisited to ensure that the efforts for REDD+ are not undermined and land-use tenure rights may need to be better defined. This undeniably places the burden for action on developing countries, although not all countries will be eligible to participate. Depending on a country's historical rate of deforestation and the amount of forest cover they have, only some developing countries may be rewarded. It is arguably unfair to countries that have kept deforestation under control previously to be excluded from any REDD+ mechanisms now. This approach could also create perverse incentives for countries with high forest cover and traditionally low rates of deforestation to negatively change their land-use practices. Such perverse incentives may compromise long-term adaptation to climate change for countries that historically made efforts to conserve their tropical forests. The social and environmental justice impacts of REDD+ across 50+ countries with tropical forests need to be carefully investigated as well (e.g. see Turnhout et al., 2017).

While the implementation policy for protecting the rights of indigenous communities is still being debated under the social safeguards, REDD+ faces a fundamental challenge from the international trade regulations mandated under World Trade Organization (WTO) arrangements; and food and agricultural subsidies provided by World Bank, regional development banks, and other international organisations promoting the standard 'Western' style of neoliberal governance policies in tropical forested developing countries under the garb of 'food security' and 'economic development' (Zia, 2013; Zia & Kaufmann, 2018). The REDD+ policy mechanism is designed on such a counterfactual basis that the calculation of opportunity costs, forest densities, and carbon densities will remain uncertain so long as free trade and economic growth policies continue to promote the spread of mono-agriculture in tropical forests. These mono-cropping agricultural practices are either promoting the replacement of old growth forests in tropical countries with food system input crops (e.g. growth of soybean and palm oil plantations in tropical forests during the last 50 years) or biofuel energy inputs (e.g. corn for ethanol). In theory, the replacement of old growth forests with mono-crops will conserve the carbon density of the forests; however, in practice, it could trade off biodiversity (as animal habitats will be lost due to mono-cropping practices) as well as indigenous communities (as their habitats will be lost), perhaps as unintended consequences, but ultimately undercutting adaptive capacity in tropical countries. Multifunctional landscape design approaches aimed at building synergies across carbon, biodiversity, and cultural conservation goals also face 'reality checks' in the face of 'business-as-usual incentives' in countries such as Peru, Ecuador, and Brazil (Lima et al., 2017). There are unavoidable valuation, governance, and distributional trade-offs with the REDD+ policy mechanism, yet REDD+ is one of the key cornerstones of the Paris Agreement and one of the critical policy mechanisms for keeping alive the likelihood of attaining the 1.5°C goal (e.g. see IPCC, 2018).

6.4 The Clean Development Mechanism vs the Adaptation Fund: Synergies and Trade-Offs between Climate Change Mitigation and Adaptation

Both the Kyoto Protocol and the Paris Agreement show the bias of the UNFCCC process towards policy mechanisms aimed at 'mitigation to climate change', such as the Clean Development Mechanism (CDM). UNFCCC policy mechanisms on adaptation to climate change have only recently started to penetrate the negotiation process, most notably leading to the establishment of the Adaptation Fund (AF), and the Loss and Damage Mechanism, under the Paris Agreement. While all of these mechanisms are being pursued in parallel for the 'rule book' that was negotiated in the UNFCCC COP25 in Madrid, Spain, in 2019, each of them have implicit synergies and trade-offs between mitigation and adaptation to climate change. For brevity of space, I am excluding discussion of loss and damage mechanism and elucidate the underlying synergies and trade-offs in the CDM and AF, respectively.

The CDM is one of the 'flexibility' mechanisms defined in the Kyoto Protocol and extended under the Paris Agreement. The CDM has two main goals: cost-effective compliance for developed countries through GHG emission reductions in developing countries, and contributing to sustainable development in developing countries (Bakker et al., 2011; Stahlke, 2019). The CDM allows industrialised countries to invest in emission reductions wherever it is cheapest globally. Between 2001 and 2012, the CDM was expected to produce some 1.5 billion tons of CO_2e in emission reductions, where most of these reductions were achieved through renewable energy, energy efficiency, and fuel. While 1.5 billion tons of CO_2e in emission reductions are significant in and of themselves, they pale in *scale* to the hundreds of billion tons of CO_2e produced by developed countries during the same period.

Dinar et al. (2011) found that with 34 investor countries and 175 potential host countries, there are 5,950 plausible pairs for the CDM to be enacted, yet only 305 of those pairs through 5,669 projects had been at work together. In an attempt to study the factors that led to existing dyads of participating countries, the authors evaluated countries on the measure of the colonial ties between two countries, the membership of host countries to international governmental organisations, the energy use and source of that energy in host countries, as well as vulnerability of, governance, and ease of doing business within the host country. Several findings were concluded to increase the likelihood of collaboration: countries with strong colonial ties or trade relationships, democratic and demilitarised governments, and involvement in international governing institutions that all contribute to the ease of doing business with the country (Dinar et al., 2011). Also worth noting is the energy use of both countries involved, as the CDM is only efficiently utilised should a country find that it is more cost-effective to lower emissions elsewhere rather than in their own industries, and many least-developed countries do not have the industry and power sectors to pollute enough for the CDM to earn an investor country enough Certified Emission Reductions (CERs) (Lederer, 2011).

The following specific challenges have been widely discussed in designing and implementing CDM projects:

1. Inadequate criteria for additionality and establishment of baseline (Cames et al., 2016).
2. Unclear empirical evidence if true reductions in global net emissions are taking place (Al Awadhi et al., 2017).
3. CDM projects are disproportionately focused on 'clean energy' (Baird & Green, 2020).
4. Inequitable displacement of responsibility and adverse impacts on local communities (Benites-Lazaro & Mello-Théry, 2019; Dirix et al., 2016).

From a governance standpoint, the CDM programme has been fraught with corruption and has experienced limited success in prompting a proliferation of sustainable technologies in the developing world (Cox, 2010). Additionally, the CDM's current structure does not incentivise GHG reductions below target levels. Schneider (2009: 95) argues that the CDM is a 'zero game to the atmosphere', meaning that any certified reduction in a developing nation can be met with an equal rise in emissions in the corresponding developed nation if it is already meeting its reduction timeline.

Because CDM projects are only monetised in terms of their total abatement of GHG emissions, the true value of projects that promote sustainable development (including adaptation to climate change) not directly related to GHG mitigation is not realised in market pricing of CERs. The sustainable development projects evaluated on a longer temporal scale will ultimately reduce the severity of pressures and consequences of continued growth. Therefore, any pricing of CERs must include considerations of the future benefits of a sustainable development project (including adaptation co-benefits) as they relate to reducing the vulnerability of future generations to climate change. This would necessitate the formation of an index or ranking system, in which a development can be evaluated based upon its environmental and social benefits, particularly poverty easement. An alternative to this more complex pricing mechanism would be to add a premium value to CERs related to high sustainable development projects, which 'might increase the share of such projects in global carbon markets' (Sutter & Parreño, 2007: 89).

From polycentric governance of the SES perspective, the CDM is a policy mechanism set into place to create a global solution for what has traditionally been seen as national or state problems in international development and energy sectors. The local and national scale politics, for example, demonstrate that CDM projects can be used on many levels and manipulated in many ways. Even at the very early stages of CDM implementation, Repetto (2001) identified several potential flaws within the CDM framework. One such fatal flaw he called the 'incentive incompatibility': 'stripped to the basics, CDM is an international payment for a service, the reduction of greenhouse gas emissions. A fundamental flaw is that neither the seller nor the buyer of the credit has a private interest in the actual delivery of the service' (Repetto, 2001: 327). It is not clear whether CDM design can ever be able to overcome this incentive incompatibility problem.

The CDM has also been criticised by participating countries for its low efficiency, complicated and inapplicable methodological requirements, lack of transparency, imbalanced regional distribution, and uncertain international rules after 2012 (Duan, 2011). The additionality is key to the validity of the CDM projects because without it the impact, and subsequent emission reductions, of the donor countries' contributions would be unknown. Yet, this additionality is difficult to prove and some officials have expressed that they feel the process is arbitrary (Cames et al., 2016; Schiermeier, 2011). Each project also has to demonstrate the maintenance of environmental integrity. The CDM has to ensure each of these requirements on a trade-by-trade basis and this process requires a lot of time and administrative resources leading to high transaction costs. The design of the system has created a trade-off between transaction costs and credibility. Fewer regulations verifying the validity of the projects, or standardisation of registration, would reduce these costs and increase efficiency but jeopardise the credibility of the CDM.

As many sceptics argue, the CDM isn't fully beneficial because of its low contribution to sustainable development, unbalanced regional and sectoral distribution of projects, and its limited contribution to global emission reductions (Benites-Lazaro & Mello-Théry, 2019; Dirix et al., 2016). More specifically, the major concerns about the functioning of the CDM are that it has often been noted that the CDM does not lead to global emission reductions but is, at best, a mechanism that offsets emission increases in industrialised countries. The contribution of the CDM to sustainable development in the host countries is widely seen as being very limited. Asian and Latin American countries make up more than 95 per cent of the projects and CERs in the CDM project pipeline, raising concerns about the equitable regional and sub-regional distribution of projects. The unequal distribution of CDM projects among sectors has also been noted, with the transport and building sectors, both key for achieving ambitious climate targets, almost completely absent from the project portfolio. Certain project types, notably the destruction of industrial gases such as HFC-23 and N, are thought to generate high windfall profits for project developers and host countries. Construction of dams under CDM compromises adaptation to climate change for local fishing communities (Baird & Green, 2020). Projects face significant transaction costs due to the institutional and governance structure of the CDM. Despite the cost effectiveness of CDM, the sheer reductions in global-scale cumulative GHGs from the CDM projects remains a very marginal, small-scale contribution that should be a big cause of concern for post-Kyoto climate governance regime under the Paris Agreement.

In contrast to CDM, the AF was established under the Kyoto Protocol as a financial instrument to support projects in developing nations vulnerable to the effects of climate change (Manuamorn et al., 2020). It has been scaled up under the Paris Agreement. Currently, the AF is funded by a 2 per cent levy on CERs, colloquially known as carbon credits, issued by qualified initiatives under the CDM. The governance linkage between CDM and AF must be noted to understand the synergies and trade-offs embedded in the UNFCCC-mediated global climate governance process.

While the exact cost of adapting to a changed climate cannot be known, the AF's projected maximum payment of $5 billion by 2020 is shy of the estimated minimum cost of $500 billion per year over the next 50 years, with many of the highest costs expecting to be incurred in the world's least-developed nations. In addition to an inadequate amount of funding, which continues to bedevil AF even after the Paris Agreement, the AF's funding scheme works to the detriment of the Clean Development Fund by taxing developed countries seeking to invest in clean technologies abroad. Therefore, it has been proposed frequently that the AF change its funding mechanism. Further, the AF also needs to establish clear criteria for eligible adaptation projects in order to adhere to its mission and promote resiliency in economically disadvantaged areas.

Whereas distributive justice has been an issue of contingency for CDM policy mechanism, it is a key concern with regards to the AF. The AF, which is funded by 2 per cent of CERs generated, as well as through private funds and donations, is specifically designed to provide the most vulnerable countries with the least adaptive capacity with compensation for the pollution that industrialised countries have caused. Grasso's (2011) work traces the meetings that gave birth to the AF as it exists today and supports that through the clashes and negotiations and revisiting of its terms, developed and developing countries have been able to equally and actively participate in its planning. As the AF is designed to be more accessible to the least-developed countries, they have distributed the power more greatly to and evenly among national governing bodies rather than multilateral agencies. In the case of the AF, negotiations continued until developing countries were satisfied that it ensured that the most vulnerable countries received a fair disbursement of funds and the management of funds would be undertaken by entities less likely to favour the developed countries.

While Grasso's assessment of the procedural ethics of designing the AF is quite positive, the operationalisation of it has not seen the level of success in disbursing funds as was planned. While the AF's interdependence from official government assistance was planned to make funding more equitable, Horstmann (2011) explains that besides the 2 per cent of CERs generated through the CDM, there were no binding financial agreements to create funding. The concept of 'direct access' for vulnerable countries to the AF has rather evolved into a set of hurdles to jump through in order to comply with the policies and procedures required to access the funds from a Global Environmental Facility (GEF) agency, although the GEF's role was diminished for that very reason during the Paris Agreement negotiation process. Horstmann (2011) also questions the lack of specificity of the initiative to particularly support the most vulnerable countries. Relevant documents regarding the AF mention the prioritisation of 'vulnerable countries', but merely in generalisations to their geographic vulnerability to climate change or the economic vulnerability to adapt themselves, and without specific language regarding who these priority countries are and whether funding needs to be provided to specific vulnerable communities, state governments, specific projects, etc. The national implementation entities in charge of the AF now face the challenge of having the capacity to consider and assess each vulnerable country through a transparent process that provides adaptation funding as the AF promises.

Because the AF sources its funds from a tax on CERs, it is essentially discouraging carbon offsets. While this tax is not particularly significantly detrimental at the 2 per cent level, the previously demonstrated need for significantly greater funding necessitates a source that will not be detrimental to the CDM. Recalling that the AF is an attempt to reconcile the inequity caused by the pollution of developing countries, it would seem prudent to adopt a transportation tax scheme. Flåm and Skjaerseth (2009) suggested that a tax on maritime and air fuel may provide the benefit of mitigating usage, thus reducing environmental impact, as well as raising revenue. They argued that a fuel tax would also not be as susceptible to repeal as a carbon tax. Furthermore, the tax could be levied without a significant burden on the individual consumer; for example, a $10 tax per flight could yield an estimated $20 billion per year (Flåm & Skjaerseth, 2009).

Zadek (2011: 1065) proposed that, 'It is national (and, perhaps in some cases, sub-national and regional) leadership and ambition that will drive progress'. Zadek (2011) did acknowledge that outside funding would be helpful, but that it is mostly a proponent for moving away from placing blame and more looking towards how to fix the problem. However, the reality of the situation is that climate change and GHG emissions are a global problem. There are also portions of the global community who have contributed huge amounts more to this problem for which everyone has to suffer the consequences. Because of this, it is important that regions of the world such as China and the United States take on the larger consequences of their larger actions. With this methodology and mentality in place, there are ways in which the industrialised nations could and even should help to aid the underdeveloped countries to prepare for adaptation to climate change.

The AF is managed by the AF Board (UNFCCC). The AF Board consists of representatives from 16 countries that adhere to the Kyoto Protocol. Climate adaptation in a country or a community is not isolated; it is connected with all other social, environmental, and economic problems in that area. Climate change will affect all aspects of life in vulnerable areas, including food availability, poverty, unemployment, access to water, sanitation education, and health care. That is why it is so important for local stakeholders to have input and decision-making power regarding what they need, and what solutions would work best in their community. The AF Board has little contact with members of civil society or stakeholders; the only contact is the allowance of accredited observers and possible formal dialogue with those observers at the end of the board meetings (Abbott & Gartner, 2011).

Despite AF's stated goal of supporting 'particularly vulnerable' communities, there is no official definition of 'vulnerability' with which to rate countries applying for aid (Horstmann, 2011). When applying for funding each country has to make a case for their vulnerability, so they are forced to define it themselves. This system demonstrates the country-driven approach of the AF. The allocation of funding to the most vulnerable communities is decided by the national government of each country and therefore responsibility and accountability for the success of the projects is placed not with the AF Board but with the national government of each country.

Many developing countries, however, currently do not even have the relevant 'absorptive capacity' – the capacity to carry out the adaptation measures needed – even if the funding were available. Most will unnecessarily have to suffer adverse impacts of climate change that could be avoided under an improved adaptation regime. The responsibility for these avoidable adverse impacts – whether due to a lack of funding or of absorptive capacity – will fall squarely on industrialised countries. Some stakeholders, mainly from the developed world, have been tempted to cite the lack of certainty about the adaptation funding needs of developing countries and their lack in absorptive capacity as reasons to postpone a debate of the rough issue of international adaptation finance. The two issues are intricately linked, and there is an urgent need to look into ways of simultaneously scaling up the provision of adaptation funds for developing countries of the appropriate kind, and the absorptive capacity to use these funds meaningfully (Flåm & Skjærseth, 2009). In the case of adaptation funding, developing country ownership and public transparency of decision-making is not only desirable but a prerequisite for success, particularly in the context of mainstreaming activities. Given this, the AF should be the main instrument for the purpose of raising and managing international adaptation finance for developing countries. Vulnerability to future climate risks, the governance of civil society, and the access modality to international climate funds are key enabling conditions for internationally financed, community-focused adaptation (Manuamorn et al., 2020). The synergies and trade-offs between mitigation and adaptation goals of CDM and AF projects can be better navigated by linking the projects in these two mechanisms. Ironically, an inter-agency linkage between CDM and AF will add to the transaction costs and likely induce additional project delays.

6.5 Conclusions, Policy Relevance, and Future Research Directions

An integrative framework to evaluate valuation, governance, and distributional trade-offs of public policies within an SES approach can be potentially used to improve the UNFCCC-mediated multilevel policy mechanisms such as REDD+, CDM, and AF. An integrative approach can elucidate and potentially mediate the synergies and trade-offs for both mitigation and adaptation to global climate change. While REDD+ has been touted as a win–win–win policy mechanism for reducing GHG emissions, conserving biodiversity, and promoting sustainable development, there are a variety of adaptation and biodiversity/cultural conservation trade-offs ensuing from the current governance structure of REDD+. Similarly, CDM and AF programmes are continually supported under the Paris Agreement, both piloted under the Kyoto Protocol with clear goals to mitigate and adapt to climate change respectively. However, both CDM and AF projects entail synergies and trade-offs for mitigation vs adaptation, which can be better mediated by linking the projects in these two policy mechanisms through inter-agency collaboration. Specific bridge organisations within the UNFCCC can also be institutionalised to link the assessment of mitigation and adaptation trade-offs ensuing from REDD+, CDM, AF, and Loss and Damage Mechanism projects. The earth system governance community can inform the development and field testing of the proposed integrative framework within an SES analytical approach. The future earth system governance research in this domain can inform the design of REDD+, CDM, AF, and other new climate policy mechanisms evolving under the Paris Agreement (e.g. cap and trade linkage mechanisms). Rigorous analyses about synergies and trade-offs between mitigation and adaptation goals for such global policy mechanisms may deepen insights about adaptive and reflexive governance of earth systems. While mitigation to climate change might also be the best adaptation to climate change, low ambitions of GHG emission reductions embedded in the Paris Agreement and high residency times of GHG concentrations in the global atmosphere imply that investments in adaptation also need to be prioritised in many vulnerable regions in the world, in particular Arctic, Small Island Developing States, Africa, South Asia, and Central America. The earth system governance community can pool their intellectual resources to inform this multilevel policy process during the next 10 to 15 years, coincidently the critical time frame that is left for humans on this planet to limit the anthropogenic warming beyond a 1.5°C increase above pre-industrial levels (IPCC, 2018).

References

Abbott, K.W. & Gartner, D. (2011). *The Green Climate Fund and the Future of Environmental Governance*. Earth System Governance Working Paper No. 16. Retrieved from https://papers.ssrn.com/sol3/papers.cfm?abstract_id=1931066.

Achard, F., Eva, H.D., Mayaux, P., Stibig, H.J., & Belward, A. (2004). Improved estimates of net carbon emissions from land cover change in the tropics for the 1990s. *Global Biogeochemical Cycles*, 18(2), 1–11.

Al Awadhi, S., Abbas, Z., & Mezher, T. (2017). Analyzing sustainable development impacts of large-scale clean development mechanism projects in host countries. *International Journal of Thermal and Environmental Engineering*, 14(2), 153–61.

Baird, I.G. & Green, W.N. (2020). The Clean Development Mechanism and large dam development: contradictions associated with climate financing in Cambodia. *Climatic Change*, 161(2), 365–83.

Bakker, S., Haug, C., van Asselt, H., Gupta, J., & Saïdi, R. (2011). The future of the CDM: same same, but differentiated? *Climate Policy*, 11(1), 752–67.

Berga, L. (2016). The role of hydropower in climate change mitigation and adaptation: a review. *Engineering*, 2(3), 313–18.

Benites-Lazaro, L.L. & Mello-Théry, N.A. (2019). Empowering communities? Local stakeholders' participation in the Clean Development Mechanism in Latin America. *World Development*, 114, 254–66.

Beymer-Farris, B.A. & Bassett, T.J. (2012). The REDD menace: resurgent protectionism in Tanzania's mangrove forests. *Global Environmental Change*, 22(2), 332–41.

Biesbroek, G.R., Swart, R.J., & van der Knaap, W.G. (2009). The mitigation–adaptation dichotomy and the role of spatial planning. *Habitat International*, 33(3), 230–7.

Boucher, D.H. (2008). *Out of the Woods: A Realistic Role for Tropical Forests in Curbing Global Warming*. Cambridge, MA: Union of Concerned Scientists.

Brunner, R.D. & Lynch, A.H. (2010). *Adaptive Governance and Climate Change*, Boston: American Meteorological Society.

Brunner, R.D., Steelman, T.A., Coe-Juell, L., Cromley, C., & Edwards, C. (2005). *Adaptive Governance: Integrating Science, Policy, and Decision Making*. New York: Columbia University Press.

Cames, M., Harthan, R.O., Füssler, J. et al. (2016). *How Additional Is the Clean Development Mechanism? Analysis of Application of Current Tools and Proposed Alternatives*. Berlin: Oeko-Institut EV CLIMA. B, 3. Retrieved from www.verifavia .com/uploads/files/clean_dev_mechanism_en.pdf.

Chhatre, A. & Agrawal, A. (2009). Trade-offs and synergies between carbon storage and livelihood benefits from forest commons. *Proceedings of the National Academy of sciences*, 106(42), 17667–70.

Cox, G. (2010). The Clean Development Mechanism as a vehicle for technology transfer and sustainable development: myth of reality. *Law Environment and Development Journal*, 6, 179.

DeFries, R.S., Houghton, R.A., Hansen, M.C. et al. (2002). Carbon emissions from tropical deforestation and regrowth based on satellite observations for the 1980s and 1990s. *Proceedings of the National Academy of Sciences*, 99(22), 14256–61.

Di Gregorio, M., Nurrochmat, D.R., Paavola, J. et al. (2017). Climate policy integration in the land use sector: mitigation, adaptation and sustainable development linkages. *Environmental Science & Policy*, 67, 35–43.

Dietz, T., Ostrom, E., & Stern, P.C. (2003). The struggle to govern the commons. *Science*, 302(5652), 1907–12.

Dinar, A., Rahman, S.M. , Larson, D.F., & Ambrosi, P. (2011). Local actions, global impacts: international cooperation and the CDM. *Global Environmental Politics*, 11(4), 108–33.

Dirix, J., Peeters, W., & Sterckx, S. (2016). Is the Clean Development Mechanism delivering benefits to the poorest communities in the developing world? A critical evaluation and proposals for reform. *Environment, Development and Sustainability*, 18(3), 839–55.

Duan, M. (2011). Reform of the Clean Development Mechanism: where should we head for? *Carbon & Climate Law Review*, 5(2), 169–77.

Flåm, K.H. & Skjærseth, J.B. (2009). Does adequate financing exist for adaptation in developing countries? *Climate Policy*, 9(1), 109–14.

Folke, C., Hahn, T., Olsson, P., & Norberg, J. (2005). Adaptive governance of social-ecological systems. *Annual Review of Environmental Resources*, 30, 411–73.

Grasso, M. (2011). The role of justice in the North–South conflict in climate change: the case of negotiations on the Adaptation Fund. *International Environmental Agreements: Politics, Law and Economics*, 11(4), 361–77.

Gunderson, L.H. & Holling, C.S. (eds.) (2002). *Panarchy: Understanding Transformations in Human and Natural Systems*. Washington, DC: Island Press.

Gupta, A., Pistorius, T., & Vijge, M.J. (2016). Managing fragmentation in global environmental governance: the REDD+ partnership as bridge organization. *International Environmental Agreements: Politics, Law and Economics*, 16(3), 355–74.

Hirsch, P.D., Adams, W.M., Brosius, J.P. et al. (2011). Acknowledging conservation trade-offs and embracing complexity. *Conservation Biology*, 25(2), 259–64.

Hirsch, P.D., Brosius, J.P., O'Connor, S. et al. (2013). Navigating complex trade-offs in conservation and development: an integrative framework. *Issues in Integrative Studies*, 31, 99–122.

Horstmann, B. (2011). Operationalizing the Adaptation Fund: challenges in allocating funds to the vulnerable. *Climate Policy*, 11(4), 1086–96.

Houghton, R.A. (2003). Revised estimates of the annual net flux of carbon to the atmosphere from changes in land use and land management 1850–2000. *Tellus B*, 55(2), 378–90.

Ingalls, M.L. & Dwyer, M.B. (2016). Missing the forest for the trees? Navigating the trade-offs between mitigation and adaptation under REDD. *Climatic Change*, 136(2), 353–66.

Intergovernmental Panel on Climate Change (IPCC) (2018). Summary for policymakers. In V. Masson-Delmotte , P. Zhai, H.O. Pörtner et al., eds., *Global Warming of 1.5°C: An IPCC Special Report on the Impacts of Global Warming of 1.5°C above Pre-Industrial Levels and Related Global Greenhouse Gas Emission Pathways, in the Context of Strengthening the Global Response to the Threat of Climate Change, Sustainable Development, and Efforts to Eradicate Poverty*. Geneva: Intergovernmental Panel on Climate Change.

Jarvis, A., Lau, C., Cook, S. et al. (2011). An integrated adaptation and mitigation framework for developing agricultural research: synergies and trade-offs. *Experimental Agriculture*, 47(2), 185–203.

Köhl, M., Neupane, P.R., & Mundhenk, P. (2020). REDD+ measurement, reporting and verification: a cost trap? Implications for financing REDD+ MRV costs by result-based payments. *Ecological Economics*, 168, 106513. doi: https://doi.org/10.1016/j.ecolecon.2019.106513.

Larson, A.M., Brockhaus, M., Sunderlin, W.D. et al. (2013). Land tenure and REDD+: the good, the bad and the ugly. *Global Environmental Change*, 23(3), 678–89.

Landauer, M., Juhola, S., & Söderholm, M. (2015). Inter-relationships between adaptation and mitigation: a systematic literature review. *Climatic Change*, 131(4), 505–17.

Lederer, M. (2011). From CDM to REDD+: what do we know for setting up effective and legitimate carbon governance? *Ecological Economics*, 70(11), 1900–7.

Lima, M.G.B., Visseren-Hamakers, I.J., Braña-Varela, J., & Gupta, A. (2017). A reality check on the landscape approach to REDD+: lessons from Latin America. *Forest Policy and Economics*, 78, 10–20.

Locatelli, B., Pavageau, C., Pramova, E., & Di Gregorio, M. (2015). Integrating climate change mitigation and adaptation in agriculture and forestry: opportunities and trade-offs. *Wiley Interdisciplinary Reviews: Climate Change*, 6(6), 585–98.

McElwee, P., Nguyen, V.H., Dung, N.V. et al. (2017). Using REDD+ policy to facilitate climate adaptation at the local level: synergies and challenges in Vietnam. *Forests*, 8(1), 11.

McShane, T.O., Hirsch, P.D., Trung, T.C. et al. (2011). Hard choices: making trade-offs between biodiversity conservation and human well-being. *Biological Conservation*, 144(3), 966–72.

Manuamorn, O.P., Biesbroek, R., & Cebotari, V. (2020). What makes internationally financed climate change adaptation projects focus on local communities? A configurational analysis of 30 Adaptation Fund projects. *Global Environmental Change*, 61, 102035. doi: https://doi.org/10.1016/j.gloenvcha.2020.102035.

Martens, P., McEvoy, D., & Chang, C. (2009). The climate change challenge: linking vulnerability, adaptation, and mitigation. *Current Opinion in Environmental Sustainability*, 1(1), 14–18.

Mata, L.J. & Budhooram, J. (2007). Complementarity between mitigation and adaptation: the water sector. *Mitigation and Adaptation Strategies for Global Change*, 12(5), 799–807.

Milne, S., Mahanty, S., To, P. et al. (2019). Learning from 'actually existing' REDD+: a synthesis of ethnographic findings. *Conservation & Society*, 17(1), 84–95.

Nabuurs, G.J., Masera, O., Andrasko, P. et al. (2007). IPCC fourth assessment report, working group III, chapter 9 (final draft). In B. Metz, O.R. Davidson, P.R. Bosch, R. Dave, & L.A. Meyer, eds., *Climate Change 2007: Mitigation: Contribution of Working Group III to the Fourth Assessment Report of the Intergovernmental Panel on Climate Change*. Cambridge, UK: Cambridge, University Press, 541–84.

Norton, B.G. (2005). *Sustainability: A Philosophy of Adaptive Ecosystem Management*. Chicago: University of Chicago Press.

Ochieng, R.M., Arts, B., Brockhaus, M., & Visseren-Hamakers, I.J. (2018). Institutionalization of REDD+ MRV in Indonesia, Peru, and Tanzania. *Ecology and Society*, 23(2), 8.

Olsson, P., Gunderson, L.H., Carpenter, S.R. et al. (2006). Shooting the rapids: navigating transitions to adaptive governance of socio-ecological systems. *Ecology and Society*, 11(1), 1–18.

Ostrom, E. (2007). A diagnostic approach for going beyond panaceas. *Proceedings of the National Academy of Sciences*, 104(39), 15181–7.

   (2009). A general framework for analyzing sustainability of social-ecological systems. *Science*, 325(5939), 419–22.

Parker, C., Mitchell, A., Trivedi, M., Mardas, N., & Sosis, K. (2009). *The Little REDD+ book*. Oxford: Global Canopy Programme.

Pistorius, T. (2012). From RED to REDD+: the evolution of a forest-based mitigation approach for developing countries. *Current Opinion in Environmental Sustainability*, 4(6), 638–45.

Ramankutty, N., Gibbs, H.K., Achard, F. et al. (2007). Challenges to estimating carbon emissions from tropical deforestation. *Global Change Biology*, 13(1), 51–66.

Repetto, R. (2001). The Clean Development Mechanism: institutional breakthrough or institutional nightmare? *Policy Sciences*, 2001(34), 303–27. doi: https://doi.org/10.1023/A:1012603007614.

Schiermeier, Q. (2011). Clean-energy credits tarnished. *Nature*, 477(7366), 517–18.

Schneider, L. (2009). A Clean Development Mechanism with global atmospheric benefits for a post-2012 climate regime. *International Environmental Agreements: Politics, Law and Economics*, 9(2), 95–111.

Scholz, J.T. & Stiftel, B. (eds.). (2010). *Adaptive Governance and Water Conflict: New Institutions for Collaborative Planning*. London: Routledge.

Schulz, A., Zia, A., & Koliba, C. (2017). Adapting bridge infrastructure to climate change: institutionalizing resilience in intergovernmental transportation planning processes in the Northeastern USA. *Mitigation and Adaptation Strategies for Global Change*, 22(1), 175–98.

Shankland, A. & Hasenclever, L. (2011). Indigenous peoples and the regulation of REDD+ in Brazil: beyond the war of the worlds? *IDS Bulletin*, 42(3), 80–8.

Shaw, A., Burch, S., Kristensen, F., Robinson, J., & Dale, A. (2014). Accelerating the sustainability transition: exploring synergies between adaptation and mitigation in British Columbian communities. *Global Environmental Change*, 25, 41–51.

Stahlke, T. (2019). The impact of the Clean Development Mechanism on developing countries' commitment to mitigate climate change and its implications for the future. *Mitigation and Adaptation Strategies for Global Change*, 1–19. doi: https://doi.org/10.1007/s11027-019-09863-8.

Stockholm Resilience Alliance (SRA). (2020) *Adaptive Governance*. Retrieved from www.stockholmresilience.org/research/research-streames/stewardship/adaptive-governance-.html.

Sunderlin, W.D., Larson, A.M., & Cronkleton, P. (2009). Forest tenure rights and REDD. In A. Angelsen, M. Brockhaus, M. Kanninen et al., eds., *Realising REDD*. Bogor: Center for International Forestry Research, 139–50.

Sunderlin, W.D., Sillis, E., Duchelle, A.E. et al. (2015). REDD+ at a critical juncture: assessing the limits of polycentric governance for achieving climate change mitigation. *International Forestry Review*, 17(4), 400–13.

Sutter, C. & Parreño, J.C. (2007). Does the current Clean Development Mechanism (CDM) deliver its sustainable development claim? An analysis of officially registered CDM projects. *Climatic Change*, 84(1), 75–90.

Thornton, T. F. & Comberti, C. (2017). Synergies and trade-offs between adaptation, mitigation and development. *Climatic Change*, 140(1), 5–18.

Turnhout, E., Gupta, A., Weatherley-Singh, J. et al. (2017). Envisioning REDD+ in a post-Paris era: between evolving expectations and current practice. *Wiley Interdisciplinary Reviews: Climate Change*, 8(1), e425. doi: https://doi.org/10.1002/wcc.425.

UN-REDD Programme (2009). *Multiple Benefits: Issues and Options for REDD*. Geneva: UN-REDD Programme.

Viguié, V. & Hallegatte, S. (2012). Trade-offs and synergies in urban climate policies. *Nature Climate Change*, 2(5), 334–7.

Weatherley-Singh, J. & Gupta, A. (2015). Drivers of deforestation and REDD+ benefit-sharing: a meta-analysis of the (missing) link. *Environmental Science & Policy*, 54, 97–105.

Wollenberg, E., Tapio-Bistrom, M.L., Grieg-Gran, M., & Nihart, A. (eds.). (2013). *Climate Change Mitigation and Agriculture*. Abingdon, UK: Routledge.

Zadek, S. (2011). Beyond climate finance: from accountability to productivity in addressing the climate challenge. *Climate Policy*, 11(3), 1058–68.

Zia, A. (2013). *Post-Kyoto Climate Governance: Confronting the Politics of Scale, Ideology and Knowledge*. Abingdon, UK: Routledge.

Zia, A., Hirsch, P., Songorwa, A. et al. (2011). Cross-scale value trade-offs in managing social-ecological systems: the politics of scale in Ruaha National Park, Tanzania. *Ecology and Society*, 16(4), 7.

Zia, A. & Kauffman, S. (2018) The limits of predictability in predefining phase spaces of dynamic social ecological systems: command and control' versus 'complex systems' based policy design approaches to conserve tropical forests. *Journal of Policy and Complex Systems*, 4(2). doi: https://doi.org/10.18278/jpcs.4.2.9.

7

Lock-Ins in Climate Adaptation Governance

Conceptual and Empirical Approaches

BERND SIEBENHÜNER, TORSTEN GROTHMANN, DAVE HUITEMA,
ANGELA OELS, TIM RAYNER, AND JOHN TURNPENNY

7.1 Introduction

After more than a decade of implementation efforts in various fields of adaptation to climate change, a growing number of scholars have expressed their concern about an apparent lack of effect on current policy and practice. In short, while the call has been for 'societal transformation' (O'Brien, 2011; Termeer et al., 2017), what we are observing is more akin to inaction or at best incrementalist 'muddling through' (Tschakert & Dietrich, 2010). Despite an almost unanimous consensus over the need – in principle – for policies to promote climate adaptation, observers identify a widening mismatch between the scientific evidence and the adaptation needs identified by academics on the one hand and, on the other hand, uninformed, ignorant, or wilful persistence of conventional practices, with increasingly vulnerable communities, infrastructures, and agriculture as a result. Even where climate adaptation has entered public debates, and related strategies and policies are being developed, they are often surprisingly un-innovative and incremental in nature. Indeed, even in regions that show relatively high levels of adaptive capacity, which means that in principle they could adapt well, the dominant approach is to postpone action, and to 'wait and see' – often referring to persistent uncertainties (see Huitema et al., 2016).

Against this background, a lively debate has emerged about *barriers to climate adaptation* (Biesbroek et al., 2013, 2014; Eisenack et al., 2014; Moser & Ekstrom, 2010) and *path dependencies* (Wise et al., 2014). This has identified an impressive, indeed 'seemingly endless' number of barriers and challenges in adaptation planning and implementation (Biesbroek et al., 2013). However, the academic literature on adaptation governance barriers remains largely descriptive, ahistorical, and lacking in conceptual clarity. Little effort has been made to develop indicators that can identify and distinguish barriers from non-barriers, identify and prioritise their importance and severity, understand their history or evolution, or more systematically identify interventions to deal with them (Biesbroek et al., 2013). Little attention has been paid to more theory-based understandings of the mechanisms at work in explaining the gaps and the underdeveloped state of adaptation policies in many countries. There is thus a need to go beyond the current context-specific and fragmented understanding of barriers, to embrace theoretical and comparative approaches, synthesising knowledge and more systematic analysis; a need that has also been identified by the Intergovernmental Panel on Climate Change (IPCC) (see Denton et al., 2014). Moreover, currently, the literature is essentially normative in its implicit assumption that barriers exist, that they are necessarily bad, and need to be overcome to allow for successful adaptation. Criticising such assumptions in the literature, Biesbroek et al. (2013: 1126) emphasise how the factors that are considered barriers are determined by 'how actors interpret and value past events, which ultimately depends on personal values, ideas, and interests (O'Brien, 2009); what might be considered a barrier to one actor could be an opportunity to other actors (Burch, 2010)'. In addition, it has been pointed out that not all the barriers are the same, with some actually serving as 'healthy selection mechanisms' (Biesbroek et al., 2013).

Building on these criticisms of the concept of barriers, and in response to calls for more nuanced understandings of why adaptation policy remains in its current, relatively underdeveloped state, this chapter focuses on *lock-ins* as a particular conceptual approach to understand path dependencies and rigidities in policy processes. Although a so far underutilised concept in terms of adaptation research (Hetz & Bruns, 2014), arguably the 'lock-in' concept represents an improvement over the concept of 'barriers' in several ways. First, it allows more insight into why most implemented adaptation actions have been incremental and not transformative. To explain this situation, Wise et al. (2014) suggest a paradigmatic shift in adaptation science and practice towards conceptualising adaptation as an element of pathways – stressing the historical dimension that means that future developments are contingent on historical pathways and difficult to change. Second, as a less normative, more social-scientific concept, 'lock-in' has potential to throw more light on the nature of particular barriers, how they emerged, relate to one another, and might be addressed. Third, although authors often use the concept with a negative connotation to highlight how decisions in the past have led to a development or path that is difficult (but not impossible) to change and that has unwanted consequences, lock-ins can be positive in their effects as well as negative.

The lack of attention paid to the lock-in concept in adaptation literature, compared to the concept of barriers, is surprising in view of the acknowledged importance of an adaptive approach to governance (see e.g. Folke et al., 2005), taking account of the possibility of surprise and acknowledging irreducible uncertainties, and thus embracing the permanent need for learning and change (see e.g. Huitema et al., 2009). Governance and policy processes often lag behind climate change impacts, with the status quo often appearing as a 'lock-in', or the rather persistent pursuit of one specific policy or technological path, potentially in the face of pressures from different actors and/or the environment for change. Or policies might change towards adaptation, but little change actually takes place. Even if the need for change is obvious, the track record of previous decisions rebels against any such change.

Interestingly, the concept of 'lock-in' receives only limited mention in the adaptation-related sections of the AR5 IPCC assessment report (IPCC, 2014), where it is linked to the concept of 'mal-adaptation'. The report states that 'some near-term responses to increasing risks related to climate change may also limit future choices. For example, enhanced protection of exposed assets *can lock in dependence on further protection measures*' (IPCC, 2014: 28, emphasis added). However, the concept remains underutilised in the current literature. According to Hetz and Bruns (2014), although there is growing interest in understanding adaptation limits, the concept of lock-ins has been 'rather marginalised' in adaptation research and in the planning literature (Hartmann, 2012).

This chapter begins to address this deficit, and map out an agenda whereby the strengths of the concept as applied in other domains can be brought to bear to better understand the dynamics at work in the governance of adaptation to climate change. It addresses and begins to set out a future research agenda for three sets of research questions. First, the chapter seeks to conceptually grasp lock-ins in climate adaptation governance and to identify indicators for lock-ins taking place and how can they be detected and described. Second, it seeks to explain lock-ins in climate adaptation governance by reference to central mechanisms originating from knowledge, discourse, and expertise; physical infrastructures; institutions and past policy tools as well as from actors. Third, in cases where they are harmful, the chapter asks how can lock-ins be overcome or abated? Accordingly, the chapter is structured in three main sections with Section 7.2 discussing the concept of lock-ins in several disciplinary contexts; Section 7.3 introducing central dimensions and explanatory avenues addressing the first and second set of research questions; and Section 7.4, by way of conclusion, focusing on the third research question.

7.2 Conceptualising Lock-Ins: Learning from Other Disciplines

Lock-in and path dependency are concepts that originate in (evolutionary) economics but that have also been picked up in political science, science and technology studies, as well as in economic geography. This section briefly reviews the literature, drawing out useful insights that may help to develop a concept of lock-ins and path dependence applicable to climate adaptation governance.

The notion of lock-in first entered currency in the discipline of *economics*, to highlight how large consequences may result from relatively 'small', often accidental events, and how particular courses of action, once introduced, can be virtually irreversible, however inefficient they may prove to be. Initially, it was closely associated with the issue of competition among technologies, identifying increasing returns to scale as the reason why one type becomes locked in (Arthur, 1989). Increasing returns to scale may result from positive information and network externalities, economies of scale in production, learning effects, and infrastructure availability. Decision makers come to be swayed by the large market share of a product or technology, rather than by its inherent properties.

Alongside the related concept of path dependence, scholars within economics and more broadly subsequently began to apply the 'lock-in' concept to companies and organisations (Schreyögg & Sydow, 2011; Sydow et al., 2009), institutions, and even consumers (Cecere et al., 2014). Unruh (2000), for example, has used the concept to explain the continuation of carbon-intensive modes of development by processes of technological and institutional coevolution (where each has a causal influence on the other).

From the perspective of *science and technology studies/sociology of knowledge*, lock-ins have latterly come to be viewed – implicitly at times – in more ontological terms (see e.g. Foxon, 2011). 'Sociological analyses highlight how new technologies have a high degree of interpretative flexibility, and so the social networks relating to these technologies only gradually reach a state of stability or "closure" in which a widely shared understanding of the technology is achieved' (Foxon, 2011: 2261).

In *political science*, Pierson (2000: 264) found Arthur's increasing returns hypothesis 'fertile territory for developing new propositions about the conditions that facilitate or impede various types of political change'. Institutions may be subject to increasing returns owing to, inter alia, political actors using their power to modify rules to their advantage. Change is possible, but remains bounded until something 'erodes or swamps the mechanisms of reproduction' (Pierson, 2000: 265). In this sense, lock-ins in policies are in sharp contrast to what has been discussed as 'policy innovation' (Jordan & Huitema, 2014).

Recent work by *economic geographers* makes a distinction between three main forms of regional industrial path development: path extension (equating to lock-in), path renewal, and new path creation (see Moodysson et al., 2016), potentially co-existing in the same region. A regional lock-in refers to a reinforcing set of well-established linkages between the production structure, the knowledge infrastructure, and the support structure that prevent, for example, industrial restructuring and manifests itself at the regional level (Moodysson et al., 2016), though it may relate to factors in other levels of governance (Hassink, 2010). For Hassink (2010: 452), policy lock-ins can be 'considered as thick institutional tissues aiming at preserving existing industrial structures and therefore unnecessarily slowing down industrial restructuring and indirectly hampering the development of indigenous potential and creativity'. Lock-ins, however, may also have 'positive' effects. The core argument put forward by Moodysson et al. (2016) is that a balance of policy change and policy continuity is required for nurturing and maintaining new path developments.

Wilson et al. (2015) highlight the usefulness of the lock-in concept in the analysis of community resilience and land degradation in Italy. Social, economic, and environmental 'lock-ins' facilitate better understanding of the challenges and opportunities for raising community resilience. Lock-in effects can be understood as 'drivers that shoehorn certain community decision-making processes into specific 'pathways' or development 'corridors' beyond which certain human decision-making actions become either 'unthinkable' or impossible to implement' (Wilson et al., 2015: 519). Wilson et al. (2015) develop lock-in variables that are 'non-directional', meaning that they can either raise or lower resilience, depending on each specific community context.

How can we define and conceptualise lock-ins in climate adaptation governance? From economic geography, we carry forward the insights that lock-ins tend to derive from an inter-related set of factors that may have their origins at multiple scales. In adaptation to climate change, a lock-in would imply that the range of conceivable options that are in principle open to decision makers is limited to a few alternatives, and that the origins of lock-in can be found in cognitive, political, infrastructure-related, and other historical paths creating specific dependencies. But we take seriously the insight that a balance of policy change and policy continuity may be required for nurturing and maintaining new path development.

7.3 Dimensions and Theory-Based Explanatory Avenues

In this section we outline a set of elements that we suggest can, often in combination, lead to 'lock-ins' and path dependencies in climate change adaptation governance. In this sense they can be regarded as explanatory variables, the presence of which can explain a lock-in. In doing so, we also highlight how they may also serve as alternative *explanations* based on different theoretical assumptions. In doing so, we refer to (a) knowledge, discourse, and expertise; (b) physical infrastructures; (c) institutions and past policy tools; as well as (d) actors.

7.3.1 Lock-Ins of Knowledge, Discourse, and Expertise

Adaptation to climate change requires knowledge about the expected climate change impacts and the range of options for adapting to them. Nyamwanza and

Bhatasara (2015: 1184) have argued that the literature on adaptation governance has failed to pay 'attention to the epistemological and ontological dimensions in climate adaptation research, yet these are the dimensions which are directly concerned with the analysis of the creation and dissemination of knowledge in any particular area of inquiry'. Accordingly, an investigation into discursive lock-ins to adaptation must start with an investigation into what constitutes legitimate knowledge on adaptation. Scientific knowledge has made the most far-ranging claims to truth and objectivity, based on methods that supposedly establish validity and replicability. 'For a long time and in many places, science held (or continues to hold) the promise of closure through fact-finding' (Mol, 2002: 177). However, it has been widely recognised that science fails to fulfil this promise. As Leipprand et al. (2017: 230) have shown in their empirical study of scientific policy advice (SPA) on the German energy transition that 'SPA operates in a context where facts and values are inextricably linked' and 'different normative starting points lead to different approaches and research aims'. Significantly, Nyamwanza and Bhatasara (2015: 1189) claim that in adaptation policy, narrow representations of reality have tended to support incrementalist approaches, since the 'methods used to plan adaptation to climate change ... have been heavily influenced by positivist scientific narratives of gradual change and economic narratives of marginal adjustments to that change'.

Mol (2002) has gone one step further and argued that we are not only seeing multiple perspectives on the same reality but actually multiple enactments of reality (i.e. multiple realities and multiple ontologies): 'reality is never so solid that it is singular. There are always alternatives' (Mol, 2002: 164). The literature on barriers to climate change adaptation has recognised this to some extent and acknowledged 'that truth is composed of multiple local realities that can only be perceived subjectively' (Biesbroek et al., 2014: 1020). However, Biesbroek et al. (2014: 1020) have interpreted the struggle between competing versions of reality as 'frame contests' that are rooted in individual values and material interests.

In this perspective, lock-ins need to be regarded as multiple realities that result from competing discourses that are a collective rather than an individual phenomenon. While discourses need to be reproduced by individual actors in order to remain stable, they are an intersubjective structure of shared meaning. A discourse is here defined as a heterogeneous ensemble of knowledge claims that creates certain visibilities, enables certain practices, incites certain forms of subjectivity, and legitimises certain power relations (Dean, 1999). Discourses are inherently linked to power relations: dominant discourses legitimise particular power relations, while those power relations define what constitutes legitimate knowledge (Foucault, 1976; Nyamwanza & Bhatasara, 2015). Foucauldian discourse analysis but also historical institutionalism thus helps to study empirically how specific framings of problems achieve dominance and become 'institutionalised' (see Carstensen & Schmidt, 2016; Hajer, 1995).

The complex nature of adaptation to climate change rules out a single objectively right answer to any given problem. In climate change adaptation, as elsewhere, struggles between competing discourses and practices are ubiquitous. Conventional adaptation practices are thus buttressed by a level of proof, provided by expert communities that are formed around existing technologies, such as hydrological engineers. These communities have developed expertise (and associated 'policy tools' – see Jordan & Turnpenny, 2015) in line with the basic notions of their paradigm. What changes over time are often the tools (i.e. technical instruments, procedures) that produce 'different versions of the object' (Mol, 1999: 77).

It follows that a *discursive lock-in* can be studied as a set of dominant practices based on a particular ontology. The opening up of a locked-in policy regime is closely linked to the rise of a new ontology that offers the rationale for a policy change based on a different set of theoretical assumptions, methods, and scientific evidence than before. Changing the horizon of what is 'thinkable' is often a precondition for policy change. Späth (2012) has investigated four cases of regional initiatives that pursue energy self-sufficiency through the use of renewable energy sources in Austria. He reports that not all transitions can be explained by networks of actors alone but require a discourse analysis to fully understand their genesis: 'If we look at their very early beginnings, even before networks were formalized and plans discussed, we can, firstly, discern a discursive shift in what was thinkable with regards to development strategies, and secondly, a merging or linking of various discourses that have previously been separate' (Späth, 2012: 1258).

It is to be expected that established expert communities with their privileged practices will not be supportive when their paradigm is challenged, and other practices become more relevant. Leipprand et al. (2017) have studied the struggle between two competing advocacy coalitions (and their scientific bases) that followed the contested introduction of the Renewable Energy Act in Germany. They identify a polarisation between two advocacy coalitions based on science, namely those pushing for more renewables (proactive) and those defending the status quo (reactive). When the nuclear catastrophe in Fukushima hit in 2011, the energy transition was significantly speeded up by a discursive U-turn of the reactive coalition. Thus, the original idea of an energy transition has been significantly transformed and reinterpreted to become mainstream policy.

Finally, discursive lock-ins are neither positive nor negative by definition. It has to be assessed empirically, what their effects are. With new policy reforms in 2014, many have asked if the German energy transition is now being dismantled. In a recent literature review, Buschmann and Oels (2019) argue that there is a (positive) discursive lock-in of the energy transition that protects it from being dismantled (see Geels et al., 2016; Hake et al., 2015; Lauber & Jacobsson, 2016; Strunz, 2014). Instead, in the face of protest, the energy transition is 'only' changing its form: from decentralised ownership back into the hands of the 'big four' energy utilities but still fully committed to the transition from nuclear-fossil to renewables (Geels et al., 2016).

7.3.2 Lock-Ins in Physical Infrastructure

The planning and construction of physical infrastructure is prone to lock-ins for various reasons, the simplest being the fact that infrastructure is usually built to last for long periods, often decades or even centuries. This means that almost any infrastructure reflects the ideas, discourses, and knowledge of a certain period and that later insights – for instance to the extent that climate change will occur – or innovations will in principle not be reflected in that design. In addition, much infrastructure is 'line infrastructure' connecting places and communities (e.g. roads, railways, but also dikes), which diminishes the possibility for local variation and experimentation. This is because communities, once the infrastructure has been built, are 'in the same boat', adjustments in one place affect the others, and maintenance will in principle be aimed at maintaining the entire infrastructure. Infrastructural lock-ins are also a matter of opportunity costs – investments made in one form, for instance large-scale dams, cannot be invested in other means of achieving an objective. This in turn has various societal side effects, notably that insights and technology are likely to develop further in the chosen direction (expert companies offering this type of solution flourish and employ staff, a centralised organisation oversees the necessary budgets) and that efficiency gains are being made – thus making it more difficult to deviate. Another societal effect concerns the expectations of those served or protected by the infrastructure – if they trust the solution is effective and will remain so, they will start counting on the protection offered, giving less consideration to private solutions, thereby becoming even more dependent on the effective function of the infrastructure. Infrastructural solutions may also become a source of (national or regional) pride, a symbol of the high technological capabilities of a society or community, making its wisdom more difficult to question.

Water governance is an area where some of these dynamics play out. Huitema and Meijerink (2010), for instance, describe how water transitions around the globe are instigated and pushed through. Often, new ways of dealing with water (droughts and floods) revolve around 'soft' solutions that focus on behavioural aspects at the individual or the household level. These include reversibility as an important design criterion, and do not require the same amount of investment. Huitema and Meijerink (2010) refer to this as the 'greening of water management'. However, quite a few of these intended transitions meet with strong resistance from interests associated with infrastructure construction. In Spain, for instance, this has led to ferocious debates about the question of whether potential droughts should be addressed by lowering the demand for water, by installing desalinisation capacity, or by simply creating infrastructure that connects the water-poor North of Spain to the water-rich South of France (see Brouwer et al., 2013).

7.3.3 Lock-Ins in Institutions and Tools

In political science, institutions, as rules, procedures, norms, and habits of policymaking, tend to be regarded as a stable or conditioning element around human interactions (see e.g. Evans et al., 1985; Hall & Taylor, 1996; Immergut, 1998; March & Olsen, 1984; Peters, 2012; Schmidt, 2008; Steinmo et al., 1992). In that sense, they influence the framing of issues, who will be involved in their resolution, and whether and how the issues should be addressed. Institutions provide an element of predictability to societal interactions and thus represent a notion of lock-in in a special sense. From that point of view, institutions are often persistent, although they can change quickly in many different ways. The rich field of study on institutions includes examining how and why they are formed; how they embody values, ideas, discourses, interests, and power relationships; how and why institutions change (e.g. how different actors may maintain, alter, or even overthrow institutions); and their role in policymaking. Lock-ins in institutions may involve situations where the maintenance work is more successful than the activities of those who seek institutional change, perhaps even in the face of strong pressures for that change. Barnett et al. (2015: 5) thus find within six case studies in Australia that 'the path-dependent nature of the institutions that govern natural resources and public goods is a deep driver of barriers and limits to adaptation. Path-dependent institutions are resistant to change. When this resistance causes the changes necessary for adaptation to be slower than changes in climate, then it becomes a limit to adaptation'.

One particular element of this locking-in process of policies as institutions are the *tools* employed by different policy actors in early phases of policy processes (i.e. policy formulation tools; Jordan & Turnpenny, 2015). With this we refer to the aides that policymakers use to prepare, implement, or evaluate policy, including cost–benefit analysis, scenarios, computer models, or participatory methods like citizens' juries. Studying how, by whom, and why such tools are designed, selected, and deployed, and for what purposes, can be done through an institutional lens, thus revealing much about the institutions, and any potential lock-ins. For example, a dominant focus on cost–benefit analyses in climate adaptation policies may become 'locked in' to only economically viable solutions with calculable payback schemes. The tool may have also shaped the policy process in a way that limits other ways of seeing other problems or solutions, either conceptually or because the tool designers form a powerful interest group. The tools themselves can therefore be seen as institutions.

7.3.4 Path Dependence and Lock-Ins through Actors

The path dependence approach holds that a historical path of choices has the character of a branching process with a self-reinforcing dynamic in which positive feedback increases, while at the same time the costs of reversing previous decisions increase, and the scope for reversing them narrows sequentially, as the development proceeds, finally leading to irreversibility and lock-ins (cf. David, 2001). Literature on path dependence and lock-ins often describes these irreversibilities and lock-ins as unexpected by the actors in charge (Hirsch & Gillespie, 2001). A decision by an actor in the system is not necessary for a lock-in to occur; instead, non-linear dynamics at the systems level generate these effects (Kline & Rosenberg, 1986). Actors with both limited understanding of the consequences of their decisions and narrow interests tend to be seen only as a marginal cause of lock-ins in path dependence literature. Generally, research on path dependence and lock-ins rarely dwells on the role of individual actors (Hirsch & Gillespie, 2001) and has been criticised for its 'very simple actor model' (Meyer & Schubert, 2007: 26).

Nevertheless, Wilson et al. (2015), in their research on community resilience, see socio-psychological lock-in effects as one of the most interesting sets of lock-ins. Research suggests that many individual actors are often reluctant to break path dependencies and change towards more resilient trajectories because of entrenched psychological conservatism, also referred to as 'cultural resistance' (Burton et al., 2008). Although adopting new technologies to 'fix' community problems may be relatively easy, developing a new attitude and shifting culture from one mental mode to another is difficult (Wilson, 2013). Thomsen et al. (2012) identify narrow-minded actors that favour short-term strategies as a reason for adverse path dependencies that lessen the likelihood of effective adaptation to climate change in future contexts. Psychological research suggests that individual actors are easily biased and selective in their information preferences and processing, that they generally seek to avoid regret and disappointment, and that they do so through, for example, denying the existence of a problem, not making decisions, delaying decisions, and not changing past decisions (Janis & Mann, 1977; Raiffa et al., 2002, cited in Hermans, 2008; Zeelenberg et al., 2000).

Table 7.1. *Cognitive frames grouped into four strategic contrasts, with examples of climate issues*

	Goal orientation and focus	
Perceptual distance	Promotion orientation	Prevention orientation
Distal view (long-term, broad categories)	*Social progress frame* Defines the issue as improving quality of life or harmony with nature	*Morality/ethics frame* Defines the issue in terms of right or wrong; respecting or crossing limits
	Middle-way frame Puts the emphasis on finding a possible compromise position between polarised views Example: plan to reconcile adaptation and mitigation	*Pandora's box frame* Defines the issue as a call for precaution in the face of possible impacts or catastrophe Example: Al Gore's movie *An Inconvenient Truth*
Proximal view (short-term, narrow categories)	*Economic development frame* Defines the issue as investment that improves competitiveness	*Scientific uncertainty frame* Defines the issue as a matter of what is known versus unknown
	Conflict/strategy frame Defines the issue as a game among elites, a battle of personalities or groups Example: climate-proof city	*Public accountability frame* Defines the issue as responsible use or abuse of science in decision-making Example: sea level discussion

Source: De Boer et al. (2010: 504).

In recent years, studies have deepened the concept of institutional path dependence to cognitive path dependence, showing that cognitive frames are also a factor in path dependence (Kaplan & Tripsas, 2008; Thrane et al., 2010). Also, in adaptation research the importance of cognitive frames is stressed (e.g. McEvoy et al., 2013). One particularly promising concept for understanding cognitive frames with regard to adaptation decision-making has been developed by De Boer et al. (2010, see Table 7.1) but has not yet been used to explain lock-ins and path dependencies in adaptation governance.

In contrast to the conceptualisation of path dependency as historically embedded, emergent processes, where specific decisive events are assumed to be the primary explanation for path development and in which actors only play a marginal role in causing lock-ins (e.g. Arthur, 1989; David, 1985), Garud and Karnøe's (2001) notion of path creation emphasises the role of strategic change and deliberate action (Meyer & Schubert, 2007). They stress the relevance of the strategic, deliberate, and mindful action of actors, who initiate the development of a path through intentional deviations from known procedures or rules. In doing so, actors tend to be seen even as potential 'unlockers' of lock-ins and as problem solvers.

In the literature on climate change adaptation this notion of path-breaking and unlocking has been taken up. Thus, Burch (2010) identifies the necessity of an explicitly articulated high-level directive and leadership that stimulates an organisational culture of innovation and collaboration as crucial enablers of action on climate change. Wejs et al. (2014) identify the presence of institutional entrepreneurs in the adaptation process as key in building legitimacy for anticipatory adaptation action. Haasnoot et al. (2013) propose a method for decision-making under uncertain global and regional changes called 'dynamic adaptive policy pathways', in which a planner should create a strategic vision of the future, commit to short-term actions, and establish a framework to guide future actions. Levin et al. (2012) turn the literature on path dependency on its head to elucidate how mindfully and deliberately generating path dependencies can foster positive policy outcomes by focusing on gaining durability, expanding covered populations, and changing behaviours through largely unexplored progressive incremental forces.

Both perspectives on the role of actors, as narrow minded and as 'mindful', have their virtue. There are cases that show how narrow-minded actors contributed to negative lock-ins and path dependencies (e.g. Burton et al., 2008; Thomsen et al., 2012). But there are also cases that show how mindful actors contributed to create new positive pathways or unlocked negative lock-ins (e.g. Burch, 2010; Wejs et al., 2014). Nevertheless, research on the role of actors regarding path dependencies, path creation, and lock-ins in adaptation governance is still in its infancy and more empirical studies are needed.

7.4 Roads Policy Analysis as a Case of Combining Dimensions of Lock-In

In this section we offer a case study of how our interests in discourse, infrastructure, institutions and tools, and actors and networks as dimensions of policy 'lock-in' have been fruitfully combined, in a way that highlights their inter-relatedness and that can potentially serve as inspiration for future analyses of the origins and importance of lock-ins in adaptation.

The case centres on the controversial UK road-building programme, extensively analysed in political science, planning, and geography literatures, using concepts ranging from policy communities, advocacy coalitions (Dudley & Richardson, 2000), and discourse (Richardson, 2001), as well as discourse institutionalisation (Rayner, 2004; Vigar, 2002). These concepts have helped to examine how, particularly after 1989, critics of the government's large-scale road-building programme challenged a dominant 'Roads for Prosperity' coalition, struggling to undo what could be termed policy 'lock-ins' that were highly resistant to change. In a range of venues, at multiple levels of governance, opponents – often characterised as a 'New Realist' advocacy coalition (Dudley & Richardson, 2000) – identified a number of central assumptions that underpinned the road-building programme, and highlighted a related set of practices (or mechanisms) through which particular policy and planning outputs, increasingly recognised to be unsustainable (socially, economically, and environmentally), were routinely produced.

Among these assumptions were: (a) that increased mobility of people and goods, particularly by road, was both inevitable and desirable, and that any attempt to restrict this would be both economically harmful and an unacceptable infringement of individual freedom; (b) that new roads necessarily promote economic competitiveness; and (c) that the implications of road building for patterns of land use and the growing number of environmental policy commitments were not the concern of transport planners. Such assumptions, encapsulated in the storyline of 'Roads for Prosperity' (the title of the 1989 policy White Paper), were reflected in particular bureaucratic divisions of responsibility, large commitments to the national road budget (which encouraged local government planners to favour road-building solutions to local problems), and officially mandated project appraisal techniques that were perceived to exclude the public and embody a 'predict and provide' bias in favour of road-based 'solutions' to selectively framed transport 'problems'. The practice dubbed 'salami slicing', whereby road upgrades along a corridor were appraised and presented piecemeal at successive public inquiries, allowed for incrementalist decision-making, and kept many cumulative environmental impacts out of the frame of assessment.

'New Realists' sought to challenge the policy lock-in in numerous ways. They posed new questions (e.g. over whether new roads generate new traffic that soon cancels out initial congestion-relieving benefits) and developed new storylines and analytical practices that could do justice to radical new transport-planning concepts that would obviate the need for road building, including demand management and modal shift. Commentators such as Vigar (2002) and Richardson (2001) used Foucauldian discourse-analytical concepts to highlight the close entanglement of policy networks, policy tools, and over-arching narratives or 'storylines' (cf. Hajer, 1995). To provide a fuller picture of how policy discourses are transmitted and become embedded in practices, and the ways in which policy networks are maintained, Vigar (2002) suggests that policy arenas – the institutional 'sites' where policy is discussed – should be a focus (cf. Dudley & Richardson, 2000). These may or may not be formally constituted, and the importance of any given arena is an empirical question. Focusing here allows the analyst to look beyond formal practices and organisational structures to the quality of relations (or networks) among stakeholders, to determine the direction of flow of influence, as ideas develop, shift, and change (Vigar, 2002).

For Richardson and collaborators, the construction of knowledge about the likely implications of different courses of action that goes to inform decision-making, whether for individual projects, plans, or strategies, is a central preoccupation (Richardson, 2001; Richardson & Haywood, 1996). The sometimes-hidden techniques and mechanisms that routinely reproduce particular institutional commitments are examined as 'practices', in the Foucauldian sense. Practices refer to the 'techniques of notation, computation and calculation; procedures of examination and assessment; the invention of devices such as surveys ... the inauguration of professional specialisms and vocabularies'; in short, the 'apparently humble and mundane mechanisms which appear to make it possible to govern' (Miller & Rose, 1993: 83).

In the UK transport policy case, these practices were particularly well 'locked-in', despite an overhaul of the official approach to appraisal (Rayner, 2004). Forecasting continued to be informed by assumptions of relatively inelastic demand for road use; cost–benefit analysis for road schemes continued to monetise all time-saving benefits enjoyed by future road users; and non-road modes often faced stricter assessment criteria. Additional and newly emerging assessment criteria and challenges such as climate change impacts thus struggled to be integrated meaningfully into the knowledge systems and discourses of the locked-in transport policies in the UK.

7.5 Conclusions

Coming back to our initial questions concerning the conceptualisation, explanation, and revision of lock-ins, we will finally summarise some basic insights and sketch some future research needs. As iterated at great length in the recent literature on barriers to climate adaptation and based on numerous case studies therein, the case can be made that in view of an increasingly transformational challenge, too many present-day adaptation policies are slow and incrementalist in nature (Wise et al., 2014) or entirely absent. In seeking to understand why that is, we suggest that there is significant potential in researching different kinds of lock-ins affecting adaptation.

From discourse analysis (and from a focus on institutions and tools) we take the insight that lock-ins may derive from a set of practices that, despite being apparently appropriate mechanisms, serve to institutionalise a dominant, incrementalist discourse (Buschmann & Oels, 2019). Particular practices of spatial planning and allocations of bureaucratic responsibility may also constitute important procedures that are tied to existing approaches to the provision of physical infrastructure. These various practices are overseen by established expert communities who are likely to be resistant when their paradigms and 'knowledge hierarchies' (Nyamwanza & Bhatasara, 2015) are challenged, and other practices become more relevant. However, when opening up to broader stakeholder groups and other communities, these actors may also be able to rethink, to become 'institutional entrepreneurs' (Wejs et al., 2014), and the extent to which this is possible is an empirical question for future research. It is thus important to know how expert communities in exchange with other knowledge-holding groups are involved in promoting or overcoming lock-ins and how they deal with proposals for transformation, which will often come about in the context of continuous negative evaluations of existing approaches (Owens et al., 2004).

From the perspective on physical infrastructures such as coastal protection measures, water and electricity grids, roads, etc., we can assume that their existence tends to underpin strong path dependencies once investment decisions have been made and measures have been implemented. Thus, innovations and changes are in principle only possible within the larger pathways of these infrastructures and can thus often not exceed incrementalist levels. More fundamental change is then only possible if the technical solutions fail to effectively abate the underlying problem or to provide the services they are expected to deliver. However, with a view to future research, it can be hypothesised that this change essentially requires also a change in discourse or the existence of alternative bodies of knowledge that provide a new paradigm or rationale for other technical or non-technical solutions.

In addition, guiding policies and the dominant choice of instruments and policy formulation tools often limit flexibility and constitute another source of lock-ins with a particular relevance in climate adaptation issues. As the case of UK roads policy demonstrates, the early focus on particular tools to guide policymaking provided for a lock-in that was then combined with an infrastructure lock-in, once heavy investments in roads had been made. However, the use of other policy formulation tools would allow for a change in perspectives and brings with it the possibility of bringing to the fore new ideas and forms of knowledge that might constitute path changes. How far this applies to climate adaptation policies on different levels is also an empirical question for future research.

This brings us to the last of our causes of lock-ins, namely the actors themselves and potential mental or cognitive lock-ins. While large parts of the economics literature are reluctant to discuss changes in preferences at all, they can be seen as pivotal for larger societal transformations and effective path changes in the field of climate adaptation. Thus, the need for more effective responses to climate impacts constitutes a strong case for individual and social learning and change (Collins & Ison, 2009; Hegger et al., 2012; Pahl-Wostl et al., 2007). While there is a wealth of knowledge and empirical evidence on small-scale learning and change processes, it is left to future research to better understand and effectively support social learning processes on larger societal scales and with broader stakeholder groups.

Regarding the actual policy implications of lock-in research on adaptation, it can be assumed that the various causes of lock-ins relate to different political approaches to effectively address them and instigate change to unlock given adaptation pathways. Infrastructural lock-ins most likely require significant governmental efforts to change given practices often with substantial investments in novel technological or organisational approaches. Also, institutional lock-ins require strong political will and commitment by governments and various governance actors to reverse them. By contrast, behavioural or actor-based lock-ins will need to be addressed by more bottom-up and social-learning-based approaches that potentially change cognitive mindsets or basic understandings and framings. In particular, this relation between reflexivity and adaptiveness is at the core of the Earth System Governance Project (ESG) Science Plan of 2018 (ESG, 2018) and constitutes a promising future research field given the slowness and limitations of conventional governmental policies and their abilities to implement actual change and social transformations.

References

Arthur, W.B. (1989). Competing technologies, increasing returns, and lock-in by historical events. *Economic Journal*, 99, 116–31.

Barnett, J., Evans, L.S., Gross, C. et al. (2015). From barriers to limits to climate change adaptation: path dependency and the speed of change. *Ecology and Society*, 20(3), 5. doi: http://dx.doi.org/10.5751/ES-07698-200305.

Biesbroek, G.R., Klostermann, J.E.M., Termeer, C.J.A.M., & Kabat, P. (2013) On the nature of barriers to climate change adaptation. *Regional Environmental Change*, 13, 1119–29.

Biesbroek, G.R., Termeer, C.J.A.M., Klostermann, J.E.M., & Kabat, P. (2014). Analytical lenses on barriers in the governance of climate change adaptation. *Mitigation and Adaptation Strategies for Global Change*, 19(7), 1011–32. doi: http://doi.org/10.1007/s11027-013-9457-z.

Brouwer, S., Rayner, T., & Huitema, D. (2013). Mainstreaming climate policy: the case of climate adaptation and the implementation of EU water policy. *Environment and Planning C: Government and Policy*, 31(1), 134–53. doi: http://doi.org/10.1068/c11134.

Burch, S. (2010). Transforming barriers into enablers of action on climate change: insights from three municipal case studies in British Columbia, Canada. *Global Environmental Change*, 20, 187–97. doi: http://doi.org/10.1016/j.gloenvcha.2009.11.009.

Burton, R.J., Kuczera, C., & Schwarz, G. (2008). Exploring farmers' cultural resistance to voluntary agri-environmental schemes. *Sociologia Ruralis*, 48(1), 16–37.

Buschmann, P. & Oels, A. (2019). The overlooked role of discourse in breaking carbon lock-in: the case of the German energy transition. *WIREs Climate Change*, 10(3), e574. doi: http://doi.org/10.1002/wcc.574.

Carstensen, M. & Schmidt, V.A. (2016). Power through, over and in ideas: conceptualizing ideational power in discursive institutionalism. *Journal of European Public Policy*, 23(3), 318–37.

Cecere, G., Corrocher, N., Gossart, C., & Ozman, M. (2014). Lock-in and path dependence: an evolutionary approach to eco-innovations. *Journal of Evolutionary Economics*, 24, 1037–65.

Collins, K. & Ison, R. (2009). Jumping off Arnstein's ladder: social learning as a new policy paradigm for climate change adaptation. *Environmental Policy and Governance*, 19(6), 358–73.

David, P.A. (1985). Clio and the economics of QWERTY. *American Economic Review*, 75, 332–7.

   (2001). Path dependence, its critics, and the quest for 'historical economics'. In P. Garrouste & S. Ioannides, eds., *Evolution and Path Dependence in Economic Ideas: Past and Present*. Cheltenham: Edward Elgar, 15–40.

De Boer, J., Wardekker, J.A., & van der Sluijs, J.P. (2010). Frame-based guide to situated decision-making on climate change. *Global Environmental Change Volume*, 20(3), 502–10.

Dean, M. (1999). *Governmentality: Power and Rule in Modern Society*. London: Sage.

Denton, F., Wilbanks, T.J., Abeysinghe, A.C. et al. (2014). Climate-resilient pathways: adaptation, mitigation, and sustainable development. In C.B. Field, V.R. Barros, D.J. Dokken et al., eds., *Climate Change 2014: Impacts, Adaptation, and Vulnerability. Part A: Global and Sectoral Aspects. Contribution of Working Group II to the Fifth Assessment Report of the Intergovernmental Panel on Climate Change*. Cambridge, UK: Cambridge University Press, 1101–31.

Dudley, G. & Richardson, J. (2000). *Why Does Policy Change? Lessons from British Transport Policy, 1945–99*. London: Routledge.

Earth System Governance (ESG) Project. (2018). *Earth System Governance: Science and Implementation Plan of the Earth System Governance Project*. Utrecht: Earth System Governance.

Eisenack, K., Moser, S., Hoffmann, E. et al. (2014). Explaining and overcoming barriers to climate change adaptation. *Nature Climate Change*, 4, 867–72.

Evans, P.B., Rueschemeyer, D., & Skocpol, T. (eds.) (1985). *Bringing the State Back In*. Cambridge, UK: Cambridge University Press. doi: https://doi.org/10.1017/CBO9780511628283.

Folke, C., Hahn, T., Olsson, P., & Norberg, J. (2005). Adaptive governance of social-ecological systems. *Annual Review of Environment and Resources*, 30, 441–73.

Foxon, T.J. (2011). A coevolutionary framework for analysing a transition to a sustainable low carbon economy. *Ecological Economics*, 70, 2258–67.

Foucault, M. (1976). *The History of Sexuality. Volume 1: The Will to Knowledge*. London: Penguin Books.

Garud, R. & Karnøe, P. (2001). Path creation as a process of mindful deviation. In R. Garud & P. Karnøe, eds., *Path Dependence and Creation*. Mahwah, NJ: Lawrence Erlbaum Associates, 1–38.

Geels, F.W., Kiern, F., Fuchs, G. et al. (2016). The enactment of socio-technical transition pathways: a reformulated typology and a comparative multi-level analysis of the German and UK low-carbon electricity transitions (1990–2014). *Research Policy*, 45(4), 896–913. doi: http://doi.org/10.1016/j.respol.2016.01.015.

Haasnoot, M., Kwakkel, J.H., Walker, W.E., & Ter Maat, J. (2013). Dynamic adaptive policy pathways: a method for crafting robust decisions for a deeply uncertain world. *Global Environmental Change*, 23(2), 485–98.

Hajer, M.A. (1995). *The Politics of Environmental Discourse: Ecological Modernization and the Policy Process*. Oxford: Clarendon Press.

Hake, J.-F., Fischer, W., Venghaus, S., & Weckenbrock, C. (2015). The German Energiewende: history and status quo. *Energy*, 92, 532–46. doi: http://doi.org/10.1016/j.energy.2015.04.027.

Hall, P.A. & Taylor, R.C.R. (1996). Political science and the three new institutionalisms. *Political Studies*, 44(5), 936–57.

Hartmann, T. (2012). Wicked problems and clumsy solutions: planning as expectation management. *Planning Theory*, 11, 242–56. doi: https://doi.org/10.1177/1473095212440427.

Hassink, R. (2010). Locked in decline? On the role of regional lock-ins in old industrial areas. In R. Boschma & R. Martin, eds., *The Handbook of Evolutionary Economic Geography*. Cheltenham: Edward Elgar, 450–68.

Hegger, D., Lamers, M., van Zeijl-Rozema, A., & Dieperink, C. (2012). Conceptualising joint knowledge production in regional climate change adaptation projects: success conditions and levers for action. *Environmental Science & Policy*, 18, 52–65.

Hermans, L.M. (2008). Exploring the promise of actor analysis for environmental policy analysis: lessons from four cases in water resources management. *Ecology and Society*, 13(1), 21.

Hetz, K. & Bruns, A. (2014). Urban planning lock-in: implications for the realization of adaptive options towards climate change risks. *Water International*, 39, 884–900.

Hirsch, P.M. & Gillespie, J. (2001). Unpacking path dependence: differential valuations accorded history across disciplines. In R. Garud & P. Karnoe, eds., *Path Creation and Dependence*, Mahwah, NJ: Psychology Press, 69–90.

Huitema, D., Adger, W.N., Berkhout, F. et al. (2016). The governance of adaptation: choices, reasons, and effects. *Ecology and Society*, 21(3), 37. doi: http://dx.doi.org/10.5751/ES-08797-210337.

Huitema, D. & Meijerink, S. (2010). Realizing water transitions: the role of policy entrepreneurs in water policy change. *Ecology and Society*, 15(2), 26.

Huitema, D., Mostert, E., Egas, W. et al. (2009). Adaptive water governance: assessing adaptive management from a governance perspective. *Ecology and Society*, 4(1), 26.

Immergut, E.M. (1998). The theoretical core of the new institutionalism. *Politics & Society*, 26(1), 5–34.

Intergovernmental Panel on Climate Change (IPCC). (2014). Summary for policymakers. In C.B. Field, V.R. Barros, D.J. Dokken et al., eds., *Climate Change 2014: Impacts, Adaptation, and Vulnerability. Part A: Global and Sectoral Aspects. Contribution of Working Group II to the Fifth Assessment Report of the Intergovernmental Panel on Climate Change*. Cambridge, UK: Cambridge University Press, 1–32.

Janis, I.L. & Mann, L. (1977). *Decision Making: A Psychological Analysis of Conflict, Choice, and Commitment*. New York: Free Press.

Jordan, A.J. & Huitema, D. (2014). Policy innovation in a changing climate: sources, patterns and effects. *Global Environmental Change*, 29, 387–94.

Jordan, A.J. & Turnpenny, J.R. (2015). *The Tools of Policy Formulation: Actors, Capacities, Venues and Effects*. Cheltenham: Edward Elgar.

Kaplan, S. & Tripsas, M., (2008). Thinking about technology: applying a cognitive lens to technical change. *Research Policy*, 37(5), 790–805.

Kline, S. & Rosenberg, N. (1986). An overview of innovation. In R. Landau & N. Rosenberg, eds., *The Positive Sum Strategy: Harnessing Technology for Economic Growth*. Washington, DC: National Academy Press, 275–306.

Lauber, V. & Jacobsson, S. (2016). The politics and economics of constructing, contesting and restricting socio-political space for renewables: the German Renewable Energy

Act. *Environmental Innovation and Societal Transitions*, 18, 147–63. doi: http://doi
.org/10.1016/j.eist.2015.06.005.

Leipprand, A., Flachsland, C., & Pahle, M. (2017). Advocates or cartographers? Scientific
advisors and the narratives of German energy transition. *Energy Policy*, 102, 222–36.
doi: http://doi.org/10.1016/j.enpol.2016.12.021.

Levin, K., Cashore, B., Bernstein, S., & Auld, G. (2012). Overcoming the tragedy of super
wicked problems: constraining our future selves to ameliorate global climate change.
Policy Sciences, 45, 123–52. doi: http://doi.org/10.1007/s11077-012-9151-0.

McEvoy, D., Fünfgeld, H., & Bosomworth, K. (2013). Resilience and climate change
adaptation: the importance of framing. *Planning Practice & Research*, 28(3), 1–14.

March, J.G. & Olsen, J.P. (1984). The new institutionalism: organizational factors in
political life. *American Political Science Review*, 78(3), 734–49.

Meyer, U. & Schubert, C. (2007). Integrating path dependency and path creation in a
general understanding of path constitution: the role of agency and institutions in the
stabilisation of technological innovations. *Science, Technology & Innovation Studies*,
3, 23–44.

Miller, P. & Rose, N. (1993). Governing economic life. In M. Gane & T. Johnson, eds.,
Foucault's New Domains. London: Routledge, 75–105.

Mol, A. (1999). Ontological politics: a word and some questions. *Sociological Review*,
47(S1), 74–89. doi: http://doi.org/10.1111/j.1467-954X.1999.tb03483.x.

  (2002). *The Body Multiple: Ontology in Medical Practice*. Durham, NC: Duke
University Press.

Moodysson, J., Trippl, M., & Zukauskaite, E. (2016). Policy learning and smart special-
ization: balancing policy change and continuity for new regional industrial paths.
Science and Public Policy, 44(3), 382–91. doi: https://doi.org/10.1093/scipol/
scw071.

Moser, S.C. & Ekstrom, J.A. (2010). A framework to diagnose barriers to climate change
adaptation. *Proceedings of the National Academy of Sciences*, 107, 22026–31.

Nyamwanza, A.M. & Bhatasara, S. (2015). The utility of postmodern thinking in climate
adaptation research. *Environment, Development and Sustainability*, 17(5), 1183–96.
doi: http://doi.org/10.1007/s10668-014-9599-5.

O'Brien, K.L. (2009). Do values subjectively define the limits to climate change adaptation? In N. Adger, I. Lorenzoni, & K.L O'Brien, eds., *Adapting to Climate Change:
Thresholds, Values, Governance*. Cambridge, UK: Cambridge University Press,
164–80.

  (2011). Global environmental change II: from adaptation to deliberate transformation.
Progress in Human Geography, 36(5), 667–76.

Owens, S., Rayner, T., & Bina, O. (2004). New agendas for appraisal: reflections on theory,
practice and research. *Environment and Planning A*, 36, 1943–59.

Pahl-Wostl, C., Craps, M., Dewulf, A. et al. (2007). Social learning and water resources
management. *Ecology and Society*, 12(2), 5.

Peters, B.G. (2012). *Institutional Theory in Political Science: The New Institutionalism*, 3rd
ed. London: Continuum.

Pierson, P. (2000). Increasing returns, path dependence, and the study of politics. *American
Political Science Review*, 94, 251–67.

Raiffa, H., Richardson, J., & Metcalfe, D. (2002). *Negotiation Analysis: The Science and
Art of Collaborative Decision Making*. Cambridge, MA: Belknap Press.

Rayner, T. (2004). Sustainability and transport appraisal: the case of the Access to Hastings
multi-modal study. *Journal of Environment Policy Planning and Assessment*, 6(4),
465–91.

Richardson, T. (2001). The pendulum swings again: in search of new transport rationalities. *Town Planning Review*, 72(3), 299–319.

Richardson, T. & Haywood, R. (1996). Deconstructing transport planning: lessons from policy breakdown in the English Pennines. *Transport Policy*, 3(1–2), 43–53.

Schmidt, V.A. (2008). Discursive institutionalism: the explanatory power of ideas and discourse. *Annual Review of Political Science*, 11, 303–26.

Schreyögg, G. & Sydow, J. (2011). Organizational path dependence: a process view. *Organization Studies*, 32, 321–35.

Späth, P. (2012). Understanding the social dynamics of energy regions: the importance of discourse analysis. *Sustainability*, 4(12), 1256–73. doi: http://doi.org/10.3390/su4061256.

Steinmo, S., Thelen, K., & Longstreth, F. (eds.) (1992). *Structuring Politics: Historical Institutionalism in Comparative Analysis*. Cambridge, UK: Cambridge University Press.

Strunz, S. (2014). The German energy transition as a regime shift. *Ecological Economics*, 100, 150–8. doi: http://doi.org/10.1016/j.ecolecon.2014.01.019.

Sydow, J., Schreyögg, G., & Koch, J. (2009). Organizational path dependence: opening the black box. *Academy of Management Review*, 34, 689–709.

Termeer, C.J.A.M., Dewulf, A., & Biesbroek, G.R. (2017). Transformational change: governance interventions for climate change adaptation from a continuous change perspective. *Journal of Environmental Planning and Management*, 60(4), 558–76.

Thomsen, D.C., Smith, T.F., & Keys, N. (2012). Adaptation or manipulation? Unpacking climate change response strategies. *Ecology and Society*, 17(3), 20. doi: http://dx.doi.org/10.5751/ES-04953-170320.

Thrane, S., Blaabjerg, S., & Møller, R.H., (2010). Innovative path dependence: making sense of product and service innovation in path dependent innovation processes. *Research Policy*, 39(7), 932–44.

Tschakert, P. & Dietrich, K.A. (2010). Anticipatory learning for climate change adaptation and resilience. *Ecology and Society*, 15(2), 11.

Unruh, G.C. (2000). Understanding carbon lock-in. *Energy Policy*, 28(12), 817–30.

Vigar, G. (2002). *The Politics of Mobility: Transport, the Environment, and Public Policy*. New York: Spon Press.

Wejs, A., Harvold, K., Vammen Larsen, S., & Saglie, I.-L. (2014). Legitimacy building in weak institutional settings: climate change adaptation at local level in Denmark and Norway. *Environmental Politics*, 23(3), 490–508.

Wilson, G.A. (2013). Community resilience, policy corridors and the policy challenge. *Land Use Policy*, 31, 298–310.

Wilson, G.A., Quaranta, G., Kelly, C., & Salvia, R. (2015). Community resilience, land degradation and endogenous lock-in effects: evidence from the Alento region, Campania, Italy. *Journal of Environmental Planning and Management*, 59(3), 518–37.

Wise, R.M., Fazey, I., Stafford Smith, M. et al. (2014). Reconceptualising adaptation to climate change as part of pathways of change and response. *Global Environmental Change*, 28, 325–33.

Zeelenberg, M., van Dijk, W.W., Manstead, A.S.R., & van der Pligt, J. (2000). On bad decisions and disconfirmed expectancies: the psychology of regret and disappointment. *Cognition and Emotion*, 14(4), 521–41.

8

Governance and Climate Change Mitigation and Adaptation in Conflict-Affected Countries of Central Africa

H. CAROLYN PEACH BROWN

8.1 Introduction

Much of the discussion related to conflict and climate change has focused on it as a cause of increased social instability due to increasing natural resource scarcity, intensification of natural disasters, and sea level rise. In January 2019, the United Nations Security Council (UNSC) convened an open debate to discuss the security implications of climate change as it is considered to be a 'threat multiplier' – having a direct impact on human security while also exacerbating existing vulnerabilities (UN News, 2019). This in turn could increase the likelihood, intensity, and length of conflict (UNSC, 2019). A review of 50 quantitative studies found strong support for a causal association between climatological changes and conflict across a range of geographies, time periods, spatial scales, and climatic events of different durations (Hsiang & Burke, 2014). Other studies of existing local conflict over natural resources have indicated that they may be exacerbated by climate change (Mwiturubani & van Wyk, 2010; Scheffran et al., 2014). The findings of Slettbbak (2012), however, suggest that climate-related natural disasters may actually reduce the risk of conflict. Other variables, such as political or economic circumstances, were found to have more predictive value in relation to increasing conflict. Scholars generally agree that the relationship between climate change and conflict is complex and interacts with contextual factors (Boas & Rothe, 2016; Buhaug et al., 2009; Gartzke, 2012; Scheffran et al., 2014; UNEP, 2011).

African populations are considered to have increased vulnerability to climate change as a result of a higher than the global average degree of change, high levels of dependence on rain-fed agriculture, and a low degree of adaptive capacity (Busby et al., 2013; Toulmin, 2009). Many African countries have also experienced or are experiencing violent civil conflict (Wig & Tollefsen, 2016; Witmer et al., 2017). In areas affected by existing conflict, people are more likely to be vulnerable to climate change due to a variety of factors that restrict their opportunities to develop long-term capacity to adapt to climate change (Buhaug et al., 2009; Busby et al., 2013; Mason et al., 2011; Stoett et al., 2016). The overlap of climate change vulnerabilities and civil conflict has led some to suggest that there needs to be more deliberate dialogue between scholars and practitioners who focus on those respective areas (Babcicky, 2013; King & Mutter, 2014; Rüttinger et al., 2015; Stoett et al., 2016). Matthew (2014) argues that given the heightened vulnerability to climate change impacts, there needs to be an integration of climate change into peacebuilding in Africa where many United Nations (UN) peacebuilding countries are located. However, the UNSC has not yet acted to bring these two aspects together (Rüttinger et al., 2015; Scott, 2015).

Many sub-Saharan African countries are considered to be fragile in that they exhibit varying levels of dysfunctions including the 'inability to provide basic services and meet vital needs, unstable and weak governance, a persistent condition of extreme poverty, lack of territorial control, and a high propensity to conflict and civil war' (Bertocchi & Guerzoni, 2012: 769). Such contextual factors not only make such countries more vulnerable to civil conflict, they also affect their response to climate change (Busby et al., 2013; Rüttinger et al., 2015; Wig & Tollefsen, 2016; Witmer et al., 2017). In such fragile countries, governance institutions are sometimes only partially representative, but are often autocratic and place restrictions on the individual political and economic freedoms of their citizens. When national and local governance institutions fail to serve the interests of the majority of citizens or actively marginalise some groups, they will not only increase the likelihood of civil conflict, they will also fail to respond to the challenges of climate change (Scheffran et al., 2014; Witmer et al., 2017). It is therefore critical that international initiatives on climate change mitigation and adaptation are cognisant of conflict risks in the countries where they are intervening and seek to integrate such awareness into their programmes on the ground.

Reducing Emissions from Deforestation and Forest Degradation (and the role of conservation, sustainable management of forests, and enhancement of forest carbon stocks in developing countries; REDD+) is one such initiative that has a large focus on countries in Africa (UNDP, 2016b). An estimated 25–60 billion metric tons of carbon is stored in the Congo Basin forest of Central Africa, the second largest contiguous tropical rainforest in the world (de Wasseige et al., 2009; Hoare, 2007; Megevand, 2013; Saatchi et al., 2017). Representing roughly 70 per cent of Africa's forests, it spans approximately 200 million hectares in the countries of Cameroon, Equatorial Guinea, Gabon, the Central African Republic (CAR), the Republic of Congo, and the Democratic Republic of Congo (DRC) (Megevand, 2013). DRC contains the largest percentage of the Congo Basin forest, accounting for approximately 23 billion tons of carbon, which represents one-third of the total carbon pool of tropical Africa (de Wasseige et al., 2009; Hoare, 2007; Saatchi et al., 2017). With REDD+, efforts are made to create a financial value for the carbon stored in these forests through offering incentives for countries to better protect and sustainably manage their forests. In this way, the greenhouse gas emissions produced from the removal and degradation of forests will be avoided and forest carbon stocks protected and enhanced (UNDP, 2016b; UN-REDD Programme, 2019). The United Nations Framework Convention on Climate Change (UNFCCC), has recognised that developing countries will need international support for capacity building and technical assistance, and coordination of results-based payments and finance in order to achieve results-based actions under REDD+ (UNDP, 2016b; UNFCCC, 2015).

A variety of international initiatives are involved in supporting developing countries to implement REDD+ with a main one being the UN-REDD Programme. This programme was developed in 2008, building on the convening role and technical expertise of the Food and Agricultural Organization of the United Nations (FAO), the United Nations Development Programme (UNDP), and the United Nations Environment Programme (UNEP) (UNDP, 2016b). The UN-REDD Programme provides advisory and technical support to developing countries' efforts to contribute to climate change mitigation while contributing to sustainable development (UN-REDD Programme, 2019). The Forest Carbon Partnership Facility (FCPF), established and administered by the International Bank for Reconstruction, is a second important initiative under the UNFCCC (International Bank for Reconstruction, 2015). The FCPF is a partnership of developed and developing country governments, businesses, civil society, and indigenous peoples, which aids developing countries through two funding mechanisms, the Readiness Fund and the Carbon Fund (FCPF, 2018c). The money administered through these funds is intended to help developing countries in their efforts to reduce deforestation and forest degradation, conserve and enhance their forest carbon stocks, and sustainably manage their forests. Outside the UNFCCC process there are other actors who are also seeking to help countries implement REDD+ (UNDP, 2016b).

Since poor governance has been identified as one of the factors that makes African countries more vulnerable to civil conflict, as well as affects their response to climate change, it is not surprising that Gizachew et al. (2017) have identified governance as one of the challenges for implementation of REDD+. Poor governance refers to deficits in accountability, transparency, citizen engagement, social inclusion, the rule of law, among others (Milabyo Kyamusugulwa et al., 2014; World Bank Group, 2019). Castro-Nunez et al. (2016) point out that the success of REDD+ initiatives in conflict-affected countries relies on the enabling conditions of social and political stability. Therefore, the incorporation of governance reform and peacebuilding activities into climate change mitigation and forest conservation policies and programmes is essential. This will involve paying attention to the process and structure of institutional arrangements that bring together state and non-state actors at local and national levels to address the common goal of mitigation of climate change (Cadman & Maraseni, 2011; Wig & Tollefsen, 2016). REDD+ has already faced some governance challenges particularly related to the institutional arrangements for effective stakeholder participation and interest representation, organisational responsibility, its decision-making processes, and the implementation of decisions (Cadman et al., 2017). Therefore, in conflict-affected countries it is important to understand how REDD+ is being implemented in order to assess if these initiatives are addressing the conflict and governance challenges.

Given the focus on the Congo Basin forest of Central Africa for REDD+ initiatives, they provide an opportunity to investigate such questions as some of these countries have a history of fragility and continue to be affected by civil conflict. This is particularly true of DRC and CAR. Therefore, a content analysis of publicly available documents of four major international initiatives for REDD+ readiness, strategy design, and pilot projects in DRC and CAR was conducted (Gizachew et al., 2017). The analysis sought to understand how conflict is being integrated into the discourse on REDD+ and its implications for the mitigation of climate change or possible co-benefits of poverty reduction and climate change adaptation. Are measures in place to address the reality of ongoing civil conflict in these countries? Given the importance of governance in addressing both climate change and conflict, do the REDD+ policies and programmes in these countries seek to address governance concerns? Are the elements of good governance being fostered through these initiatives? Following a presentation of results, the intersection of governance, peacebuilding, and climate change response is discussed.

8.2 Context of Focal Countries: DRC and CAR

Endowed with vast forest and mineral resources, DRC has the potential to become one of the richest countries in Africa. Yet its population of 81 million people mired in poverty, ranking among the lowest countries in the world on the Human Development Index (UNDP, 2018; World Bank, 2018c). Considered to be one of the countries in Africa most vulnerable to climate change (Busby et al., 2013), global climate models predict an increase in the frequency and intensity of extreme heat events in the Great Lakes region where some of the world's poorest and most vulnerable people reside (Asefi-Najafabady et al., 2018), and where there is ongoing instability.

DRC has a complex history of political violence and although a new president was recently elected, governance in the vast country is weak (Busby et al., 2013; International Crisis Group, 2019b; Mushi, 2013). The country has also been recovering from a series of conflicts that occurred during the 1990s, which have had an extremely negative effect on the population and economy and that continue to influence ongoing instability in some areas (World Bank, 2018c). A UN peacekeeping force has been on the ground in DRC for two decades (United Nations, 2019). While the last decade has been relatively stable, leading to political and economic reforms, this stability is threatened by rebel groups in the centre and east (International Crisis Group, 2019b; World Bank, 2018c). The country also faces a humanitarian crisis with 3.8 million internally displaced persons, particularly in some regions, the most in Africa. It is also dealing with a steady flow of refugees from neighbouring countries – Burundi, CAR, and South Sudan (United Nations, 2017). Furthermore, an Ebola epidemic has claimed more than 1,200 lives and risks spreading to other provinces in the eastern region (United Nations, 2019).

Similar to DRC, CAR, a landlocked country of 4.6 million people, has rich forest and mineral resources (World Bank, 2018b). However, it ranks near the bottom of the 2018 Human Development Index report (188th out of 189 countries) (UNDP, 2018). Given its social, political, and geographic context, CAR is considered to be among the most vulnerable African countries to climate change (Busby et al., 2013). According to the World Bank (2010), during the period 1978–2009, CAR experienced an average temperature increase of about $0.3°C$ per decade and an average decrease in rainfall of about 19 mm/year. Projections show a temperature increase of $1.5°C–2.75°C$ by 2080, accompanied by a slight increase in annual precipitation that may be less frequent, but more intense.

While CAR has been described as an 'extreme example of the lack of viability of a state in general, and democracy in particular' (Mehler, 2011: 115), in 2016 for the first time in its history, a president and parliament were democratically elected (World Bank, 2018b). This transition to democracy came after a long, complex history of political instability and civil conflict with numerous internal and external rebel groups (Gapia & Bele, 2012; World Bank Group, 2018). The motivation of these groups is diverse, with some being self-defence groups fighting for specific ethnic or territorial constituencies, others for political independence, and many are implicated in controlling mineral resources and trade in some areas (Spittaels & Hilgert, 2009; World Bank Group, 2018). The extended period of conflict has had a devastating effect on the population with many human rights abuses and over a million people becoming internally displaced or fleeing to neighbouring countries (Glassius, 2008; Potts et al., 2011; World Bank, 2018b). While the economy is recovering, over half of the population was still in need of humanitarian assistance in 2018. CAR is not yet a post-conflict country as the government only controls 40 per cent of the country and many armed groups remain (International Crisis Group, 2019a; World Bank Group, 2018).

8.3 Methods

The following initiatives were chosen for analysis as they are the primary initiatives involved in implementing the REDD+ mechanism or in providing funds for Congo Basin countries to implement policies and projects related to the mechanism (Gizachew et al., 2017; for a general summary of the approaches of each of these four initiatives, see Brown 2017: tab. 1):

- UN-REDD Programme (2019);
- FCPF (2018c);
- Central African Forest Initiative (CAFI, 2019);
- World Bank Forest Investment Program (FIP, 2018).

A search was conducted of the websites of each of the previously named four initiatives for publicly available documents, in English and French, related to their approach to implementation of REDD+ in general and in DRC and CAR in particular. Website searches took place until May 2019. In total 193 documents (DRC – 143, CAR – 50) were downloaded from the sites and analysed using the NVivo 10 qualitative data analysis software. In order to gain an understanding of the more recent evolution of the REDD+ interventions in DRC and CAR, emphasis was placed on analysing documents from the last five years. Key founding documents for some institutions were also included in the analysis as they provided descriptions of the initiatives. General information from the web pages of these institutions that described the initiatives and their interventions in DRC and CAR was also included in research. In the content analysis, the themes explored related to conflict, instability, and governance.

8.4 REDD+ Activities

Four elements must be in place for countries to implement REDD+ and to access results-based payments and results-based finance. These are a national strategy or action plan, a national forest reference level, a robust and transparent national forest monitoring system, and a safeguard information system (UNDP, 2016b). Activities take place in three phases, the 'readiness phase', the 'implementation phase', and the 'results-based action phase'. The national governments play a central role in designing and implementing these systems and programmes, with the full engagement of all relevant stakeholders, including all those who benefit from forests or whose activities impact forests. The expectation is that this would include political and customary leaders at various levels of governance, as well as the private sector, civil society, and indigenous peoples (UNDP, 2016b).

The UN-REDD Programme and the FCPF seek to harmonise their approaches of provision of technical assistance and finance to build national capacity to implement REDD+ (FCPF, 2018c; UN-REDD Programme, 2015). To accomplish these goals, they often collaborate with the other two initiatives examined as well as other partners. The FCPF provides grant funding as well as technical assistance, as countries develop strategies, policies, and institutional capacity and progress through the readiness stages of development of Readiness Planning Idea Notes and Readiness Preparation Plans. The Carbon Fund also provides financing for emissions reduction programmes, which are designed to pilot performance-based payments for emission reductions from REDD+ (FCPF, 2018c; UN-REDD Programme, 2015).

DRC was one of the first UN-REDD partner countries to progress through both the planning and implementation stages of REDD+ preparedness (DRC, 2015; UNDP, 2016b; UN-REDD Programme, 2019). The National UN-REDD Programme has been officially launched including the completion of key studies and in-country consultation processes, testing of REDD+ pilot projects, and the training of personnel. It was the first country to have finalised its readiness package and among the first to be selected for Carbon Fund financing, with support from the FCPF (DRC, 2015; FCPF, 2015). The government developed the Mai Ndombe Emissions-Reduction Programme as a first step in implementing the country's national REDD+ strategy, as a model for green development in the Congo Basin, and for REDD+ results-based payments on climate action. Through provision of alternatives to deforestation and rewarding performance to mitigate climate change, the programme aims to implement the country's green development vision, reduce poverty, sustainably manage natural resources, and conserve biodiversity (FCPF and UN-REDD Programme, 2012; World Bank, 2017). In 2018, DRC signed an Emissions Reduction Agreement to reward community efforts in tackling deforestation and forest degradation (World Bank, 2019).

CAR is also one of the 65 countries that are part of the UN-REDD Programme (UN-REDD Programme, 2011, 2016b). By 2013, it had advanced through the readiness process and completed its Readiness Preparation Plan (FCPF, 2018b). While the civil conflict delayed the process for five years, preparation of the readiness package is currently underway. The goal of the grant funding is to sustainably manage forests so as to contribute to the country's crisis response and early recovery, address the principal drivers of deforestation and forest degradation, support the sustainable management of forests to aid in the successful recovery of the state, and support basic livelihoods of the population (World Bank, 2018a). These REDD+ readiness activities are being implemented with CAFI funding.

The goal of CAFI is to recognise and preserve the value of these forests for mitigating climate change, reducing poverty, and contributing to sustainable development in the region (CAFI, 2015). The intention is to finance one national investment framework per eligible country, based on a country's strong commitment to national reforms to address the drivers of deforestation and forest degradation. DRC was the first country in Central Africa to sign a letter of intent for funding from CAFI (UNDP, 2016a). The government stated that it would use this contribution to its REDD+ national fund, as well as financing from other international initiatives, to finance its national strategy framework adopted in 2012. The strategy states that it will put the preservation of forests at the centre of its country's economic and human development (DRC, 2015; FCPF and UN-REDD Programme, 2012; UNDP, 2016a). In February 2016, the CAFI executive board approved a grant to the International Bank for Reconstruction and Development to support the development of CAR's national investment framework (CAFI, 2016). Given that the finalisation of this framework is taking longer than expected, in November 2018 the preparatory grant period was extended until the end of 2019 (CAFI, 2018).

With funding from the Climate Investment Fund, FIP provides grants and low-interest loans to support developing countries in REDD+ implementation. These direct investments are channelled through partner multilateral development banks and designed to benefit the forest, development, and the climate (Climate Investment Funds, 2016). In DRC, money is channelled through the African Development Bank for projects in three subnational programmes, Kinshasa, Kisangani, and Kanaga/Mbuji-Mayi (FCPF and UN-REDD Programme, 2012; World Bank, 2014). The development objective of these projects is to empower indigenous peoples, who are often marginalised, and local communities to benefit from and engage in REDD+ polices and projects (World Bank, 2014). At the present time, FIP is not engaged in projects in CAR.

8.5 Conflict and REDD+

Recognition of conflict was integrated into the discourse on REDD+ in several different ways across the four initiatives (Table 8.1). While it was acknowledged that civil conflict had an impact on forests and would have an impact on the implementation of REDD+, there was little concrete discussion of how it could be addressed. While there were common themes in both countries, there were some differences in the findings.

All the initiatives recognised the reality of historical and ongoing conflict in both countries, particularly in some regions. This historical and current civil conflict had resulted in deforestation and environmental degradation, particularly

Table 8.1. *Characterisation of conflict in DRC and CAR across the four initiatives*

Conflict	Description
Source of deforestation	• Historical and current civil conflict is recognised as a driver of deforestation
Resulting from insecurity of tenure system	• The land is the exclusive property of the state, but the existence of customary and other land-use regimes is a potential source of local conflict among stakeholders
Across economic sectors	• Different sectors (forestry, agriculture, and mining) impact the forest differently • Initiatives in one sector may affect forest outcomes in another sector
Civil conflict	• Violence can be a result of the current political instability, which increases deforestation due to break down in effective forest governance • Conflict can sometimes have a protective role for the forest • Conflict has led to delays in the implementation of REDD+

when that conflict led to the internal displacement of people. In the eastern part of DRC, the large concentration of people in internally displaced people camps has put pressure on the surrounding forests. Some later documents did state that historical conflict had played a protective role due to constraining business development in the forest in some cases. Documents for DRC often referred to it as being in a post-conflict situation, particularly since 2003, and there was only occasional mention of the ongoing instability and conflict in some areas. The relative political stability over the past 15 years was seen as having contributed to investment in DRC, which had also resulted in increased deforestation and greenhouse gas emissions. While some initiatives in DRC did recognise the continuing fragility of the country, this recognition was more evident in the initiatives in CAR. This is probably due to the fact that open conflict is more recent and widespread in CAR, with the government still controlling only about 40 per cent of the country (World Bank Group, 2018).

Given their vastness, forest resources are seen as an opportunity for economic development and livelihood improvement in a post-conflict situation. In fact, inclusive and economic development is considered to be an essential part of the necessary conditions for breaking the cycle of instability and conflict in CAR (World Bank Group, 2018). Persistent insecurity is one of the most critical obstacles to poverty reduction. Despite the relative stability throughout much of DRC, there was concern raised that any increase in political instability or conflict would lead to an increased rate of deforestation. This would then reduce any mitigation or co-benefits from REDD+ activities. More recent conflict had in fact delayed a REDD+ workshop. There was some limited discussion of how political and governance risks are being mitigated in the design of one project (FCPF, 2016). In CAR, despite delays in the REDD+ implementation process due to conflict and ongoing uncertainty, some initiatives were still forging ahead in providing funding and technical assistance (CAFI, 2018).

Another characterisation of conflict in both countries concerned conflict between different stakeholders at the local level. In CAR, mention was made of the conflict among agriculturalists and livestock herders. This inter-ethnic local conflict has been magnified by the civil conflict and become more widespread throughout the country. In DRC, while the land is the exclusive property of the state, the existence of customary and other land-use regimes was also seen as a potential source of conflict. In all four initiatives there was an emphasis on mechanisms to ensure the inclusion of all stakeholders and their concerns in discussions on the reform of DRC's land law. REDD+ initiatives are considered to be an important part of this process as tenure security is recognised as an enabling condition for REDD+ (UN-REDD Programme, 2015). Some initiatives include a specific conflict resolution, grievance, and appeals mechanism as one aspect of their safeguard measures (World Bank, 2011).

Different uses of the forest by indigenous, local people and various sectors including mining, forestry, and agriculture, were also mentioned as sources of conflict in both countries. In the early stages of the REDD+ process, research on the drivers of deforestation and forest degradation is essential (UNDP, 2016b). Analysis of documents indicated consensus on direct drivers of deforestation including agriculture, logging, fuel wood, mining, and bushfires. Therefore, a multi-sectoral approach is seen as being essential to the success of REDD+ initiatives. However, there were few specifics on how conflict would influence such an approach. It is important to note that in some regions of both countries, the exploitation of natural resources, particularly minerals, is fuelling ongoing conflict (Global Witness, 2015, 2019).

8.6 Governance and REDD+

Governance is a cross-cutting theme for the UN-REDD Programme (UN-REDD Programme, 2015). Under the UNFCCC, a safeguard information system is an essential element with one of those safeguards being that REDD+ actions complement or be consistent with the objectives of the national forest programme (UNDP, 2016b). Furthermore, transparent and effective national forest governance structures need to be put in place, including enforcement of the rule of law, coherence of national and subnational legal, policy and regulatory frameworks for transparent and effective forest governance, the institutional capacity for sustainable forest management, among others. Tenure security is also recognised as an enabling condition for REDD+ (UN-REDD Programme, 2015).

Given the history of weak governance and lack of institutional capacity in both countries, it is not surprising that the REDD+ initiatives emphasise some aspects of good governance. As weak governance is an underlying cause of deforestation, all the initiatives seek to build institutional and technical capacity to address its primary drivers and strengthen governance going forward. Since 2002, DRC has been reviewing its forest code, and REDD+ initiatives have been involved in that process, while also seeking to build inter-sectoral coordination. Since 2018, some REDD+ initiatives have been collaborating with a natural resources governance project in CAR that seeks to improve governance and strengthen capacity in the forestry and mining sectors (World Bank, 2018d). In DRC, one programme (funded by FIP) seeks to combine activities to strengthen governance, build capacity, address local-level land-use planning, secure land tenure, as well as sectoral activities such as improved agricultural practices, reduced impact logging, fire management, and charcoal production.

Besides reform of forest codes, other elements of good governance promoted by REDD+ initiatives include strategies to engage all relevant stakeholders in programme and project planning, including all those who benefit from forests or whose activities impact forests. This includes promoting the rights and participation of local and indigenous communities and both men and women. Efforts to address concerns of secure land tenure and access to forests are ongoing. Given its technical and institutional complexities, REDD+ requires substantial capacity at all levels – national, provincial, and local. In DRC, the initiatives have fostered the capacity of civil society groups to play an overseeing role for REDD+. While there has been some progress, REDD+ is still very much focused on the capital of Kinshasa, with little capacity developed at the provincial or local levels, except where there are pilot projects.

Given the conflict in CAR and the fact that the government is not in control of the entire country, REDD+ initiatives are at a much earlier stage. Safeguards and monitoring are therefore needed to prevent the derailment of fledgling projects. Besides instability, corruption and lack of transparency are ongoing concerns in both countries, so REDD+ initiatives place an emphasis on providing support to ensure good governance, improvement of public finance, and transparency in the management of REDD+ funds and public and natural resources. According to the UN-REDD Programme (2016a), the goals of REDD+ in DRC are ambitious, but if the country continues to improve its governance, promoting sustainable use of forest resources, forest-based livelihoods, and the national REDD+ Programme, then social, economic, and environmental benefits can be realised.

8.7 Discussion

In the four REDD+ initiatives examined for this study, the reality of conflict was explicitly recognised either in reference to historical conflict or current conflict. Despite this acknowledgement, there was not a lot of discussion of how it is affecting forests or the REDD+ initiatives or how it might do so in the future. Nor was there much specific discussion of climate change response more broadly. Given the widespread instability in CAR and the regional instability in DRC, a more concrete discussion of approaches to address the conflict would have been expected. Discussions about how ongoing instability and open conflict will affect REDD+ initiatives and outcomes may be taking place, but the evidence of that in the public documents is limited.

The cross-cutting governance reform and institutional capacity building emphasis of the REDD+ initiatives in both countries is playing an important role in trying to address some of the sources of conflict. It has been shown that good governance is associated with a lower probability of conflict-related violence at the subnational level (Wig & Tollefsen, 2016). Research in post-conflict Sierra Leone suggested that in order to enhance political trust governments must demonstrate real concern for the needs of local people and engage them in policymaking (Wong, 2016). Therefore, by working with national governments to reform the forest code, address issues of tenure security, engage all stakeholders, and require accountability and transparency in the REDD+ process, these four initiatives promote essential elements of good governance. Such approaches can help to mitigate or prevent conflict. This is critical, as well-intentioned policies and programmes that are poorly designed and implemented can contribute to political instability and undermine climate related goals and their co-benefits (Rüttinger et al., 2015). Unfortunately, larger studies of REDD+ governance quality have raised concerns, particularly related to the capacity and resources that would facilitate meaningful stakeholder participation, and its efforts in securing tenure rights of indigenous peoples and local communities (Angelsen et al., 2018; Cadman et al., 2017). REDD+ interventions have also had minimal influence on enhancing women's participation in decision-making and protecting their rights (Angelsen et al., 2018; Samndong & Kjosavik, 2017). Others have suggested that the market-based approach of REDD+ has led to increased conflict in some areas (Dunlap & Fairhead, 2014). Since positive impacts have been limited and mixed, it is imperative that international institutions continue to address governance concerns so that REDD+ can meet its environmental, economic, and social goals (Angelsen et al., 2018; Cadman et al., 2017).

Addressing the complexity of conflict, poor governance and climate change is an immense challenge. As mentioned previously, the overlap of climate change vulnerabilities and civil conflict has led some to call for deliberate integration of climate change into peacebuilding in Africa (Babcicky, 2013; King & Mutter, 2014; Matthew, 2014; Rüttinger et al., 2015; Scott, 2015). Additionally, social, political, and military stability are enabling conditions for climate mitigation activities (Castro-Nunez et al., 2016). Unless addressed, those countries with fragility and conflict may be disadvantaged in accessing resources for climate change response due to the limits of their internal capacity (Rüttinger et al., 2015). Others have suggested that in order for REDD+ to be effective, forest-based mitigation needs to be incorporated into national and climate action plans (Angelsen et al., 2018). Given the sectoral silos of government, Central African leaders and researchers have called for urgent intersectoral coordination to establish links between economic development and climate change mitigation and adaptation (Eba'a Atyi, 2018). There is some evidence that international partners are beginning to address these concerns. For example, the National Recovery and Peacebuilding Plan for CAR does mention the potential role of REDD+ in climate change mitigation and economic recovery in a post-conflict situation (CAR, 2016). In its 2011–15 growth and poverty reduction strategy paper, DRC jointly identified protecting the environment and combating climate change as one of the four pillars of development, alongside strengthening governance and peacebuilding (FCPF, 2018a). Since climate change initiatives, peacebuilding, and development initiatives are often funded by the same institutions, organisations, and countries, dedicated long-term funding and explicit integration of these goals is critical.

While not framed specifically as peacebuilding in the initiatives analysed, the forest governance reform emphasis of REDD+ is consistent with the emphases of international initiatives to help countries move beyond conflict. Lessons learned from some post-conflict African countries demonstrate the importance of fostering a robust civil society to promote democracy, strengthen public accountability, and enhance transparency, while building the capacity of the public administration (World Bank Group, 2018). Understanding the local context and adjusting to the local realities of the population is also critical in post-conflict recovery and reconstruction (Maxwell et al., 2017; Milabyo Kyamusugulwa et al., 2014). In Liberia, international peacebuilders placed forest governance reform high on the agenda, leading to a reduced likelihood that timber revenues would reignite conflict. However, they did not address concerns of unfair land tenure and lack of rights to land and resources, or genuine inclusion in decision-making (Beevers, 2015b). While there are many factors that determine whether a conflict-affected country can return to long-term peace, studies in Sierra Leone and Liberia have demonstrated that it is imperative that international actors understand historical dynamics and address how natural resources are governed (Beevers, 2015a). Neglect of this important area will not only undermine the underlying conditions for peace but also impede actions to mitigate and adapt to climate change.

8.8 Conclusion

The case study presented in this chapter examined external interventions on climate change and how they interact with governance processes in countries that are experiencing conflict. Weak governance institutions contribute to conflict and increase the vulnerability of the local population to climate change by limiting their capacity to adapt and potentially benefit from external interventions. It is essential that international institutions understand the complex history and reality of the local governance context so that appropriate strategies and activities are undertaken to address the multiple challenges. The changing nature of these situations requires interveners to anticipate the difficulties and adapt their approaches. This is not easy for large international institutions not known for being nimble, as it requires the ability to critically reflect on their performance and the humility to learn from their mistakes and reshape their values, goals, and practices. While there are increasing attempts to bring climate change mitigation and adaptation together, a greater focus is needed on integrating climate change into strategies for governance reform in conflict-affected situations. Given the commonality of institutions, organisations, and countries that fund such initiatives, climate change should be a cross-cutting issue in all development and peacebuilding interventions. With a changing climate, its complex interactions with conflict will only increase, so further research will be needed to see if it is possible for international institutions to better integrate such issues and what such interventions would look like. What role should the UN or other international institutions play in bringing these concerns together? How should interventions be structured and adapted to the context? How will marginalised groups be affected? Ultimately, what will be the outcomes for people and the planet? These questions have strong resonance with many of the dimensions of the new Earth System Governance research framework (ESG, 2018).

References

Angelsen, A., Martius, C., Duchelle, A.E. et al. (2018). Conclusions: lessons for the path to a transformational REDD+. In A. Angelsen, V. De Sy, A.E. Duchelle, A.M. Larson, & P.T. Thuy, eds., *Transforming REDD+*. Bogor, Indonesia: CIFOR, 203–14.

Asefi-Najafabady, S., Vandecar, K.L., Seimon, A., Lawrence, P., & Lawrence, D. (2018). Climate change, population, and poverty: vulnerability and exposure to heat stress in countries bordering the Great Lakes of Africa. *Climatic Change*, 148(4), 561–73. doi: https://doi.org/10.1007/s10584-018-2211-5.

Babcicky, P. (2013). A conflict-sensitive approach to climate change adaptation. *Peace Review: A Journal of Social Justice*, 25(4), 480–8.

Beevers, M.D. (2015a). Governing natural resources for peace: lessons from Liberia and Sierra Leone. *Global Governance*, 21, 227–46.

(2015b). Peace resources? Governing Liberia's forests in the aftermath of conflict. *International Peacekeeping*, 22(1), 26–42.

Bertocchi, G. & Guerzoni, A. (2012). Growth, history, or institutions: what explains state fragility in sub-Saharan Africa? *Journal of Peace Research*, 49(6), 769–83.

Boas, I. & Rothe, D. (2016). From conflict to resilience? Explaining recent changes in climate security discourse and practice. *Environmental Politics*, 25(4), 613–32.

Brown, H.C.P. (2017). Implementing REDD+ in a conflict-affected country: a case study of the Democratic Republic of Congo. *Environments 2017*, 4(3), 61. doi: https://doi .org/10.3390/environments4030061.

Buhaug, H., Gleditsch, N.P., & Theison, O.M. (2009). Implications of climate change for armed conflict. In R. Mearns & A. Norton, eds., *Social Dimensions of Climate Change*. Washington, DC: World Bank, 75–101

Busby, J.W., Smith, T.G., White, K.L., & Strange, S.M. (2013). Climate change and insecurity: mapping vulnerability in Africa. *International Security*, 37(4), 132–72.

Cadman, T. & Maraseni, T. (2011). The governance of climate change: evaluating the governance quality and legitimacy of the United Nations REDD-plus programme. *International Journal of Climate Change: Impacts and Responses*, 2(3), 103–23.

Cadman, T., Maraseni, T., Ok Ma, H., & Lopez-Casero, F. (2017). Five years of REDD+ governance: the use of market mechanisms as a response to anthropogenic climate change. *Forest Policy and Economics*, 79, 8–16.

Castro-Nunez, A., Mertz, O., & Quintero, M. (2016). Propensity of farmers to conserve forest within REDD+ projects in areas affected by armed-conflict. *Forest Policy and Economics*, 66, 22–30.

Central African Forest Initiative (CAFI). (2015). *Central African Forest Initiative-CAFI Joint Declaration*. Retrieved from www.cafi.org/content/cafi/en/home/our-work/gov ernance/the-cafi-declaration.html.

(2016). *CAFI Executive Board Decision*. Retrieved from www.cafi.org/content/cafi/en/ home/partner-countries/central-african-republic.html.

(2018). *No Cost Extension of the Preparatory Grant for the Central African Republic*. Retrieved from www.undp.org/content/dam/cafi/docs/Executive%20Board/CAFI_ EB_Decisions/English/EB.2018.24-%20Extension% 20CAR.pdf.

(2019). *Central African Forest Initiative*. Retrieved from www.cafi.org/.

Central African Republic (CAR). (2016). *Central African Republic: National Recovery and Peacebuilding Plan 2017–2021*. European Union, World Bank Group, United Nations. Retrieved from https://eeas.europa.eu/headquarters/headquarters-homepage/12902/ national-plan-for-recovery-and-peacebuilding—central-african-republic_en.

Climate Investment Funds. (2016). *Forest Investment Program Fact Sheet*. Washington, DC: World Bank.

de Wasseige, C., Devers, D., de Marcken, P. et al. (2009). *Les Forêts du Bassin du Congo – État des Forêts 2008*. Luxembourg: Publications Office of the European Union.

Democratic Republic of Congo (DRC). (2015). *REDD+ Investment Plan (2015–2020)*. Retrieved from: www.unredd.net/documents/un-redd-partner-countries-181/africa-335/democratic-republic-of-the-congo-189/15895-drc-national-redd-investment-plan-2015-2020.html.

Dunlap, A. & Fairhead, J. (2014). The militarisation and marketisation of nature: an alternative lens to 'climate-conflict'. *Geopolitics*, 19, 937–61.

Earth System Governance (ESG) Project. (2018). *Earth System Governance: Science and Implementation Plan of the Earth System Governance Project*. Utrecht: Earth System Governance. Retrieved from www.earthsystemgovernance.org/wp-content/uploads/ 2018/11/Earth-System-Governance-Science-Plan-2018.pdf.

Eba'a Atyi, R. (2018). *Contributions of Central African Countries to Combat Climate Change.* COMIFAC. Retrieved from www.observatoire-comifac.net/docs/policy_brief/OFAC-Brief-02-en-web.pdf.

Forest Carbon Partnership Facility (FCPF). (2015). *Forest Carbon Partnership Facility Information Card.* Washington, DC: FCPF.

(2016). *Emissions Reduction Program Document.* Washington, DC: FCPF.

(2018a). *Advancing Green Development in the Democratic Republic of Congo.* Retrieved from www.forest carbonpartnership.org/country/congo-democratic-republic.

(2018b). *Central African Republic.* Retrieved from www.forestcarbonpartnership.org/country/central-african-republic.

(2018c). *Forest Carbon Partnership Facility.* Retrieved from www.forestcarbonpartnership.org/.

Forest Carbon Partnership Facility (FCPF) and UN-REDD Programme. (2012). *National REDD+ Framework Strategy of the Democratic Republic of Congo: Summary for Decision-Makers.* Kinshasa, DRC: FCPF and UN-REDD.

Gapia, M. & Bele, Y. (2012). *Adaptation et atténuation en République centrafricaine: Acteurs et processus politiques.* Bogor: CIFOR.

Gartzke, E. (2012). Could climate change precipitate peace? *Journal of Peace Research, 49* (1), 177–92.

Gizachew, B., Astrup, R., Vedeld, P., Zahabu, E.A., & Duguma, L.A. (2017). REDD+ in Africa: contexts and challenges. *Natural Resources Forum, 41,* 92–104.

Glassius, M. (2008). 'We ourselves, we are part of the functioning': the ICC, victims and civil society in the Central African Republic. *African Affairs,* 108(430), 49–67.

Global Witness. (2015). *Conflict Minerals in Eastern Congo.* Retrieved from www.globalwitness.org/fr/campaigns/conflict-minerals/conflict-minerals-eastern-congo/.

(2019). *Central African Republic.* Retrieved from www.global witness.org/en/campaigns/central-african-republic-car/.

Hoare, A.L. (2007). *Clouds on the Horizon: The Congo Basin Forests and Climate Change.* London: Rainforest Foundation.

Hsiang, S.M. & Burke, M. (2014). Climate, conflict, and social stability: what does the evidence say? *Climatic Change, 123,* 39–55.

International Bank for Reconstruction. (2015). *Charter Establishing the Forest Carbon Partnership Facility.* Washington, DC: World Bank Group.

International Crisis Group. (2019a). *Central African Republic.* Retrieved from www.crisisgroup.org/crisiswatch.

(2019b). *Democratic Republic of Congo.* Retrieved from www.crisisgroup.org/crisiswatch.

King, E. & Mutter, J.C. (2014). Violent conflicts and natural disasters: the growing case for cross-disciplinary dialogue. *Third World Quarterly,* 35(7), 1239–55.

Mason, M., Zeitoun, M., & El Sheikh, R. (2011). Conflict social vulnerability to climate change: lessons from Gaza. *Climate and Development, 3,* 285–97.

Matthew, R. (2014). Integrating climate change into peace-building. *Climatic Change, 123,* 83–93.

Maxwell, D., Mazurana, D., Wagner, M., & Slater, R. (2017). *Livelihoods, Conflict and Recovery: Findings from the Secure Livelihoods Research Consortium.* London: Secure Livelihoods Research Consortium.

Megevand, C. (2013). *Deforestation Trends in the Congo Basin.* Washington, DC: World Bank.

Mehler, A. (2011). Rebels and parties: the impact of armed insurgency on representation in the Central African Republic. *Journal of Modern African Studies,* 49(1), 115–39.

Milabyo Kyamusugulwa, P., Hilhorst, D., & van der Haar, G. (2014). Capacity builders for governance: community-driven reconstruction in the eastern Democratic Republic of Congo. *Development in Practice*, 24(7), 812–26.

Mushi, F.M. (2013). Insecurity and local governance in Congo's South Kivu. *IDS Bulletin*, 44(1), 15–29.

Mwiturubani, D.A. & van Wyk, J.-A. (2010). *Climate Change and Natural Resources in Africa*. Pretoria, SA: Institute for Security Studies.

Potts, A., Myer, K., & Roberts, L. (2011). Measuring human rights violations in a conflict-affected country: results from a nationwide cluster survey in Central African Republic. *Conflict and Health*, 5(1), 4. doi: https://doi.org/10.1186/1752-1505-5-4.

Rüttinger, L., Smith, D., Stang, G., Tänzler, D., & Vivekananda, J. (2015). *A New Climate for Peace: Taking Action on Climate and Fragility Risks*. Retrieved from www.newclimateforpeace.org/.

Saatchi, S., Xu, A., Meyer, V. et al. (2017). *Carbon Map of DRC*. Los Angeles: University of California.

Samndong, R.A. & Kjosavik, D.J. (2017). Gendered forests: exploring gender dimensions in forest governance and REDD+ in Equateur Province, Democratic Republic of Congo (DRC). *Ecology and Society*, 22(4). doi: https://doi.org/10.5751/ES-09753-220434.

Scheffran, J., Ide, T., & Schilling, J. (2014). Violent climate or climate of violence? Concepts and relations with focus on Kenya and Sudan. *International Journal of Human Rights*, 18(3), 369–90.

Scott, S.V. (2015). Implications of climate change for the UN Security Council: mapping the range of potential policy responses. *International Affairs*, 91(5), 1317–33.

Slettebak, R.T. (2012). Don't blame the weather! Climate-related natural disasters and civil conflict. *Journal of Peace Research*, 49(1), 163–76.

Spittaels, S. & Hilgert, F. (2009). *Mapping Conflict Motives: Central African Republic*. Antwerp: International Peace Information Service (IPIS). Retrieved from https://ipisresearch.be/wp-content/uploads/2014/11/IPIS-CAR-Conflict-Mapping-November-2014.pdf.

Stoett, P., Daszak, P., Romanelli, C. et al. (2016). Avoiding catastrophes: seeking synergies among the public health, environmental protection, and human security sectors. *Lancet Global Health*, 4(10), e680–1. doi: https://doi.org/10.1016/S2214-109X(16)30173-5.

Toulmin, C. (2009). *Climate Change in Africa*. London: Zed Books.

United Nations. (2017). *United Nations Relief Chief Appeals for Urgent Funds for People in Need in the DR Congo*. Retrieved from http://reliefweb.int/report/democratic-republic-congo/united-nations-relief-chief-appeals-urgent-funds-people-need-dr.

    (2019). *United Nations Organization Stabilization Mission in the Democratic Republic of Congo*. Retrieved from https://monusco.unmissions.org/en.

United Nations Development Programme (UNDP). (2016a). Major agreement between CAFI and the DRC sets best practices to prevent tree loss and ensure sustainable development [Press release]. Retrieved from www.undp.org/content/undp/en/home/press center/pressreleases/2016/04/22/major-agreement-between-cafi-and-the-drc-sets-best-practices-to-prevent-tree-loss-and-ensure-sustainable-development.html.

    (2016b). *Towards a Common Understanding of REDD+ under the UNFCCC*. Technical Resource Series 3. Geneva: UN-REDD.

    (2018). *Human Development Data (1990–2018)*. Retrieved from http://hdr.undp.org/en/data/trends/.

United Nations Environment Programme (UNEP). (2011). *Livelihood Security: Climate Change, Migration and Conflict in the Sahel*. Geneva: UNEP. Retrieved from https://reliefweb.int/sites/reliefweb.int/files/resources/UNEP_Sahel_EN.pdf.

United Nations Framework Convention on Climate Change (UNFCCC). (2015). *Warsaw Framework for REDD-Plus*. Retrieved from https://unfccc.int/topics/land-use/resources/warsaw-framework-for-redd-plus.

United Nations Security Council (UNSC). (2019). *Letter Dated 2 January 2019 from the Permanent Representative of the Dominican Republic to the United Nations Addressed to the Secretary-General*. New York: United Nations Security Council.

UN News. (2019). Climate change recognized as threat multiplier, UN Security Council debates its impact on peace. Retrieved from https://news.un.org/en/story/2019/01/1031322.

UN-REDD Programme. (2011). *Joint Declaration of Intent on REDD+ in the Congo Basin between Central African and Donor Countries*. South Africa: United Nations.

(2015). *UN-REDD Programme Strategic Framework 2016–2020*. Washington, DC: United Nations.

(2016a). *Modelling REDD+ in the Democratic Republic of Congo*. Nairobi, Kenya: UNEP.

(2016b). *UN-REDD Programme*. Retrieved from www.un-redd.org/partner-countries.

(2019). *The United Nations Collaborative Programme on Reducing Emissions from Deforestation and Forest Degradation in Developing Countries*. Retrieved from www.un-redd.org/.

World Bank. (2010). *République Centrafricaine: Analyse Environnementale de Pays: Gestion environnementale pour une croissance durable*. Washington, DC: World Bank.

(2011). *Climate Investment Funds: Investment Plan Democratic Republic of Congo*. Washington, DC:World Bank. Retrieved from www.climateinvestment funds.org/sites/cif_enc/files/fip_4_ dcr_ip_0.pdf

(2014). *Project Information Document (PID) Concept Stage*. Washington, DC: World Bank. Retrieved from http://documents.worldbank.org/curated/en/5587514%2068015027713/pdf/PID-Print-P145634–08-11-2014-1407772091132.pdf.

(2017). *Forest and Climate-Smart Development in the Democratic Republic of Congo*. Retrieved from http://blogs.worldbank.org/climatechange/forest-and-climate-smart-development-democratic-republic-congo.

(2018a). *CAR REDD+ Readiness Preparation Support*. Washington, DC: World Bank. Retrieved from www.forestcarbonpartnership.org/system/files/documents/GRM%20CAR%20FY18%20Progress%20Report.pdf.

(2018b). *Central African Republic Overview*. Retrieved from www.worldbank.org/en/country/centralafricanrepublic/overview.

(2018c). *Democratic Republic of Congo Overview*. Retrieved from www.worldbank.org/en/country/drc/overview.

(2018d). *International Development Association Project Appraisal Document on a Proposed Grant to the Central African Republic for a Natural Resources Governance Project*. Retrieved from http://documents.worldbank.org/curated/en/823091521079287934/pdf/CAR-PADnew-02212018.pdf.

(2019). Mozambique and Democratic Republic of Congo sign landmark deals with World Bank to cut carbon emissions and reduce deforestation [Press release]. Retrieved from www.worldbank.org/en/news/press-release/2019/02/12/mozambique-and-democratic-republic-of-congo-sign-landmark-deals-with-world-bank-to-cut-carbon-emissions-and-reduce-deforestation.

World Bank Forest Investment Program. (2018). *Forest Investment Program.* Retrieved from www.climateinvestmentfunds.org/fund/forest-investment-program.

World Bank Group. (2018). *Central African Republic Economic Update: Breaking the Cycle of Conflict and Instability.* Washington, DC: World Bank Group. Retrieved from http://documents.worldbank.org/curated/en/444491528747992733/pdf/127056-WP-PUBLIC-BreakingTheCycleOfConflitAndInstabilityInCAR.pdf.

(2019). *Worldwide Governance Indicators.* Retrieved from https://info.worldbank.org/governance/wgi/#home.

Wig, T. & Tollefsen, A.F. (2016). Local institutional quality and conflict violence in Africa. *Political Geography*, 53, 30–42.

Witmer, F.D., Linke, A.M., O'Loughlin, J., Gettelman, A., & Laing, A. (2017). Subnational violent conflict forecasts for sub-Saharan Africa, 2015–65, using climate-sensitive models. *Journal of Peace Research*, 54(2), 175–92.

Wong, P.-H. (2016). How can political trust be built after civil wars? Evidence from post-conflict Sierra Leone. *Journal of Peace Research*, 53(6), 772–85.

9

Policy Tools and Capacities for Adaptiveness in US Public Land Management

ZACHARY WURTZEBACH AND COURTNEY SCHULTZ

9.1 Introduction

In an era of rapid social and ecological change, a key goal for earth system governance research is to understand the governance attributes that allow social actors to respond and proactively adapt to changing social and ecological conditions in complex institutional settings (Burch et al., 2019). A central problem is the issue of scale and boundaries. Mismatches between the temporal and spatial scales of assessment and management, along with epistemic and organisational boundaries, often impede planning and action over large enough spatial and temporal extents to affect change, and limit the co-production and exchange of useable knowledge decision-making (Allen & Gunderson, 2011; Cash et al., 2006; Schultz et al., 2019). Another challenge is capitalising on the capacity inherent in local, participatory, and emergent processes, which scholars have observed are essential for implementing collaborative adaptive management, and the customisation of policies and governance to local contexts (Armitage et al., 2009; DeCaro et al., 2017; Lemos & Agrawal, 2006).

Addressing these challenges requires governance regimes that balance tensions between stability and flexibility across scales and levels of socio-ecological organisation (Burch et al., 2019). While institutional flexibility (i.e. the ability to change rules) is essential for learning and adaptation to change, elements of stability, such as democratic accountability and legitimacy, are essential for the achievement of long-term and systemic goals (Beunen et al., 2017). Scholars of adaptive governance note that multilevel and polycentric governance systems with linkages via social networks and bridging organisations may provide a needed balance between flexibility and stability (DeCaro et al., 2017; Huitema et al., 2009; Schultz et al., 2019). Specifically, these institutional structures are thought to provide sufficient flexibility and coordination for adaptive management, and enable the emergence of novel governance regimes that can effectively address scalar mismatches between institutions and socio-ecological systems (Chaffin et al., 2014; Folke et al., 2005).

Despite its normative appeal for practitioners and scholars, however, legal and policy frameworks and approaches are needed to operationalise elements of adaptive governance in practice (Decaro et al., 2017; Sharma-Wallace et al., 2018). This consideration is especially relevant in contexts where state bureaucracies retain significant authority for natural resource governance (Cosens et al., 2017). In such settings, a key challenge for policymakers is how to design legal tools that provide sufficient flexibility and stability for more adaptive forms of governance (Beunen et al., 2017; Burch et al., 2019; DeCaro et al., 2017). Indeed, the design and implementation of novel policy tools is not without its challenges. Scholars of public policy have long noted the limitations of statutory law in structuring governance outcomes, particularly in complex networked governance settings (Pressman & Wildavsky, 1973; Sabatier, 1986). New policies and authorities are not introduced into vacuums. They are often 'layered' on to existing policy structures, creating challenges for coherence and coordination across scales of governance (Howlett & Rayner, 2007). While adaptive governance theorists have outlined candidate legal tools for improved adaptiveness, less attention has been given to the resources and capacities needed to design and operationalise policy tools for adaptiveness.

In this chapter, we synthesise insights from our empirical research on the design and implementation of novel policy tools for adaptiveness in the context of federal forest management in the United States. Our goal is to contribute to debates around legal and policy frameworks for adaptive governance by examining policy tools and capacities needed to support more adaptive forest governance. In the next section, we outline our conceptual framework, rooted in recent scholarship on adaptive governance and policy design, and provide an overview of recent developments in US federal forest management. We then discuss findings from our research, focusing on two areas of policy change: multilevel monitoring and collaborative forest restoration. For each topic, we discuss their importance for building adaptive capacity in the forest management regime, key policy tools, and complementary capacity needs. We conclude with a discussion of key lessons of relevance for policy and practice, contributions to existing debates around policy tools and adaptive governance, and knowledge gaps needed to inform the future development of the earth system governance framework.

9.2 Conceptual Framework: Policy Tools and Capacities for Adaptive Governance

Collaborative adaptive management and adaptive governance are key paradigms for improved adaptiveness in the context of natural resource governance. Adaptive management is a structured decision-making paradigm that emphasises 'learning while doing' in natural resource management; management activities are treated as hypotheses to be tested, with monitoring information used to inform and adapt future activities iteratively over time (Walters & Holling, 1990). Collaboration among scientists, managers, and stakeholders is essential for minimising conflict, integrating diverse interests, articulating goals and hypotheses, and improving the knowledge base for implementation (Armitage et al., 2009; Gregory et al., 2006). Yet adaptive management has often failed to meet its promise in practice due to inflexible bureaucratic structures, inadequate resources and monitoring strategies, and temporal and spatial mismatches between jurisdictions, political cycles, and ecological processes (Allen & Gunderson, 2011; Stankey et al., 2003; Westgate et al., 2013).

Adaptive governance refers to governance regimes that can enable and coordinate collaborative adaptive management across spatial and temporal scales of socio-ecological organisation (Cosens & Williams, 2012). Multilevel poly-centric governance regimes are theorised to provide sufficient flexibility for adaptive management and facilitate the emergence of novel governance regimes that can more effectively match the temporal and spatial scales of socio-ecological systems (Huitema et al., 2009). Social networks and bridging organisations facilitate the co-production and exchange of knowledge across epistemic communities and organisations operating at different levels, build social capital for collaborative decision-making and adaptive management, and reduce transaction costs for collective action (Cash et al., 2006; Folke et al., 2005; Termeer et al., 2010). While the emergence of adaptive governance may be spurred by focusing on events or governance failures, recent scholarship highlights the importance of legal tools for enabling more adaptive forms of governance. Candidate legal tools include flexible standards rather than prescriptive rules, authority for participatory and collaborative decision-making at meaningful scales for ecological governance, legal sunsets, and the provision of tangible resources (Craig et al., 2017; DeCaro et al., 2017). However, there has been limited empirical research on policy tools for adaptiveness in state bureaucracies, or the capacities needed to tailor and implement them in specific contexts (Wyborn & Dovers, 2014).

Recent scholarship on policy design provides a useful lens for investigating attributes of policies and policy capacities needed to support more adaptive forms of governance. Policies are conceived as multilevel and nested mixes of goals and policy tools, which are 'the identifiable means through which collective action is structured to address a policy problem' (Salamon & Elliot, 2002: 12). Policy tools are often categorised by the governing resource they utilise (i.e. state authority, financial incentives, bureaucratic organisation), or the embedded assumptions they make about the behaviours of policy targets (i.e. resources, mandates, or incentives needed to support collective action) (Howlett, 2009; Schneider & Ingram, 1990). Substantive policy tools directly affect the delivery of goods and services in the public sphere, while procedural policy tools, such as steering committees or collaborative decision-making structures, shape policy processes. Policy design is often conceptualised as both a noun and verb. It refers to both the package or 'mix' of goals and policy tools contained within a policy, and the iterative and adaptive process in which policy goals and tools are formulated at higher levels of governance and tailored for implementation in specific contexts. At the macro level of governance, the selection of policy tools is constrained by prevailing sociopolitical 'implementation preferences' for specific types of policy tools and service delivery mechanisms (Howlett, 2009). Market-based tools, and networked and voluntary service delivery mechanisms, for instance, are implementation preferences often associated with the neoliberal governance paradigm. At the 'meso' and 'micro' levels of governance, agents in state organisations and partner networks operationalise and tailor higher-level policy tools for specific contexts, developing new practices and procedures to structure implementation by street-level bureaucrats and co-operating partners (Howlett, 2009; Moulton & Sandfort, 2016). Policy design and implementation may also be adaptive; information about implementation outputs and outcomes may be disseminated through policy networks and used to refine or change policy tools across levels of governance (Lynn et al., 2000). The design, implementation, and adaptive refinement of policy tools across levels of governance, however, is dependent upon the presence of policy capacity.

Policy capacity refers to the competencies, capabilities, and resources needed to perform policy functions (i.e. policy design, decision-making, implementation, and monitoring and evaluation) (Wu et al., 2015). Competencies and capabilities associated with policy capacity are categorised into three interrelated types (analytical, operational, and political) at three nested levels of analysis (individual, organisational, systemic) (Table 9.1). They may be present in state institutions with authority for policy or in external organisations and networks (Moulton & Sandfort, 2016). Analytical capacity encompasses the competencies needed to generate, acquire, and integrate useable knowledge into policy processes. Operational capacity refers to the competencies and capabilities needed for policy implementation and service delivery. Political capacity undergirds both analytical and operational capacity. It refers to the capabilities needed to marshal political resources for policy functions. Each type of capacity exists and interacts across different system levels. Systemic-level capacities, for instance, reflect the aggregate of organisational-level capacities across the governance system. At the same time, attributes of systemic-level capacity, such as public trust in state institutions, likewise heavily influence organisational-level capacities. Similarly,

Table 9.1. *Dimensions of policy capacity*

Competency type	Analytical level		
	Individual	Organisational	Systemic
Analytical	Technical domain expertise; skills in data management and analysis; skills in leveraging external sources of data and information	Organisational culture that supports learning/ evidence-informed decision-making; IT infrastructure; organisational structures dedicated to knowledge management	General availability of individuals and organisations with analytical skills and competencies
Operational	Communication, budgeting, and financial management skills; leadership and networking competencies	Funding, staffing, technology, infrastructure, and human resource management for implementation; inter-organisational relationships/social capital	Accountability mechanisms; presence of individuals and organisations with operational capacity; systemic human, financial, and technological resources
Political	Skills in outreach and communication; strategic messaging; political acumen; leadership	Communication and negotiation skills; relationships with stakeholders and stakeholder management abilities	Public trust; political legitimacy

Source: Adapted from Wu et al. (2015).

organisational-level capacities, such as human resource management and information technology (IT) infrastructure, are essential for exploiting individual-level capacities (Wu et al., 2015).

Multilevel dimensions of policy capacity are a critical consideration for the design and implementation of policy tools for adaptiveness. At local scales, attributes of individual- and organisational-level policy capacity are essential for tailoring policy tools for specific contexts, and implementing different aspects of collaborative adaptive management (e.g. facilitating collaboration, implementing monitoring, committing to and implementing changes in management). Across broad scales, the adoption and coordination of adaptive policies across organisational and jurisdictional boundaries likewise requires organisational-level and systemic-level policy capacities (e.g. leadership commitment and inter-organisational relationships). A policy tools and capacities framework can therefore be used to characterise and evaluate policies and capacities needed to pursue more adaptive forms of governance across multiple levels of socio-ecological organisation.

9.3 Federal Forest Management in the United States

The US Forest Service (USFS) is a large federal bureaucracy responsible for the management of 193 million acres, the majority of which lies in the Western United States. For much of the twentieth century, the agency retained significant administrative discretion for forest management and decision-making. It utilised this discretion to emphasise timber production and fire suppression – activities that provided tangible benefits to local communities and allowed the agency to secure political support and budgetary increases from members of Congress (Hirt, 1994). Challenges for the agency's orientation to timber production and limitations on its administrative discretion emerged with the birth of the national environmental movement in the 1960s, and the passage of the National Environmental Policy Act of 1969, the Endangered Species Act of 1973, and the National Forest Management Act of 1976. These laws required the agency to adopt a rational-comprehensive planning paradigm; provide opportunities for public comment and engagement; and place a greater emphasis on wildlife, recreation, and other non-timber resources. The laws of the environmental era also provided significant opportunities for stakeholders and organised interests to litigate agency decisions (Hoberg, 2001). In 1991 a court ruling forced the agency to suspend timber harvesting in the Pacific Northwest until it developed a plan to protect the northern spotted owl (*Strix occidentalis*). The resulting controversy led the agency to adopt an ecosystem management paradigm that emphasised integrated resource planning, ecological restoration, adaptive management, collaboration, and cross-boundary coordination (Schultz et al., 2012). Despite changing management paradigms, however, statutory laws and administrative structures that govern federal forest management have remained largely unchanged since the 1970s. The practice of linking annual budgetary allocation to timber production targets, and the agency's aggressive approach to fire suppression, for example, represent long-standing institutional legacies that often conflict with more recent goals for holistic resource management on individual forests (Nie, 2008; Stephens et al., 2016).

Today, there are several factors that influence adaptiveness in the context of federal forest management. One is a significant decline in human and financial resources within the USFS. As the extent and severity of wildfires in the Western United States has increased, resources allocated for fire suppression have increasingly consumed funding and staffing for other resource programmes and management objectives (Stephens et al., 2016). With the decline in timber production, many regions of the USFS have also seen a concomitant reduction in funding and capacity (Maier & Abrams, 2018). Mirroring neoliberal policy preferences at national and international levels, federal forest policy is increasingly characterised by an emphasis on networked governance arrangements that elevate the role of private and non-state actors in forest management, with less funding and authority for agents in federal institutions (Abrams, Davis et al., 2017; Abrams, Huber-Stearns et al., 2017). At the same time, stakeholder demands for greater participation and involvement in forest management on local landscapes have increased in response to declining trust, and as an alternative to adversarial and litigious conflict. Today, collaboration and network governance are often essential for leveraging external resources and securing a 'social licence' for forest management activities (Schultz et al., 2012). And, as in other forested regions around the world, forest governance in the United States increasingly emphasises 'landscape' approaches that emphasise collaboration, integrated planning, and cross-sectoral coordination at meaningful scales, and the co-production of useable knowledge among scientists, managers, and stakeholders (Arts et al., 2017). In this arena, long-standing challenges have included failures to honour collaboratively forged agreements, plan activities that were strategically coordinated across landscapes to affect ecological processes, and implement monitoring and adaptive management (Biber, 2011; Schultz et al., 2012). Given these challenges, new policy tools have emerged in the past decade to build capacity for evidence-informed and adaptive planning, and forest restoration.

9.4 Policy Experiments in Forest Management

Policy is changing within the USFS along multiple pathways. For instance, the Trump administration has been emphasising timber harvest and partnership with state entities as primary goals, utilising several policy tools to achieve these objectives (USFS, 2018). Another major effort was to update the regulations (i.e. administrative law) that govern land and resource management planning on US national forests. Restoring natural processes and increasing resilience in light of climate change is a primary focus of these regulations (Wurtzebach & Schultz, 2016). In addition, across multiple spatial and organisation levels the agency has been investing in forest restoration activities, including thinning of small trees to reduce fuel loads and the reintroduction of fire, as restoration is largely an activity meant to restore fire as a natural and essential ecological process in dry forest ecosystems (USFS, 2012). Herein we focus on two areas where we have conducted empirical work on policies for improved adaptiveness in the face of social and ecological change: improving multilevel monitoring and facilitating collaborative forest restoration. In both arenas, we explore policy design and capacities, with an eye towards understanding strategies to increasing adaptiveness.

9.4.1 Multilevel Monitoring

Ecological monitoring (i.e. the iterative collection and analysis of ecological data) is a fundamental source of knowledge for adaptive land management planning and decision-making. Monitoring conducted over a variety of spatial and temporal scales is essential for evaluating the effectiveness of management actions and measuring progress towards conservation goals, providing early warnings of 'state shifts' in ecosystem dynamics, and evaluating trends in landscape patterns and processes at ecoregional scales (Hutto & Belote, 2013; Lindenmayer & Likens, 2010; Williams, 2011). Despite its importance for adaptive decision-making, there are often significant institutional challenges for monitoring implementation in the context of public land management. Agency staff often lack the analytical capacity needed to design monitoring strategies that can generate credible and relevant information at appropriate temporal and spatial scales, or to analyse and interpret monitoring data and information produced by other actors (Deluca et al., 2010). Budget cuts, turnover, IT issues, and problematic incentives represent organisational-level policy capacity challenges that complicate consistency and coordination for data collection and analysis (Biber, 2011). Mismatches between the spatial scales of monitoring and decision-making and problematic communication strategies often complicate the use of monitoring information in planning and decision-making contexts (Bennetts & Gross, 2007; Guerrero et al., 2013).

Emerging strategies for supporting multilevel monitoring design, implementation, and communication are evident in the USFS 2012 National Forest Management Act (NFMA) regulations for national forest planning. Under these, the USFS is required to monitor socio-economic variables and 'key characteristics' of ecological integrity or attributes of ecological structure, function, process, and composition associated with ecosystem resilience and the persistence of biodiversity. There are also two complementary tiers of ecological monitoring in the new planning rule: monitoring plans on each national forest within the land management plan, and, in addition, 'broader-scale monitoring programmes' developed by each of the nine USFS regions, the administrative level above national forests. Broader-scale monitoring is a novel policy requirement intended to generate efficiencies and complement forest plan monitoring; it is specifically meant to be applicable for resources that should be assessed consistently and at a scale greater than the individual national forest (Federal Register, 2012: § 219.12 (b)). The rule also calls on the agency to collaborate with 'other Forest Service units, Federal, State or local government agencies, scientists, partners, and members of the public' (Federal Register, 2012: § 219.12 (b)), to utilise 'best available scientific information' (Federal Register, 2012: § 219.3), and to ensure that monitoring results are integrated back into planning and decision-making cycles through biennial reporting cycles (Federal Register, 2012: § 219). The intent of the new regulations is to foster reflexivity through a planning process that 'informs integrated resource management and allows the Forest Service to adapt to changing conditions, including climate change, and improve management based on new information and monitoring' (Federal Register, 2012: § 219.5).

We conducted research looking at the early years of interpretation and implementation of these new requirements through qualitative interviews with over 90 respondents from the USFS and partner organisations (Wurtzebach, Schultz et al., 2019). Respondents in our research highlighted several challenges, benefits, and opportunities for implementing monitoring requirements associated with the new planning rule. The most widely cited challenge was resource scarcity. On individual forests, staff often lack the time, resources, and expertise needed to design and implement forest plan monitoring strategies that can inform adaptive forest planning processes. Given the absence of standardised procedures for data collection and data management, and cumbersome data management infrastructure, challenges for analysis and aggregation across units are extensive (Wurtzebach, Schultz et al., 2019). Because of funding and staffing shortages, and the agency's decentralised decision-making structure, national forest-level decision makers often use their discretion (or 'flexibility') to prioritise resource allocation for management implementation rather than monitoring. Agency staff indicated that regional leadership is often unwilling to invest in new regional broader-scale monitoring strategies unless it is associated with regulatory requirements and legal commitments. Indeed, while broader-scale monitoring represents a new policy commitment, there is no additional provision of funding to support implementation (Wurtzebach, Schultz et al., 2019).

Despite these challenges, the regulations have fostered deliberation and evaluation about the feasibility and utility of existing monitoring strategies on individual forests, and additional opportunities for leveraging external sources of data. Legal requirements have compelled staff within the USFS to deliberate about the scale at which particular management questions should be addressed and with what data sources, setting the stage for collective learning (Waltz et al., 2017). To address capacity gaps, agency staff and partners highlighted the importance of leveraging external policy capacity through collaboration and partnerships with other state, federal, research, and non-governmental organisations (NGOs) that will allow the USFS to leverage capabilities and expertise for monitoring implementation that it does not have 'in-house' (Wurtzebach, Schultz et al., 2019). Multi-year funding agreements for partner monitoring at regional levels allow the USFS to ensure consistent funding over multiple budgetary cycles, and consistent implementation data collection, data management, analysis, and communication across multiple units. Interviewees also highlighted several administrative tools associated with successful examples of broader-scale monitoring. In the Pacific Northwest, shared interagency funding and staffing structures, and staff dedicated to full-time monitoring implementation, have supported regional and cross-boundary monitoring strategies for over 20 years (Ringold et al., 1999). In addition to generating useable information for decision-making at multiple scales, we found that regionally coordinated approaches leverage economies of scale for data management and analysis to generate efficiencies for implementation. However, the development of such approaches requires proof of concept to managers responsible for funding allocation, and leadership commitment (i.e. political capacity). While innovative strategies have been developed in some regions, systematic implementation across the USFS will require funding and increased organisational-level analytical capacity to coordinate monitoring across resource and programme areas; 'translate' externally produced broader-scale data so that it is relevant for end users; and provide technical assistance, accountability, and oversight for unit-level monitoring implementation (Wurtzebach, Schultz et al., 2019).

9.4.2 Collaborative Forest Restoration

In the United States forest restoration efforts typically are designed to restore natural ecological processes, such as fire, in degraded systems. As a result of climate change and the legacy of a century of fire suppression in fire-adapted ecosystems, fire extent and severity have increased in the last 20 years substantially, threatening homes, lives, watersheds, and other valued resources in the Western United States (Schultz et al., 2019). This presents a profound social-ecological systems governance challenge, and there is need for changes in policy and governance that allow for adaptiveness on multiple fronts, including planning and acting over larger spatial extents and time frames. Additionally, restoration requires an iterative approach, grounded in adaptive management, which means planning, monitoring, re-evaluating, and re-entering sites sequentially to accomplish restoration goals (DeLuca et al., 2010). And, there is a critical need to work across jurisdictions, leveraging capacity and agreement across diverse actions in order to undertake actions at a large-enough scale to affect an ecological process such as fire (Schultz et al., 2012).

In the US public lands context, collaborative governance efforts emerged as a predominant approach to management in the 1990s, typically at a community or town scale, to build agreement around how to prioritise between conservation and commodity production; forest restoration is an iteration of ecosystem-based management in this era of heightened ecological disturbance (Cortner & Moore, 1999; Predmore et al., 2008; Schultz et al., 2012). Traditional agency funding cycles and approaches to planning through environmental impact analysis are at odds with the integrated goals of ecological restoration implemented through an adaptive management paradigm (Biber, 2011; Nie & Schultz, 2012). Despite these challenges, collaborators highlight the need to scale up collaborative efforts to address larger ecological issues and landscapes (Schultz et al., 2012).

In recent years, the federal government, often in response to demand from community-based forestry groups, has promulgated new policies to support collaborative participation in forest restoration processes. These policy changes create new opportunities to plan and implement projects at flexible scales, capitalise on partnerships and networks, and overcome persistent challenges that limit adaptiveness within the system. In 2009, Congress passed a law establishing the Collaborative Forest Landscape Restoration Program (CFLRP, P.L. 111-11), which allocates funding through a competitive process to landscape-scale restoration projects that have been proposed jointly by the USFS and a group of collaborators. The law requires that projects propose a programme of work over a landscape of a minimum of 50,000 acres, and proposals must explain the ecological need for restoration across the landscape and discuss economic and social factors that make that landscape a priority for investment. Collaboration with external partners is required throughout planning, implementation, and monitoring. There are 23 CFLRP projects across the United States that were awarded 10 years of funding; these projects vary in size and scale depending on collaborative history, societal or political factors, available infrastructure, capacity, and ecological vulnerability and necessity (Schultz et al., 2012). The enabling law, while requiring some scale matching to ecological processes, allows for considerable flexibility based on these variables and for funding to be used for a variety of activities. The CFLRP creates new space for longer-term and larger-scale planning and formally expands opportunities for stakeholders to play a direct role in federal forest management. The 10-year commitment of flexible funding allows groups to have certainty that the government will support a 10-year coordinated programme of work across a landscape, which facilitates groups' ability to leverage funding, prioritises investment to support landscape-scale restoration and increases opportunities for industry, and also provides certainty that projects will have out-year monitoring funds, thereby overcoming some of the traditional challenges of sustaining monitoring efforts in the face of annual budgeting cycles (Schultz et al., 2014). Another programme to support restoration at larger scales than in the past, called the Joint Chiefs Landscape Restoration Partnership, was established in 2014 internally by the USFS and the Natural Resource Conservation Service, two different administrative agencies with the US Department of Agriculture. This programme competitively awards funding for up to three years of work to support fuels reduction and the improvement of water quality and wildlife habitat across both public and private forest lands, again focusing on larger landscapes and collaboration with a multi-year funding commitment.

These programmes raise a number of questions about the emerging role of policy innovations to support adaptive management, create a greater space for collaboration with private landowners and other actors, and encourage longer-term and larger-scale planning. Indeed, these policies have much in common with proposed design principles for supporting more adaptive forms of governance, and we were interested in their efficacy in practice (DeCaro et al., 2017). We have found in our empirical work on these programmes, including over 150 interviews and surveys of over 425 personnel, that mandates to collaborate with non-state actors, multi-year commitments of funding, and mandates to work at a landscape scale have led to greater collective action and planning across larger spatial extents and longer time frames (Schultz, McIntyre et al., 2018). At the same time, a lack of operational capacity in the industry sector to support this work was a major limitation, as were outdated USFS staffing models that left projects without adequate, enduring leadership and capacity.

Key lessons from our work are that these policy tools, which integrated proposed design principles for adaptiveness, are effective at improving scale-fit and support collective action (Schultz et al., 2019). At the same time, new operational capacities are needed as part of the policy mix to maximise the utility of these new tools. In addition, we found that despite larger-scale planning and implementation of vegetation management activities, projects still struggled to apply controlled burns (i.e. intentionally ignited fires) as planned. Our subsequent research revealed that a lack of adequate human resource and funding capacity are limiting the application of these burns, particularly given that qualified fire management personnel are increasingly in demand to fight wildland fires (Schultz, Huber-Stearns et al., 2018). Broader adaptiveness within the social-ecological systems of forest in the American West is going to require significantly increased operational capacity to work with fire, to collaborate at multiple levels of the governance system, and political capacity to improve implementation and policy tools for controlled burning. In summary, our work is finding that innovative policy changes are allowing for novel and more adaptive governance approaches to scale, but there is a need to further understand how new institutions interact with old ones and where new capacities are needed to further progress.

9.5 Discussion

9.5.1 Implications for Policy and New Challenges

Our research reveals several practical and policy relevant considerations for adaptiveness in the context of forest management, particularly in the United States, where most forests are managed by the federal government as national forests. The two policies we discussed are interrelated and involve mandates for collaborative monitoring, planning, and implementation. Within the CFLRP and Joint Chiefs Partnership Program, new policy tools have allowed agency actors to leverage collaborative processes and partner capabilities and increase the pace and scale of restoration planning and implementation activities. The collaborative monitoring requirements in the CFLRP and 2012 planning regulations have led agency actors and collaborators to develop and consider new monitoring approaches that can inform adaptive decision-making at appropriate scales and re-evaluate existing practices and procedures.

One important lesson learned from both examples is that policies, through a mix of tools, can improve scale matching, whether it is by including multi-year funding commitments to overcome the volatility that comes with annual appropriations and evaluations, or through mandates to explicitly consider scale issues (Schultz et al., 2019). In both cases we found that partnerships are critical for maintaining commitments to planning processes, creating forums to bridge across actors across levels and jurisdictions, and connecting science to management (Schultz et al., 2019). Improving scale-fit and addressing other types of scale mismatches is critical to adaptiveness, as it allows for working at a variety of spatial extents, leveraging scale-specific comparative advantages of different institutions, over-coming ignorance of scale-related challenges, and addressing the long-standing mismatch between political and administrative decision-making cycles and the timelines of ecological processes and response. These policy approaches highlight some potentially positive changes for adaptiveness with regard to scale-related challenges and considerations.

The other critical lesson learned from our work is that the implementation of novel policy tools for adaptive forest governance is dependent upon the presence of diverse policy capacities. In terms of analytical capacity, boundary organisations and science-focused NGOs are often essential for facilitating collaboration between managers and scientists, and providing expertise and capabilities for activities such as monitoring design, data collection, data management, and analysis. Partners also represent an important source of operational capacity and political capacity. Within the CFLRP and Joint Chiefs Program, partner funding, participation in planning, and capacity for management implementation were identified as important facilitators of success (Butler & Schultz, 2019). Likewise, by conducting outreach and education activities with local stakeholders and serving as boundary-spanning 'trust ambassadors', external actors can build buy-in for collaboration, and provide legitimacy for agency planning and management activities (Coleman & Stern, 2018; Cyphers & Schultz, 2019). Indeed, pre-existing collaborative relationships were one of the most significant variables affecting success in the CFLRP and Joint Chiefs Program (Schultz, McIntyre et al., 2018). However, the availability of external individual- and organisational-level policy capacity is highly variable across scales and contexts. Within the context of forest plan monitoring, limited external analytical capacity and stakeholder constituencies for monitoring are barriers for implementation on many remote and under-resourced forests. Market variables and limited infrastructure have created challenges for leveraging private sector operational capacity for forest restoration implementation on many CFLRP and Joint Chiefs projects (Cyphers & Schultz, 2019; Schultz, McIntyre et al., 2018).

A cross-cutting challenge and capacity gap is organisational-level policy capacity management institutions. Leadership, turnover, expertise, staffing shortages, inadequate funding, and other aspects of operational and analytical capacity have been common challenges for with the implementation of the CFLRP, Joint Chiefs, and monitoring requirements of the 2012 planning rule. Indeed, while partnerships and collaboration are essential for leveraging external resources and capabilities, state capacity is typically needed to steer networks, and channel flows of 'policy energy' needed to achieve policy goals (McGuire & Agranoff, 2011). A critical role for state agents in this respect is the development of substantive and procedural administrative policy tools, either internally or with partners, that can support implementation. Investment in staff dedicated to knowledge management and networking, steering committees and formal collaborative structures, resource allocation prioritisation processes and pre-ignition, collaborative fire planning processes (Schultz et al., 2019) represent important tools in this respect. However, the development of such tools often requires leadership commitment and political capacity, which is difficult to secure given top-down political pressures for meeting management targets under conditions of resource scarcity. Indeed, organisational scholars note that 'slack' resources are often needed to generate knowledge needed to explore and proactively change organisational structures and procedures in the face of change. When organisational policy capacity is limited, as in the USFS, public organisations are often reactive; they are forced to exploit existing structures and scarce resources for emergent problems, compliance with legal requirements, and management activities associated with future resource allocation (Berends et al., 2003; March, 1999). In sum, despite the presence of individual and organisational policy capacity in many contexts, limited organisational policy capacity within the USFS and spatial variability in systemic policy capacity across inter-organisational networks represents a challenge for systematically implementing collaborative and adaptive forest management across scales.

Our research also reveals the importance of integrating policy capacity into conceptualisations of flexibility and stability. Legal tools that provide authority and discretion for participatory decision-making, or delineate guidelines rather than rigid standards, for example, are theorised to provide a balance of flexibility and stability. However, the effectiveness of these tools is predicated on the assumption that governance actors have the analytical capacity to tailor and adapt policy tools for specific contexts, the political capacity to negotiate agreement among diverse stakeholders, and the operational capacity to implement policy actions (Schneider & Ingram, 1990). Flexibility in action is a function of both rules and resources. The ability to adaptively change rules, practices, and procedures and implement policy actions requires the authority and discretion to do so (i.e. regulatory flexibility), but also the requisite competencies and capabilities. This consideration has important implications for policy design for adaptiveness because similar symptoms of maladaptive institutional behaviour may have different root causes that require unique policy prescriptions. Calls for legal reform, for instance, may be misplaced if the underlying problem is limited operational and analytical capacity in state institution, rather than regulatory 'rigidity'. The assertion that legal flexibility will facilitate the emergence of novel collaborative or network governance arrangements is likewise predicated on the assumption that diverse institutional actors have the requisite resources and commitment to singular policy goals, and won't pursue their own parochial interests or create veto points that complicate decision-making and implementation (Maier & Abrams, 2018; Pressman & Wildavsky, 1973). Mandates for collaboration and competitive funding processes are innovative procedural and substantive policy tools in this respect. They allow higher-order authorities to make assumptions about organisational-level policy capacity in specific settings, prioritise the allocation of scarce resources, incentivise collaboration, and build operational capacity for implementation.

As we consider the role of policy tools designed to facilitate and support emergent participatory processes, we also must continue to critically question whether such approaches will exacerbate entrenched inequities. In the United States, resources under programmes like the CFLRP are directed to locations where collaborators have already organised and accomplished some degree of planning. These locations are likely to be places where the population is concentrated and where there is existing expertise and capacity in non-profit organisations and scientific or educational organisations. More rural and impoverished areas may be less likely to compete for investments and become systematically left behind, regardless of their need for ecological restoration. Even given civil society capacity, limited resources in state institutions nonetheless represents a critical challenge in the context of forest management. In contrast to other policy regimes, such as water governance, implementing proactive adaptation strategies such as forest restoration requires significant operational capacity. Indeed, the challenges increase on private land ownership as a result of increased transaction costs, and the diverse values and decision-making behaviours (Cyphers & Schultz, 2019). In such contexts, financial incentives tools might be more appropriate for shaping policy target behaviours, but they too entail public expenditures and may exacerbate existing disparities and inequities.

Though our research is drawn from the relatively unique context of US public land management, there are several findings that are generalisable to other contexts. One is the importance of policy capacity for tailoring policy tools for specific contexts, and the implications of existing policy capacity for tools that provide authority and discretion to institutional actors at different scales and levels of governance (Fukuyama, 2013). In resource contexts such as climate change adaptation and mitigation policy in Vietnam, for instance, bureaucratic politics and limited state and civil society policy capacity have challenged the ability of governance actors to tailor and implement policy tools at provincial levels of governance (Phuong et al., 2018; Wurtzebach, Casse et al., 2019). Efforts to substantively devolve authority to actors at lower levels of governance in Australia have run aground for similar reasons (Harrington et al., 2008). The importance of capacity-building policy tools (i.e. funding and resources), managerial capacity in state institutions for steering network governance, and procedural tools for coordination and collaboration are also widely acknowledged in the public administration literature (Howlett, 2009; McGuire & Agranoff, 2011; May, 2012). However, the specific packages of policy tools described in our research likely lack relevance in other contexts. Variance in socio-ecological contexts, political dynamics, policy target behaviours, vulnerabilities to climate change, and state architectures mean policy tools and policy processes associated with adaptiveness will necessarily differ from those found in the US context.

9.5.2 Remaining Gaps

The themes and issues highlighted by our research point to several knowledge gaps of relevance for the future development of the earth systems governance framework. Specifically, our research underscores the importance of research that investigates the role of innovative policy tools, the architecture of state agencies, and the agency of administrative actors for adaptiveness. While existing research on adaptive governance often focuses on top-down laws, systemic-level structures (i.e. polycentric governance regimes), and bottom-up processes of emergent organisation, less attention has been given to the 'meso level' of state bureaucracies (Morrison et al., 2017; Wyborn & Dovers, 2014). Indeed, as the locus of second-order policymaking and implementation, state bureaucracies the world over play a critical role in environmental governance (Peters, 2010). One important knowledge gap in this respect is around the organisational structures and processes in state agencies that represent enablers, rather than barriers, for adaptiveness in specific contexts. To the extent that organisational change in state agencies is needed to support adaptiveness, research on administrative rather than legislative policy design therefore represents an important area for further inquiry. The importance of administrative policy design is particularly important in the US context given seemingly intractable political gridlock in legislative venues (Klyza & Sousa, 2010). Rather than wait for more adaptive policy tools to emerge through legislation on already-crowded agendas, our research suggests there are opportunities for change that may be pursued now through bureaucracies.

Given these considerations, the agency and interests of actors in state bureaucracies is another important topic for future research. In 'thick' institutional settings, in which new policy tools, goals, and management paradigms are layered on to existing authorities and administrative structures, individuals at executive and middle-management levels of state agencies are often essential for performing the 'institutional work' needed to operationalise novel policy tools and facilitate organisational change (Cloutier et al., 2016; Lawrence & Suddaby, 2006; Rutherford & Schultz, 2019). In undertaking institutional work, administrative agents must mediate the 'bottom-up' interests of street-level bureaucrats and local stakeholders, the top-down priorities and interests of political principals, and sideways competition for scarce resources from other state agencies. Understanding how bureaucratic politics and power dynamics shape policy change, and the tools and resources that administrative actors leverage to address entrenched interests, therefore represent an important avenue for future research on adaptiveness (Cloutier et al., 2016).

Beyond state architectures and agency, our research also underscores the challenge of building systemic policy capacity for adaptiveness in an era of neoliberal governance. With its emphasis on regulatory flexibility and legal reform, networks and non-state actors, devolved authority for resource governance, and emergent (i.e. voluntary) forms of collaboration, adaptive governance is perfectly compatible with the implementation preferences of the neoliberal governance paradigm. From a pragmatic point of view, this is not necessarily a weakness. It suggests there are feasible opportunities for facilitating adaptive governance in certain contexts through purposive policy design. Yet this consideration raises questions we suggest require attention from earth systems governance scholars over the next five years. First, given the emphasis on external actors and organisations in adaptive governance and neoliberal paradigms, how do institutional actors build civil society and network governance capacity in areas where it is lacking? Can this be fostered through public policy, or is it inherently dependent upon 'emergent' forms of civil society organisation? Second, to what extent can elements of adaptive governance be 'scaled up' under existing institutional governance paradigms? Can transformational change be achieved from the bottom up? Or are systemic structural changes in political economy, including resource redistribution and investment in state institutions, an essential pre-requisite for building policy capacity for more adaptive forms of governance? If the latter is true, political reform in constitutional venues may be needed to address structural features of political institutions that privilege entrenched interests and the status quo. The larger question, in other words, is if adaptive governance can precipitate transformational change, or if transformational changes to existing institutions, achieved through social and political mobilisation, are needed to support more adaptive forms of governance and substantively build adaptive capacity for an era of rapid change.

References

Abrams, J.B., Davis, E.J., Moseley, C., & Nowell, B. (2017). Building practical authority for community forestry in and through networks: the role of community-based organisations in the U.S. West. *Environmental Policy and Governance*, 27(4), 285–97.

Abrams, J.B., Huber-Stearns, H., Bone, C., & Moseley, C. (2017). Adaptation to a landscape-scale mountain pine beetle epidemic in the era of networked governance: the enduring importance of bureaucratic institutions. *Ecology and Society*, 22(4), 22.

Allen, C.R. & Gunderson, L.H. (2011). Pathology and failure in the design and implementation of adaptive management. *Journal of Environmental Management*, 92(5), 1379–84.

Arts, B., Buizer, M., Horlings, L. et al. (2017). Landscape approaches: a state-of-the-art review. *Annual Review of Environment and Resources*, 42(1), 439–63.

Armitage, D.R., Plummer, R., Berkes, F. et al. (2009). Adaptive co-management for social–ecological complexity. *Frontiers in Ecology and the Environment*, 7(2), 95–102.

Bennetts, R.E. & Gross, J. (2007). Linking monitoring to management and planning: assessment points as a generalized approach. *George Wright Forum*, 24(2), 59–77.

Berends, H., Boersma, K., & Weggeman, M. (2003). The structuration of organizational learning. *Human Relations*, 56(9), 1035–56.

Beunen, R., Patterson, J., & van Assche, K. (2017). Governing for resilience: the role of institutional work. *Current Opinion in Environmental Sustainability*, 28, 10–16.

Biber, E. (2011). The problem of environmental monitoring. *University of Colorado Law Review*, 83, 1–82.

Burch, S., Gupta, A., Inoue, C.Y. et al. (2019). New directions in earth system governance research. *Earth System Governance*, 1, 100006.

Butler, W.H. & Schultz, C.A. (2019). *A New Era for Collaborative Forest Management: Policy and Practice Insights from the Collaborative Forest Landscape Restoration Program*. Abingdon, UK: Routledge.

Cash, D.W., Adger, W.N., Berkes, F. et al. (2006). Scale and cross-scale dynamics: governance and information in a multilevel world. *Ecology and Society*, 11(2), 8–19.

Chaffin, B.C., Gosnell, H., & Cosens, B.A. (2014). A decade of adaptive governance scholarship: synthesis and future directions. *Ecology and Society*, 19(3), 56.

Cloutier, C., Denis, J.-L., Langley, A., & Lamothe, L. (2016). Agency at the managerial interface: public sector reform as institutional work. *Journal of Public Administration Research and Theory*, 26(2), 259–76.

Coleman, K. & Stern, M.J. (2018). Boundary spanners as trust ambassadors in collaborative natural resource management. *Journal of Environmental Planning and Management*, 61(2), 291–308.

Cortner, H.J. & Moore, M.A. (1999). *The Politics of Ecosystem Management*. Washington, DC: Island Press.

Cosens, B.A., Craig, R.A., Hirsch, S.L. et al. (2017). The role of law in adaptive governance. *Ecology and Society*, 22(1), 30.

Cosens, B.A. & Williams, M. (2012). Resilience and water governance: adaptive governance in the Columbia River basin. *Ecology and Society*, 17(4), 3.

Craig, R.K., Garmenstani, A.S., Allen, C.R. et al. (2017). Balancing stability and flexibility in adaptive governance: an analysis of tools available in U.S. environmental law. *Ecology and Society*, 22(2), 3.

Cyphers, L.A. & Schultz, C.A. (2019). Policy design to support cross-boundary land management: the example of the Joint Chiefs Landscape Restoration Partnership. *Land Use Policy*, 80(10), 362–9.

DeCaro, D.A., Chaffin, B.C., Schlager, E., Garmestani, A.S., & Ruhl, J.B. (2017). Legal and institutional foundations of adaptive environmental governance. *Ecology and Society*, 22(1), 1689–99.

DeLuca, T.H., Aplet, G.H., Wilmer, B., & Burchfield, J. (2010). The unknown trajectory of forest restoration: a call for ecosystem monitoring. *Journal of Forestry*, 108, 288–95.

Elliott, O.V. & Salamon, L.M. (2002). *The Tools of Government: A Guide to the New Governance*. Oxford: Oxford University Press.

Federal Register (2012). *Electronic Code of Federal Regulations (CFR), Title 36. Parks, Forests, and Public Property, Subpart A – National Forest System Land Management Planning (§§219.1–219.19). 77 FR 21260*. Washington, DC: US Department of Agriculture, Forest Service.

Folke, C., Hahn, T., Olsson, P., & Norberg, J. (2005). Adaptive governance of social-ecological systems. *Annual Review of Environment and Resources*, 30(1), 441–73.

Fukuyama, F. (2013). What is governance? *Governance*, 26(3), 347–68.

Gregory, R., Ohlson, D., & Arvai, J. (2006). Deconstructing adaptive management: criteria for applications to environmental management. *Ecological Applications*, 16(6), 2411–25.

Guerrero, A.M., McAllister, R.R., Corcoran, J. et al. (2013). Scale mismatches, conservation planning, and the value of social-network analyses. *Conservation Biology*, 27(1), 35–44.

Harrington, C., Curtis, A., & Black, R. (2008). Locating communities in natural resource management. *Journal of Environmental Policy & Planning*, 10(2), 199–215.

Hirt, P.W. (1994). *A Conspiracy of Optimism: Management of the National Forests Since World War Two*. Lincoln: University of Nebraska Press.

Hoberg, G. (2001). The emerging triumph of ecosystem management: the transformation of federal forest policy. In C. Davis, ed., *Environmental Politics and Western Public Lands*. New York: Routledge, 55–86.

Howlett, M. (2009). Governance modes, policy regimes and operational plans: a multi-level nested model of policy instrument choice and policy design. *Policy Sciences*, 42(1), 73–89.

Howlett, M. & Rayner, J. (2007). Design principles for policy mixes: cohesion and coherence in 'new governance arrangements'. *Policy and Society*, 26(4), 1–18.

Huitema, D., Mostert, E., Egas, W. et al. (2009). Adaptive water governance: assessing the institutional prescriptions of adaptive (co-)management from a governance perspective and defining a research agenda. *Ecology and Society*, 14(1), 26.

Hutto, R.L. & Belote, R.T. (2013). Distinguishing four types of monitoring based on the questions they address. *Forest Ecology and Management*, 289, 183–9.

Klyza, C.M.G. & Sousa, D. (2010). Beyond gridlock: green drift in American environmental policymaking. *Political Science Quarterly*, 125(3), 443–63.

Lawrence, T.B. & Suddaby, R. (2006). Institutions and institutional work. In S.R. Clegg, C. Hardy, T.B. Lawrence, & W. R. Nord, eds., *The SAGE Handbook of Organization Studies*. London: Sage, 215–54.

Lemos, M.C. & Agrawal, A. (2006). Environmental governance. *Annual Review of Environment and Resources*, 31(1), 297–325.

Lindenmayer, D.B. & Likens, G.E. (2010). The science and application of ecological monitoring. *Biological Conservation*, 143(6), 1317–28.

Lynn, L.E., Jr, Heinrich, C.J., & Hill, C.J. (2000). Studying governance and public management: challenges and prospects. *Journal of Public Administration Research and Theory*, 10(2), 233–62.

Mcguire, M. & Agranoff, R. (2011). The limitations of public management networks. *Public Administration*, 89(2), 265–84.

Maier, C. & Abrams, J.B. (2018). Navigating social forestry: a street-level perspective on national forest management in the US Pacific Northwest. *Land Use Policy*, 70(11), 432–41.

March, J.G. (1999). Exploration and exploitation in organizations. *Pursuit of Organizational Intelligence*, 2(1), 114–36.

May, P.J. (2012). Policy design and implementation. In J. Aguilera, ed., *The Sage Handbook of Public Administration*. London: Sage, 279–91.

Morrison, T.H., Adger, W.N., Brown, K. et al. (2017). Mitigation and adaptation in polycentric systems: sources of power in the pursuit of collective goals. *Wiley Interdisciplinary Reviews: Climate Change*, 8(5), 1–16.

Moulton, S. & Sandfort, J.R. (2016). The strategic action field framework for policy implementation research. *Policy Studies Journal*, 45(1), 144–69.

Nie, M.A. (2008). *The Governance of Western Public Lands*, Lawrence: University Press of Kansas.

Nie, M.A. & Schultz, C.A. (2012). Decision-making triggers in adaptive management. *Conservation Biology*, 26(6), 1137–44.

Peters, B.G. (2010). *The Politics of Bureaucracy: An Introduction to Comparative Public Administration*, Abingdon, UK: Routledge.

Phuong, L.T.H., Biesbroek, G.R., & Wals, A.E.J. (2018). Barriers and enablers to climate change adaptation in hierarchical governance systems: the case of Vietnam. *Journal of Environmental Policy and Planning*, 20(4), 518–32.

Predmore, A.S., Copenheaver, C.A., & Mortimer, M.J. (2008). Ecosystem management in the US forest service: a persistent process but dying discourse. *Journal of Forestry*, 106(6), 339–45.

Pressman, J.L. & Wildavsky, A.B. (1973). *Implementation: How Great Expectations in Washington Are Dashed in Oakland*. Berkeley: University of California Press.

Ringold, P.L., Mulder, B., Alegria, J. et al. (1999). Establishing a regional monitoring strategy: the Pacific Northwest forest plan. *Environmental Management*, 23, 179–92.

Rutherford, T.K. & Schultz, C.A. (2019). Adapting wildland fire governance to climate change in Alaska. *Ecology and Society*, 24(1), 27.

Sabatier, P.A. (1986). Top-down and bottom-up approaches to implementation research: a critical analysis and suggested synthesis. *Journal of Public Policy*, 6(1), 2148.

Schneider, A. & Ingram, H. (1990). Behavioral assumptions of policy tools. *Journal of Politics*, 52(2), 510–29.

Schultz, C.A., Coelho, D.L., & Beam, R.D. (2014). Design and governance of multiparty monitoring under the USDA Forest Service's Collaborative Forest Landscape Restoration Program. *Journal of Forestry*, 112(2), 198–206.

Schultz, C.A., Huber-Stearns, H., McCaffrey, S. et al. (2018). *Prescribed Fire Policy Barriers and Opportunities: A Diversity of Challenges and Strategies across the West*. Eugene: Ecosystem Institute, University of Oregon. Retrieved from https://ewp .uoregon.edu/sites/ewp.uoregon.edu/files/WP_86.pdf.

Schultz, C.A., Jedd, T., & Beam, R.D. (2012). The Collaborative Forest Landscape Restoration Program: a history and overview of the first projects. *Journal of Forestry*, 110(7), 381–91.

Schultz, C.A., McIntyre, K.B., Cyphers, L. et al. (2018). Policy design to support forest restoration: the value of focused investment and collaboration. *Forests*, 9(9), 512.

Schultz, C.A., Timberlake, T.J., Wurtzebach, Z., et al. (2019). Policy tools to address scale mismatches: insights from US forest governance. *Ecology and Society*, 24(1), 21.

Sharma-Wallace, L., Velarde, S.J., & Wreford, A. (2018). Adaptive governance good practice: show me the evidence! *Journal of Environmental Management*, 222(3), 174–84.

Stankey, G.H., Bormann, B.T., Ryan, C. et al. (2003). Adaptive management and the northwest forest plan rhetoric and reality. *Journal of Forestry*, 101(1), 40–6.

Stephens, S.L., Collins, B.M., Biber, E., & Fulé, P.Z. (2016). U.S. Federal fire and forest policy: emphasizing resilience in dry forests. *Ecosphere*, 7(11), 1–19.

Termeer, C.J.A.M., Dewulf, A., & van Lieshout, M. (2010). Disentangling scale approaches in governance research: comparing monocentric, multilevel, and adaptive governance. *Ecology and Society*, 15(4), 4.

United States Forest Service (USFS) (2012). *Increasing the Pace of Restoration and Job Creation on Our National Forests*. Retrieved from www.fs.fed.us/sites/default/files/ media/ types/publication/field_pdf/increasing-pace-restoration-job-creation-2012.pdf.

(2018). *Toward Shared Stewardship across Landscapes: An Outcome-Based Investment Strategy*. Retrieved from www.fs.usda.gov/sites/default/files/toward-shared-stewardship .pdf.

Walters, C.J. & Holling, C.S. (1990). Large-scale management experiments and learning by doing. *Ecology*, 71(6), 2060–8.

Waltz, A., Wurtzebach, Z., Esch, B., Wasserman, T., & Schultz, C. (2017). *Developing a Framework for the U.S. Forest Service Broader-Scale Monitoring Strategy: Processes and Outcomes*. Flagstaff: Northern Arizona University Ecological Restoration Institute.

Westgate, M.J., Likens, G.E., & Lindenmayer, D.B. (2013). Adaptive management of biological systems: a review. *Biological Conservation*, 158, 128–39.

Williams, B.K. (2011). Adaptive management of natural resources framework and issues. *Journal of Environmental Management*, 92(5), 1346–53.

Wu, X., Ramesh, M., & Howlett, M. (2015). Policy capacity: a conceptual framework for understanding policy competences and capabilities. *Policy and Society*, 34(3–4), 165–71.

Wurtzebach, Z., Casse, T., Meilby, H., Nielsen, M.R., & Milhoj, A. (2019). REDD+ policy design and policy learning: the emergence of an integrated landscape approach in Vietnam. *Forest Policy and Economics*, 101(11), 129–39.

Wurtzebach, Z. & Schultz, C. (2016). Measuring ecological integrity: history, practical applications, and research opportunities. *BioScience*, 66(6), 446–57.

Wurtzebach, Z., Schultz, C., Waltz, A.E.M., Esch, B.E., & Wasserman, T.N. (2019). Broader-scale monitoring for federal forest planning: challenges and opportunities. *Journal of Forestry*, 117(3), 244–55

Wyborn, C. & Dovers, S. (2014). Prescribing adaptiveness in agencies of the state. *Global Environmental Change*, 24(1), 5–7.

10

Adaptiveness in Earth System Governance

Synthesis, Policy Relevance, and the Way Forward

BERND SIEBENHÜNER, RIYANTI DJALANTE, NICOLAS W. JAGER,
AND JULIE P. KING

10.1 Introduction: Adaptiveness in Dynamic Earth System Governance

This chapter concludes the volume by reflecting our quest of harvesting the conceptual development of adaptiveness, as proposed by the first Science Plan of the Earth System Governance (ESG) Project. Here, adaptiveness is understood as one of the key attributes and goals of governance to anticipate, manage, and help steer complex societal, technological, and environmental changes to a path of more sustainable trajectories. It has been coined an 'umbrella term embracing a set of related concepts, vulnerability, resilience, adaptation, robustness, adaptive capacity, and social learning', referring 'to governance of adaptation to social-ecological change as well as the processes of change and adaptation within governance systems' (Biermann et al., 2009: 45). Reiterating the main question of the book – 'How has adaptiveness, as an umbrella concept, been developed and applied in the context of earth system governance in the first decade after its inception, and what insights and practical solutions has it yielded?' – we find that the use of adaptiveness as an umbrella concept implies potentials for the analysis of environmental governance. However, does this render the notion of adaptiveness futile and should we revert back to these possibly more specific concepts? If not, what can we learn from it and what does it tell us for governance practice as well as future research in the field?

By way of summarising and synthesising key insights from this book, in this chapter, we provide answers to these questions. In particular, we will first, in Section 10.2, bring together some findings from Chapter 2 reviewing the past discussions in the literature and addressing the four central questions of the first ESG Science Plan as of 2008. Section 10.3 will thus continue to reflect on the term of adaptiveness as we present the related insights linked to the so-called Utrecht Questions on the implications of conceptual progress on adaptiveness. The latter were developed during the 2018 ESG conference in Utrecht, the Netherlands, where authors of this book and other researchers discussed the political and societal relevance of adaptiveness (see the Preface). The Utrecht Questions seek to synthesise conceptual approaches and the background of the adaptiveness-related knowledge so far. They also address the generalisability, policy relevance, and practicality of the current knowledge on adaptiveness as well as the gaps and future research agendas. Finally, in Section 10.4, we revert to the ESG Science Plan presented in 2018 and conclude the book by discussing its implications with regard to future research agendas and for a broader societal transformation towards global sustainability.

10.2 Synthesis of Findings on Adaptiveness

Drawing from a systematic literature review, Siebenhüner and Djalante (Chapter 2) addressed four guiding questions of the 2008 ESG Science Plan that explored (a) the politics of adaptiveness; (b) the nature of governance processes that foster adaptiveness; (c) which attributes of governance systems enhance capacities to adapt; and finally (d) how, when, and why does adaptiveness influence, and ultimately change, earth system governance. By and large, the reviewed literature demonstrates the uses and benefits of an overarching concept of adaptiveness despite the fact of there being far more elaborate and more rigorously explored concepts included in it. However, by bringing these discourses on socio-ecological resilience, climate adaptation, social learning, or robustness, the umbrella concept makes them speak together and carve out the commonalities and the complementarities. A synthesis of the knowledge from these communities, their concepts, and bodies of knowledge allows to shift the focus on larger dynamics in governance systems and their connectedness to socio-ecological system dynamics at various scales. This synthesis work, however, is far from being concluded and this book is merely a starting point rather than the culmination of this harvesting endeavour.

In our review, we found that the politics of adaptiveness are driven by the political nature and the conflicts of adaptiveness, recognising that responses to massive changes in the ecological systems substantially impact political relations and power structures on different governance levels. Only if socio-ecological dynamics are monitored and understood well, can governance processes be designed in an adaptive manner. Thereby governance systems will learn and reverse course based on knowledge and new insights, such as through collaborative governance, adaptive governance, etc. While there is an abundance of literature assessing tools and indicators for vulnerability, resilience, and adaptive capacity, the conflictive and distributed effects of these at times abrupt and fast changes still require further scrutiny. In particular, the impacts of socio-ecological system dynamics and related governance adaptations on poverty, marginalisation, and communities left behind require more research in the future.

When looking into what exactly these adaptive governance processes are, we identified a number of promising approaches. Among the most prominent are social learning concepts that emphasise the role of knowledge in governance, acknowledging that this knowledge is highly dynamic, disputed, and diverse. The related governance processes thus need to be able to bring together different bodies of knowledge, recognise their relevance, reflect upon solutions, and cautiously or experimentally implement them. Thus experiments play a central role in adaptive governance. They bring together novel constellations of actors and facilitate innovative solutions in an error-friendly manner to allow for corrections based on new insights and findings of side effects or unintended, but severe consequences. In most cases these experiments need to be restricted to local or regional scales and decentral levels of governance. Therefore, polycentric and decentralised governance processes have been hailed as well-suited for adaptiveness vis-à-vis highly dynamic socio-ecological systems. However, coordination and scaling up then become crucial challenges for larger socio-ecological transformations of societies and governance systems that many existing ones have not yet found answers to.

These governance processes that allow for adaptiveness tend to have key attributes such as participation, multilayered institutions, and knowledge-based deliberative governance approaches. They are oftentimes supported by structured and well-moderated multi-actor processes. These bring together different framings and perspectives that allow for learning and error detection. In this sense, they allow for error-friendly governance processes; but knowledge integration and decision-making in the situation of a vast diversity of viewpoints and pieces of knowledge remain challenging.

The influence of these insights and the larger adaptiveness discourse on earth system governance at large is difficult to assess. In the literature, the question has rather been turned around by asking what barriers keep governance processes from being adaptive. One related hypothesis suggests lock-in mechanisms to counteract adaptive governance dynamics. According to this concept, many governance systems build on stability and have created path dependencies and self-reinforcing mechanisms that keep development trajectories in very narrow boundaries such as in the case of UK roads policies described in Chapter 7. In this case, the dominance of conventional foresight instruments such as cost–benefit analysis did not allow policymakers to proactively consider novel challenges such as climate change in the new roads policies.

Through these intense debates and insights, researchers continually advance their understanding of adaptiveness and adaptive governance including the processes and characteristics that promote or hinder it. They also increasingly understand its necessity for a dynamic, flexible, and responsive notion of sustainable development and problem-solving that refers to concepts of diversity and interconnected ecosystems of water, land, marine, and in particular climate change or cities (Birkmann et al., 2010; Boyd & Juhola, 2015), including emerging issues of plastic and biodiversity. More and more cross-sector connections, linkages, and trade-offs are being explored (e.g. with nexus concepts; Allan et al., 2015; Boas et al., 2016) and in the research on governance through the UN Sustainable Development Goals (SDGs; e.g. Kanie & Biermann, 2017). There is emerging literature examining the coherence and synergies between global frameworks and national development plans (e.g. Collste et al., 2017; Stafford-Smith et al., 2017) or their alignments at different governance levels (e.g. Biermann & Kim, 2020; Northrop et al., 2016; Persson et al., 2016). The multiple interlinkages bring to the fore an additional dimension of dynamics since changes in one field often impact on others, creating an ever-changing and often unstable web of interactions. Here, effective governance processes have to be dynamic and adaptive to allow for some minimal stability.

10.3 Framing, Generalisation, Policy Relevance, and Future Research Directions: Responding to the Utrecht Questions (2018)

The Utrecht Questions ask the broader conceptual and societal implications of adaptiveness. For each of the questions, we discuss the most relevant findings from different chapters in the book, we then elaborate the discussion with the latest conceptual discussion in the literature.

10.3.1 What Are the Conceptual Frames Used? What Is the Basis of the Statements/Knowledge Presented?

The book illustrates a significant advancement of the knowledge on adaptiveness, and the preconditions and drivers of adaptation. From the outset, adaptiveness has mainly served as an umbrella term for various concepts and frames, such as resilience, adaptive governance, social learning, and robustness. All of these concepts refer to dynamic developments in governance systems or in the socio-ecological systems as subjects of governance processes. In addition, in all concepts there is a potential for a sustainable future that is long-lasting and serves human as well as nature's well-being.

As such, it does not come as a surprise that the actual term adaptiveness is rarely used in the earth system governance literature. Instead, we observe a rather dispersed field of research, in which multiple terms are used and each have gathered momentum, especially around adaptive management, vulnerability, or resilience, as Chapter 2 highlights. The chapters in this volume are exemplary in this respect, employing multiple frames including adaptive capacities (Chapters 3 and 4), social-ecological systems (Chapter 6), a multidiscipline/nexus approach (Chapter 5), and multilevel policy capacity (Chapter 9).

This plurality of frames employed is also reflected in the research modes subsumed under the umbrella of adaptiveness. While several studies exist, approaching the aspects of adaptiveness from a rather disciplinary perspective (e.g. political science, psychology), the field is characterised by an inherent interdisciplinarity combining approaches from several disciplines. Even the individual concepts that comprise adaptiveness add to the diversity and richness of concepts. For instance, Montpetit et al. (Chapter 3) present the polysemy of adaptive capacity, explaining how the term is nuanced depending on the research niche and operational application. Also, transdisciplinary research, actively involving non-academic stakeholders in the research process (Siebenhüner, 2018), is observed to be prevalent – in particular when it comes to the implementation of adaptive governance approaches. Again, the contributions to this volume serve as a case in point relying on a range of disciplines and perspectives including public policy, systems sciences, economics, environmental law, and natural science.

While this plurality of frames and perspectives has a strong potential to generate a colourful diversity of insights around different aspects of adaptiveness, it also complicates their synthesis. Hence, we can observe a trade-off between the plurality of perspectives in the field and the generation of a coherent and emergent body of adaptiveness scholarship. As such, studies often cluster around specific aspects of adaptiveness such as resilience or adaptive capacities, while the links between these remain under-explored. This pattern is corroborated by some chapters in this volume. For example, Siebenhüner and Djalante (Chapter 2) found in their review that social learning serves at the same time as a precondition for and a crucial element of adaptiveness. However, efforts to address and utilise this diversity are under way, as Chapter 3 by Montpetit et al. highlights. Here, the authors link conceptualisations of adaptive capacities to different perspectives of adaptiveness, such as resilience or development.

10.3.2 *How Generalisable Are the Findings? How Confident Can We Be? What Are the Knowledge Gaps?*

Adaptiveness, as umbrella term for the 'changes made by social groups in response to, or anticipation of, challenges created through environmental change' (Biermann et al., 2009: 45), is an inherently context-dependent perspective. More often than not, varying environmental and societal circumstances require different responses, making widely generalisable findings and principles difficult to achieve. This sentiment is echoed throughout several of the contributions in this volume, stressing the pivotal role that context plays in the study of adaptiveness and its different related perspectives (e.g. Chapters 4 and 9).

This context-sensitive perspective is also reflected in the methods employed. As Siebenhüner and Djalante (Chapter 2) found in their review chapter in this volume, case studies, often on a local scale, are the main method to study adaptiveness. This trend also becomes apparent within the chapters of this volume, five of which rely on case studies. While these allow for an in-depth and contextualised understanding of the various aspects and mechanisms of adaptiveness within a given context, they only offer limited opportunities for generalisability of findings (Flick, 2009; Gerring, 2007; Yin, 2009).

That said, such inherent context-dependency does not preclude conclusions of a wider scope to be drawn altogether. One strategy to design adaptiveness research geared towards wider generalisability may lie in embedding these inquiries, both empirically and conceptually. Empirically, combining within-case research, tracing causal pathways, and striving for an in-depth understanding of cases with comparative, cross-case analyses that explore the scope of findings can offer a way to increase generalisability (Goertz, 2017). Additionally, embedding case studies within existing conceptual frames, including explicit assumptions about the role of context, may provide a fruitful channel for a dialogue between theory and practice, and as such may help to broaden the scope of studies conceptually. This understanding of context is also to be found within the 2018 ESG Science Plan, which explicitly calls for ongoing research about the role of political, economic, and social factors in constraining or fostering adaptiveness (ESG, 2018). It would also benefit substantially from synthesis and works that integrate various findings, frames, and context-specific as well as generic facts. Thereby, a more coherent set of enabling or hindering conditions of adaptive governance could ultimately be identified.

10.3.3 What Is the Policy Relevance? How Much Is It Grounded in Practical Evidence?

Through its strong problem focus and the grounding of case research through means of inter- and trans-disciplinary methods, practical relevance is often a central component of studies of adaptiveness. The contributions in this volume may serve to further illustrate this point. For example, in her document-based analysis of international forestry development programmes in the Democratic Republic of Congo (DRC) and the Central African Republic (CAR), Peach Brown (Chapter 8) concludes by emphasising the importance of the adaptiveness of large international organisations intervening in volatile countries with histories of internal conflict and poor governance. These organisations and instruments, such as the World Bank and REDD+, must approach development projects with anticipatory, reflexive, and sensitive approaches, in order to be more effective in capacity building, promoting good governance, and reducing deforestation.

This example also highlights that practitioners and decision makers have a crucial role in interpreting scientific frames and findings and operationalising these into action on the ground. We have seen a growing number of contributions to the literature discussing how key concepts related to adaptiveness such as resilience, vulnerability, and adaptive capacity have been identified, interpreted, and implemented in policies and practices. Applying adaptiveness through building resilience and reducing vulnerability is the common approach shared by the SDGs, the Paris Agreement on climate change, and the Sendai Framework for Disaster Risk Reduction.

10.3.4 What Are the New Challenges and Remaining Gaps That Are Relevant to Inform Future Development of the Earth System Governance Framework?

As the contributions of this book highlight, the study of adaptiveness has already come a long way and provides a variety of approaches, perspectives, and insights. Although Siebenhüner et al. (Chapter 7) propose the concept of lock-ins as a set of phenomena hindering adaptation practices and adaptiveness in governance processes, their chapter brings renewed attention to the idea that the dynamics behind barriers to adaptation remain under-researched and thus under-explained (Eisenack et al., 2014). That said, a number of blind spots and research gaps remain, comprising mainly the political and societal factors around adaptiveness, the question of 'what works' and under which conditions, and also the limits to adaptation (Adger et al., 2009).

The role of power relations and the surrounding dynamics are identified as a research gap in the study of adaptiveness by Siebenhüner and Djalante (Chapter 2). Currently, a strong focus in the literature is put on technical and managerial aspects of adaptiveness that tend to leave aside questions of power and politics. However, adaptiveness is a genuinely political phenomenon and as such consequently subject to constant capture and recapture through actors with varying levels of power (Cannon & Müller-Mahn, 2010; Sovacool et al., 2015). This concerns the process of adaptation itself, as well as its wider consequences. Pertinent questions arise about who benefits in which ways from adaptiveness in its different forms, spurring important debates about social justice, distribution of costs and benefits, vulnerability, and marginalisation. Peach Brown (Chapter 8) picks up this issue, calling for more attention to be paid to the ways in which adaptive governance can be designed to help vulnerable populations in volatile, conflict-riddled settings.

A second block of challenges concerns the question of what works under which conditions in adaptiveness. Adaptiveness is not an end in itself but can be perceived as means for a more sustainable, just, and liveable Anthropocene. Can adaptiveness be an emergent property of a system consisting of reflexive but at times path-dependent and boundedly rational actors? Exactly how and through which governance strategies, instruments, and exact mechanisms this can be reached is still subject to debate, while evidence remains scattered (Koontz et al., 2015). For example, Wurtzebach and Schultz (Chapter 9) point to the need to pay further attention to the role of governance modes and designs, and of public administration to enable adaptiveness. Past research flags elements of adaptiveness-related governance processes including participatory approaches, polycentric designs, and social learning. These questions are also echoed by the 2018 ESG Science Plan that explicitly asks about the adaptive potential of specific governance arrangements and their relation to knowledge and reflexivity, as well as the environmental impact of those (ESG, 2018).

Finally, adaptiveness is by no means a panacea, and there may be limits to it in the design and implementation of governance processes. One of these adaptation limits is related to specific levels of adaptive capacity that cannot be exceeded (Dow et al., 2013). Socially, it is contingent upon ethics, knowledge, attitudes to risk, and culture (Adger et al., 2009). Efficiency hailed by numerous conventional economic approaches and corporate strategists can also constitute a limit to adaptive and resilient structures and governance processes (Gupta et al., 2010; Korhonen & Seager, 2008). There is also a limit to adaptiveness through the need for stability of central institutions, as Beunen et al. (2017) posit. These types of limits, soft and hard, will influence the type of adaptation options chosen by actors, and if these limits are passed, loss and damages are to occur (De Coninck et al., 2018; Mechler et al., 2020). It will also be interesting to study maladaptation cases where the way a system adapts is not the way individual actors want it to (e.g. Magnan et al., 2016).

10.3.5 What Are the Questions That We Need Answers to in Five Years, and Why?

Against the backdrop of mixed and limited results of the REDD+ programme in the DRC and CAR, Peach Brown (Chapter 8) poses questions regarding the role of the United Nations and other international institutions in framing climate change as a cross-cutting issue, which should be integrated into development and peacebuilding initiatives: 'How should interventions be structured and adapted to the context? How will marginalised groups be affected?' Ultimately, how will international interventions affect populations and the planet?

Post-2018 literature on adaptiveness particularly asks the questions: What are the fairness, justice, and equity implications on the policies and programmes on climate change adaptation and mitigation? How can we identify and address trade-offs and synergies in climate adaptation and mitigation policies, and particularly how can we ensure no one is left behind? Studies examine vulnerability to climate change and its relations to impacts, social injustice, and fundamental human rights, through distributive justice, procedural justice, and intergenerational equity (Venn, 2019), winners and losers in climate-compatible development (Ellis & Tschakert, 2019), transformative adaptation for vulnerable groups (Stringer et al., 2020), or bridging indigenous knowledge into global climate research (Reyes-Garciá et al., 2019). We are also seeing increasing research on the role of cities in experimentation in sustainability (e.g. Castán-Broto & Westman, 2009; Fuenfschilling et al., 2019; Madsen & Hansen, 2019), and environmental migration (e.g. Krieger et al., 2020; McLeman & Gemenne, 2018). Lastly, the 2018 ESG Science Plan section on adaptiveness and reflexivity further proposes questions on assessing the contents, governance attributes, complex risks, and enabling conditions for successful adaptation and reflexivity.

10.4 Adaptiveness, Reflexivity, and toward Broader Societal Transformation and Achieving the Global Sustainability Agendas

As part of the ESG Project Harvesting Initiative, this book has attempted to harvest the conceptualisations of adaptiveness as analytical themes in earth system governance studies over a decade after the publication of the ESG 2009 Science Plan. As discussed in Chapter 1, a new Science Plan was developed in 2018 (see also Burch et al., 2019). This ESG Science Plan (ESG, 2018) adopts adaptiveness together with reflexivity as one of the analytical concepts. While adaptiveness focuses on the ability to anticipate, manage, and help steer changes, reflexivity concerns the 'ability of actors to critically reflect on one's actions and performance, and to reshape their goals, practices and values accordingly in order to wisely navigate complex, contested and changing human-environmental systems' (ESG, 2018: 68). In this notion, adaptiveness is understood to concern primarily responses to changes (coordinated, self-organised, or emergent), while reflexivity is about rethinking values and practices in managing and governing the changes. Based on the understanding that knowledge, social learning, and critical re-evaluation call for adaptive governance processes to implement them, both notions are highly complementary and in parts overlapping. Three research directions are subsequently proposed: navigating tensions between stability and flexibility, dealing with globally networked risks, and reshaping governance systems in the Anthropocene (ESG, 2018). All of them provide avenues for specific conceptually inspired research topics that would call for empirical case study as well as synthesising studies. What is more, the research lens combining adaptiveness and reflexivity also promotes novel topics on what processes and instruments may help reflection and adaptive governance responses; how stability, decision-making, and implementation can be possible under conditions of permanent change; and scrutiny as required by reflexivity. Research may guide ways out of this dilemma potentially leading to governance innovations and flexible and adaptive solutions to the complex and interconnected problems of socio-ecological change and transformations. In addition, a theoretically informed analysis of adaptive governance phenomena is important as it potentially leads to entirely different sets of explanations as to how different adaptiveness outcomes can be explained, and what can be done to improve the adaptiveness of governance systems.

During this time, the landscape of earth system governance has changed substantially. In particular, the emergence and the almost unilateral agreement over the SDGs to be achieved by 2030 marks a turning point in the political and societal efforts to bring together the numerous problem arenas of sustainable development and to kick-start a global transformation process with the highest ambitions. This shift in governance calls for rapid and transformative strategies that essentially need to be implemented in an adaptive manner due to the system complexities, the interconnectedness of goals and issue areas, as well as the hitherto unknown speed required.

First, the insights into the inextricable connectedness of social and ecological systems and our fundamental dependence on functioning ecosystems for the survival and well-being of humankind imply vast complexities. The research community is only beginning to understand socio-ecological systems and their dynamics. Surprises will therefore rather be the norm than the exception. Transformative changes will challenge existing functions and will have side effects that need to be addressed as well. Governance processes therefore, will essentially need to be error-friendly, often decentralised, and cognisant of the unknown and uncertain in these hyper-complex systems. What is essential is a governance approach that builds on these system dynamics and reflects about its progress as well as the backlashes and newly created or emerging problems.

Second, earth system governance towards the SDGs will need to be integrative at all levels. The Agenda 2030 brought together numerous policy areas under one initiative and acknowledged the fact that many of these are essentially interconnected. Fighting poverty oftentimes requires strong ecosystem functions to sustainably provide goods and services for humans. In the research communities, the nexus approaches reflect this interconnectedness and emphasises the repercussions of action in one area to others (one example is provided by Stoett & Vince in Chapter 5). If governance processes in one area expectedly will have implications for others, they need to be adaptive and ready to change course. This requires effective monitoring and intense integrative communication across the boundaries of the specific issue areas. Health policies, for instance, need to be understood and advanced in their connectedness to biodiversity, climate change, and, for instance, air and water pollution.

Third, speed is of the essence in the transformative processes required under the Agenda 2030. If humankind should have only a slight chance to meet most of the ambitious goals, we will need to be fast in the changes considering the vastness of the tasks and the indolence of many social and economic structures and routines. However, the speed required almost on all scales of governance creates new challenges at times contradicting the call for thorough reflection, systematic evaluation, and intense scrutiny in the adaptiveness literature. Thus increasing pressures to achieve transformative change in a short time, as flagged by the climate change research community, will require pragmatic and smart approaches to adaptiveness. Easy and simple monitoring systems will be part of this as well as rapid communication and the use of the immensely fast means of the digital world.

In conclusion, it will remain essential to continue research efforts on adaptiveness in these transformative governance processes to achieve the 2030 Agenda of the SDGs and broader sustainable development. This also implies that this research needs to be highly connected and adaptive to real-world governance processes. It will also require significant efforts by the research as well as the governance communities to bring experiences together, exchange about problems and their solutions, and to engage in their scaled implementation. Thus, the Agenda 2030 is a common journey that builds on the contributions by everyone, including adaptive changes in the research communities and in academia.

References

Adger, W.N., Dessai, S., Goulden, M. et al. (2009). Are there social limits to adaptation to climate change? *Climatic Change*, 93(3–4), 335–54.

Allan, T., Keulertz, M., & Woertz, E. (2015). The water–food–energy nexus: an introduction to nexus concepts and some conceptual and operational problems. *International Journal of Water Resources Development*, 31(3), 301–11.

Beunen, R., Patterson, J., & van Assche, K. (2017). Governing for resilience: the role of institutional work. *Current Opinion in Environmental Sustainability*, 28, 10–16.

Biermann, F., Betsill, M.M., Gupta, J. et al. (2009). *Earth System Governance: People, Places, and the Planet. Science Implementation Plan of the Earth System Governance Project.* Bonn: International Human Dimensions Programme on Global Environmental Change.

Biermann, F., Kanie, N., & Kim, R.E. (2017). Global governance by goal-setting: the novel approach of the UN Sustainable Development Goals. *Current Opinion in Environmental Sustainability*, 26, 26–31.

Biermann, F. & Kim, R.E. (eds.) (2020). *Architectures of Earth System Governance: Institutional Complexity and Structural Transformation.* Cambridge, UK: Cambridge University Press.

Birkmann, J., Garschagen, M., Kraas, F., & Quang, N. (2010). Adaptive urban governance: new challenges for the second generation of urban adaptation strategies to climate change. *Sustainability Science*, 5(2), 185–206.

Boas, I., Biermann, F., & Kanie, N. (2016). Cross-sectoral strategies in global sustainability governance: towards a nexus approach. *International Environmental Agreements: Politics, Law and Economics*, 16(3), 449–64.

Boyd, E. & Juhola, S. (2015). Adaptive climate change governance for urban resilience. *Urban Studies*, 52(7), 1234–64.

Burch, S., Gupta, A., Inoue, C.Y.A. et al. (2019). New directions in earth system governance research. *Earth System Governance*, 1, 100006. doi: http://doi.org/10.1016/j.esg .2019.100006.

Cannon, T. & Müller-Mahn, D. (2010). Vulnerability, resilience and development discourses in context of climate change. *Natural Hazards*, 55(3), 621–35.

Castán-Broto, V. & Westman, L. (2009). *Urban Sustainability and Justice: Just Sustainabilities and Environmental Planning.* London: Zed Books.

Collste, D., Pedercini, M., & Cornell, S.E. (2017). Policy coherence to achieve the SDGs: using integrated simulation models to assess effective policies. *Sustainability Science*, 12(6), 921–31.

De Coninck, H., Revi, A., Babiker, M. et al. (2018). Strengthening and implementing the global response. In V. Masson-Delmotte, P. Zhai, H.O. Pörtner et al., eds., *Global Warming of 1.5°C: An IPCC Special Report on the Impacts of Global Warming of 1.5°C above Pre-Industrial Levels and Related Global Greenhouse Gas Emission Pathways, in the Context of Strengthening the Global Response to the Threat of Climate Change.* Geneva: Intergovernmental Panel on Climate Change.

Dow, K., Berkhout, F., Preston, B.L. et al. (2013). Limits to adaptation. *Nature Climate Change*, 3(4), 305.

Earth System Governance (ESG) Project (2018). *Earth System Governance: Science and Implementation Plan of the Earth System Governance Project.* Utrecht: Earth System Governance Project.

Eisenack, K., Moser, S.C., Hoffmann, E. et al. (2014). Explaining and overcoming barriers to climate change adaptation. *Nature Climate Change*, 4(10), 867–72. doi: http://doi .org/10.1038/nclimate2350.

Ellis, N.R. & Tschakert, P. (2019). Triple-wins as pathways to transformation? A critical review. *Geoforum*, 103, 167–70.

Flick, U. (2009). How to design qualitative research: an overview. In U. Flick, ed., *An Introduction to Qualitative Research*, 4th ed. London: Sage, 127–45.

Fuenfschilling, L., Frantzeskaki, N., & Coenen, L. (2019). Urban experimentation & sustainability transitions. *European Planning Studies*, 27(2), 219–28. doi: http://doi .org/10.1080/09654313.2018.1532977.

Gerring, J. (2007). *Case Study Research: Principles and Practices.* Cambridge, UK: Cambridge University Press.

Goertz, G. (2017). *Multimethod Research, Causal Mechanisms, and Case Studies: An Integrated Approach.* Princeton, NJ: Princeton University Press.

Gupta, J., Termeer, C., Klostermann, J. et al. (2010). The Adaptive Capacity Wheel: a method to assess the inherent characteristics of institutions to enable the adaptive capacity of society. *Environmental Science & Policy*, 13(6), 459–71.

Kanie, N. & Biermann, F. (eds.). (2017). *Governing through Goals. Sustainable Development Goals as Governance Innovation*. Cambridge, MA: MIT Press.

Koontz, T.M., Gupta, D., Mudliar, P. et al. (2015). Adaptive institutions in social-ecological systems governance: a synthesis framework. *Environmental Science and Policy*, 53(B), 139–51. doi: http://doi.org/10.1016/j.envsci.2015.01.003.

Korhonen, J. & Seager, T.P. (2008). Beyond eco-efficiency: a resilience perspective. *Business Strategy and Environment*, 17(7), 411–19.

Krieger, T., Panke, D., & Pregernig, M. (eds.). (2020). *Environmental Conflicts, Migration and Governance*. Bristol: Bristol University Press.

McLeman, R. & Gemenne, F. (eds.) (2018). *Routledge Handbook of Environmental Displacement and Migration*. London: Routledge.

Madsen, S.H.J. & Hansen, T. (2019). Cities and climate change: examining advantages and challenges of urban climate change experiments. *European Planning Studies*, 27(2), 282–99.

Magnan, A.K., Schipper, E.L.F., Burkett, M. et al. (2016). Addressing the risk of maladaptation to climate change. *Wiley Interdisciplinary Reviews: Climate Change*, 7(5), 646–65. doi: http://doi.org/10.1002/wcc.409.

Mechler, R., Singh, C., Ebi, K. et al. (2020). Loss and damage and limits to adaptation: recent IPCC insights and implications for climate science and policy. *Sustainability Science*, 15, 1245–51.

Northrop, E., Biru, H., Lima, S., Bouye, M., & Song, R. (2016). *Examining the Alignment between the Intended Nationally Determined Contributions and Sustainable Development Goals*. Washington, DC: World Resources Institute.

Persson, Å., Weitz, N., & Nilsson, M. (2016). Follow-up and review of the Sustainable Development Goals: alignment vs. internalization. *Review of European, Comparative & International Environmental Law*, 25(1), 59–68.

Reyes-García, V., Garcia del Amo, D., Benyei, P. et al. (2019). A collaborative approach to bring insights from local observations of climate change impacts into global climate change research. *Current Opinion in Environmental Sustainability*, 39, 1–8. doi: https://doi.org/10.1016/j.cosust.2019.04.007.

Siebenhüner, B. (2018). Conflicts in transdisciplinary research: reviewing literature and analysing a case of climate adaptation in northwestern Germany. *Ecological Economics*, 154, 117–27. doi: https://doi.org/10.1016/j.ecolecon.2018.07.011.

Sovacool, B.K., Linnér, B.-O., & Goodsite, M.E. (2015). The political economy of climate adaptation. *Nature Climate Change*, 5(7), 616–18.

Stafford-Smith, M., Griggs, D., Gaffney, O. et al. (2017). Integration: the key to implementing the Sustainable Development Goals. *Sustainability Science*, 12(6), 911–19.

Stringer, L.C., Fraser, E.D.G., Harris, D. et al. (2020). Adaptation and development pathways for different types of farmers. *Environmental Science & Policy*, 104, 174–89. doi: https://doi.org/10.1016/j.envsci.2019.10.007.

Venn, A. (2019). Social justice and climate change. In T. Letcher, ed., *Managing Global Warming*. London: Academic Press, 711–28. doi: http://doi.org/10.1016/B978-0-12-814104-5.00024-7.

Yin, R.K. (2009). How to know whether and when to use case studies as a research method. In R.K. Yin, ed., *Case Study Research Designs and Methods*, 4th ed. London: Sage, 3–21.

Index

Printed in the United States
by Baker & Taylor Publisher Services